FIREBRAND FEMINISM

FIREBRAND FEMINISM

THE RADICAL LIVES OF TI-GRACE ATKINSON KATHIE SARACHILD ROXANNE DUNBAR-ORTIZ AND DANA DENSMORE

BREANNE FAHS

UNIVERSITY OF WASHINGTON | *Seattle*

UNIVERSITY OF WASHINGTON PRESS
www.washington.edu/uwpress

LIBRARY OF CONGRESS CATALOGING-IN-PUBLICATION DATA
Names: Fahs, Breanne, author.
Title: Firebrand feminism : the radical lives of Ti-Grace Atkinson, Kathie Sarachild,
     Roxanne Dunbar-Ortiz, and Dana Densmore / Breanne Fahs.
Description: Seattle : University of Washington, [2018] | Includes bibliographical
     references and index. |
Identifiers: LCCN 2017048934 (print) | LCCN 2017053559 (ebook) |
     ISBN 9780295743172 (ebook) | ISBN 9780295743158 (hardcover : alk. paper) |
     ISBN 9780295743165 (pbk. : alk. paper)
Subjects: LCSH: Feminism. | Radicalism.
Classification: LCC HQ1155 (ebook) | LCC HQ1155 .F34 2018 (print) |
     DDC 305.42—dc23
LC record available at https://lccn.loc.gov/2017048934

For my mother, for wanting willful daughters—
May all mothers be so brave and generous.

It is well to note that from radicalism has flowed all that makes life better today than yesterday. It is now, as in the past, the only force capable of leading the world out of its night of hunger, hatred and fear. Humanity advances over a path blazed by radicals and stained with their blood. So long as there is injustice there will be radicals. The name itself is the proudest title of free men and women.

—INDUSTRIAL WORKERS OF THE WORLD

CONTENTS |

PREFACE |

I first met each of these women—Ti-Grace, Kathie, Roxanne, and Dana—
when I contacted them in 2008 for an interview for my biography of
SCUM Manifesto author and would-be assassin Valerie Solanas. As radical
feminists, they had a certain fondness for Valerie's writings, particularly
her anger toward men and "Daddy's girls" and her ongoing insistence on
the twin impulses of destruction and revolution. We began our intergenerational conversations with a shared vision for a feminism full of fire, one
defined not by careful institutional progress but by hot-temperedness,
impatience, outrage, and willfulness.

During our many conversations, I realized fairly quickly that each of
these women was a force of nature in her own right, defining and shaping decades worth of thinking and theorizing about radical feminism
from its inception in the late 1960s through today. Their astonishing
bravery, hilariously dry humor, unabashed intensities, curious overlaps
and disagreements with each other, and fresh insights about feminism,
politics, and sexuality ignited an urgent feeling in me that more readers
needed to experience their world—the world as it could be, as it might
be, with full-frontal firebrand feminism at the helm. And so, this book
is an extension of, and reflection on, parts of their lives and works. It is a
testament to the collective energies of second-wave radical feminist organizing and to these women's unique roles in shaping what would become
a powerhouse social movement with deep implications for today's feminist politics.

The five of us have become, perhaps unwittingly, fellow travelers over these past decades, as their friendships span fifty years, while my friendship with them spans a mere three presidencies (and many hours of emails, phone calls, and conversations). That they have given far more to me than I have given to them is evident in every page of this book; I am the younger radical, trying to absorb their lessons, at times foolish or hasty or full of blind spots, seeing their words and works through my own privileged lens of a women's studies undergraduate and graduate education and a long-term tenured women's studies professorship. I have spent years sitting and listening, writing down, recording, transcribing, wondering about, laughing with, studying, and thinking about these women. Their uncommon generosity of time and spirit, of humor and energy, of goodwill and insight, permeates the stories they tell here. They remind us that academic feminist work must ground itself in the lived realities of women's lives (and can never refuse self-criticism and the push to listen more to activists), that marching on the streets and barricading doorways matters as much as—if not more than—speech and text, that women's studies began as the scholarly wing of an *activist* movement and thus cannot constantly seek institutional approval and stories of "respectability."

Directly or indirectly, they have taught me many lessons: Cowardice is one of the most dangerous forces in the world (and cowardly liberals should always be treated with suspicion). One must always write with blood or else not write at all. Sisterhood is far more than a pithy term for female bonding—it can, and has, changed the world. All revolutions require fun and laughter. Learning across generations not only sustains us but ensures that we don't have to reinvent the wheel every time. Radical change requires risk, loss, defiance, sacrifice, and setbacks, and is rarely recorded by historians in any depth or nuance (especially for the tales of radical women). And the stories we already know about feminism—and radical feminism in particular—are wholly, permanently incomplete.

To tell the stories in this volume, I have chosen to foreground their first-person accounts in the form of oral history. Because oral history seeks to both record and preserve oral testimony of historical events experienced firsthand, and because oral histories rely upon people's accounts of the past as connected to the present, this book relies heavily on the preservation of these women's words in order to craft a narrative of radical feminism and its relevance to contemporary feminisms. Oral histories allow for free-flowing conversations and long passages of verbatim quotes that showcase these women speaking in their own words about their histories; thus, the impressions, ideas, verbiage, tone, and conversation styles are determined by them rather than me.[1] These methods provide a unique framework for viewing the stories and testimonies of radical feminists active during the second wave (late 1960s and early 1970s).

Nevertheless, the relationship between their stories and my framing of their stories remains fraught with possibilities for misunderstandings and misinterpretations, though I have worked to minimize these whenever possible. Oral histories ask that we become *listeners*, letting people tell their stories. I embrace here the notion that these following chapters reflect the way that people select, recall, and reframe their experiences in light of current sociopolitical and biographical contexts; they speak here to us forty to fifty years after the second wave. As Susan Geiger wrote, "There is an interesting parallel, I think, between Jacqueline Hall's call 'for a historical practice that turns on partiality, that is self-conscious about perspective' and the stories and life stories oral historians relate, which are themselves partial, perspectival, and self-conscious. Feminist oral history methodology reflects and values these parallel activities— the practice of the researcher, the practice of the oral historian. Neither practice stands for the other, but if she is careful, the feminist historian's own interpretive product will encompass radical, respectful, newly accessible truths, and realities about women's lives."[2] These accounts are always partial, always shifting, always subject to revision and reframing, but they are still stories worth telling, arguably more necessary now than ever before.

While there is a small (and mighty) literature on the radical wing of second-wave feminism,[3] most of the historical studies use archival and written documents as sources of information and only a few pieces rely on a mixture of archival and interview techniques to trace the tactics, goals, and structures of radical feminist organizations. These works typically do not place central importance on the words, ideas, impressions, and sentiments of individual activists.[4] This book uniquely integrates a look at some of the early documents of radical feminism with extended oral histories. For ten years, I have interacted with these women in multiple ways: lengthy interviews, conversations in private between pairs of them and me, public forums where we debated radical feminism together, their public lectures at recent conferences, and keynote speeches delivered to university audiences. These multiple layers of interactions have led to fruitful discussions in a wide variety of contexts. I have also engaged in follow-up emails and phone calls to clarify and fact-check, thus enriching this book with a variety of conversations in a variety of times and places. The richness of these transcripts cannot be overstated; we are, the five of us, thinking together, making sense of the immensity of the past fifty years.

While I could have chosen many different women to give oral histories of early radical feminism, I selected these four women for multiple reasons. First, each of them contributed substantially to the birth of US radical feminism in the late 1960s and early 1970s, and each has an extensive body of provocative written work—mostly in the form of transcribed speeches and short essays—from which I can establish context for their archive of radical feminist thought. Second, as I had originally asked to interview them as part of a larger biographical project on Valerie Solanas—now published as *Valerie Solanas: The Defiant Life of the Woman Who Wrote SCUM (and Shot Andy Warhol)* with Feminist Press (2014)—I knew that they had all supported someone who symbolized and embodied women's rage. They did not shy away from difficult women and the transformational power of anger. Third, I wanted them to have a preexisting relationship with each other so that the four of them had some shared contexts during the second wave (e.g., overlaps in cities, organizations, and time-frames). Roxanne Dunbar-Ortiz and Dana Densmore were, and continue to be, good friends, and this bond led to interesting conversations when I interviewed them together. Similarly, Ti-Grace Atkinson and Kathie Sarachild had a history together that allowed for much mutual affection and a stimulating conversation based on that history. The dialogue contained in this book enriches the stories and narratives they provide, as they riff on each other's perspectives and debate different events. Finally, each of them, to differing degrees, rarely gave interviews to researchers or journalists and had some sense of wariness about appearing in the public eye despite each of them having major roles in radical feminist organizations. I had to earn their trust (a difficult process at times), but the result is that we hear in this book from crucial voices of the early radical feminist movement. This unprecedented access to their lives and thoughts provided stories, texts, and conversations that help to fill in some of the gaps of second-wave radical feminist history, while also showcasing how their reflections provide a useful bridge to today's feminist dialogues.

This book could be used as a roadmap for early second-wave radical feminist thinking, and in that sense, it provides signposts for moving between scholarship and activism; maps the terrain of many key issues like sex, love, and memory; provides warning labels for what to not repeat in the future; and gives a topography of the highs and lows of early radical feminist organizing. We learn about tactical decisions and major shifts in theoretical and philosophical thinking about rage, radicalism, and refusal, allowing us to better map out our next moves in light of this history. The book highlights ways to use old tools differently (e.g., exploring the utility of anger) and new tools more creatively (e.g., reimagining trans rights). We can better see the many miles traveled by older radical feminists, giving younger radical feminists better insight into how to prepare, what to avoid, what to expect, and how to archive and document these journeys. Most importantly, these stories have deep reverberations in the troubling political times we find ourselves in today. They remind us that change is not only possible but necessary; that we have an obligation to fight for and alongside each other; and that bravery, anger, and disobedience are values we must cultivate in ourselves and in future generations if we are to prevail over the ever-strengthening forces of misogyny, white supremacy, and patriarchy.

FIREBRAND FEMINISM

Introduction

The Necessity of Radical Feminism

Imagine a world—or summon it back to memory—when a husband
was required to countersign a wife's application for a credit card, a
bank loan, or automobile insurance, when psychiatrists routinely
located the cause of an unsatisfactory sex life in the frigid, castrating,
ballbreaking female partner, when abortion was an illegal, back-alley
procedure, when rape was the woman's fault, when nobody dared
talk about the battery that went on behind closed doors, or could file
a complaint about sexual harassment. And remember the hostile
humor that reinforced the times: the endless supply of mother-in-law
jokes, the farmer's daughter, the little old lady in tennis shoes, the
bored receptionist filing her nails, the dumb blond stenographer
perched on her boss's lap, the lecherous tycoon chasing his buxom
secretary around the desk. A revolution was brewing, but it took a
visionary to notice.

—SUSAN BROWNMILLER, *In Our Time: Memoir of a Revolution*

"LET'S ORDER THE ONE WITH TEN SCOOPS! WE NEED TO GO ALL
in," Ti-Grace Atkinson says gleefully to Kathie Sarachild. We sit together
at a Cajun restaurant (an homage to Ti-Grace's roots in Louisiana) in late
March of 2013 in Phoenix, Arizona, where three of us have, for the last
two hours, covered a dizzying array of subjects: disappointments about
politics, getting old, adorable cats with tumors, the importance (or unim-
portance) of orgasms, class action lawsuits, the best and worst of New
Orleans cooking, why I should no longer read or trust the *New York Times*,
ideal masturbation techniques, and the horrors of marriage.

There are times, in conversations like these, when I find it unimag-
inably confusing to merge the radicalness of these activists' lifetime

commitment to politics with their rather unassuming and nonthreatening physical appearances. These are old women, after all, with small statures, worries about osteoporosis, fears about paying their bills with limited Social Security income, and rather finicky schedules and preferences. In this country, we invisibilize, trivialize, and discard the lives of older women who look like them. But, as this book shows, these women are also still radicals with powerhouse minds, outrageous courage, blunt and sarcastic ways of speaking, and at times shockingly prescient and astute observations about the world. They are cat ladies, sure, but the cat is named Ruthless.[1]

Dessert has now arrived. The server delivers an absurd-looking sundae, ten scoops wide, slathered with chocolate and caramel sauce. Ti-Grace and Kathie, side by side in the booth, dive in, laughing and grinning. I sit across from them with a surreal sense of contradiction and awe. Earlier that day we sat together in a public forum discussing and debating the institutionalization of feminism, abortion rights, violence, radicalism, and revolution. I can rightly argue that I have rarely encountered two more serious women—serious about their work, serious about activism, serious about social change and the heavy price each has paid for trying to enact such change, serious about radical feminism and women's liberation. These are women who have put their bodies on the front lines of protests, screamed in the faces of authority and power, undermined and "unworked," and organized and recruited women from diverse backgrounds to care about the status of women in the world. They have been bullied, harassed, and imprisoned for their words and actions.

Historians of radical feminism have often highlighted divisions, infighting, conflicts, and struggles for coherence between and within different "waves" of feminist movements.[2] They have emphasized the many ways that the women's movement fractured and split apart (and, arguably, fell into disrepair and sputtered out). They have sought to understand why so many different groups emerged as offshoots and offspring of other groups, why so many groups imploded or became irrelevant, and the benefits and weaknesses of having a unified or splintered women's movement.[3] This is not my interest. On the contrary, I am interested in the kinds of provocative conversations I had at that Cajun restaurant, and the ways that these women—different in their approaches to thinking but deeply respectful of each other's positions—came together to share such affection and joy over their rather extreme dessert. I am interested in the delight I feel when I speak to them, the profound and moving stories they have told me, and the ways in which their narratives highlight the central relevance of radical feminism to contemporary feminist politics. They shaped their own history, took matters into their own hands; consequently, they matter in a *historical* sense, but they are also living subjects of their own stories, driven to imagine beyond their time and place. Their ideas continue to pulsate with vitality and audacity.

RADICAL FEMINISM AND ITS ORIGINS

> It is incredible to me that any woman should consider the fight for full equality won. It has just begun. There is hardly a field, economic or political, in which the natural and unaccustomed policy is not to ignore women. . . . Unless women are prepared to fight politically they must be content to be ignored politically.
>
> —ALICE PAUL, "WOMEN'S PARTY TO CALL A CONVENTION"

Radicalism means, most basically, "going to the roots," or looking to dig deeper and deeper into the foundations of something in order to understand its system, structure, or core. Radical *feminism*, then, seeks to look at the roots of the structural and systemic qualities of patriarchy and sexism, paying particular attention to how seemingly private experiences (e.g., sexuality, the body, the family, emotions, or spirituality) connect to broader structures that disempower women and limit their freedom and autonomy. Radical feminists of the 1970s took on, for example, topics as diverse as abortion, love, domestic housework, sexuality and celibacy, lesbianism, self-defense, media representation, daycare centers, and, in one famous episode, the eroticism of the Virgin Mary. (Ti-Grace was physically assaulted by Patricia Buckley Bozell, sister of noted conservative William F. Buckley, in March 1971 at Catholic University, for discussing the Virgin Mary's sexuality and suggesting that the Virgin Mary was more "used" than if she had participated in a sexual conception.[4]) Second-wave radical feminists in the early 1970s were, as this example showed, interested in challenging the core foundations of sexism, and were largely unafraid of confrontation, personal risk, and challenges to traditional thinking about gender and sexuality.

While the material in chapter 2 ("Radicalism and Refusal") illuminates this complexity between radical and liberal feminism in far more nuance and detail, it is crucial to note that radical feminism differs quite dramatically from its more liberal counterpart.[5] Liberalism in general focuses on individual equality and liberty, with special attention to concepts like freedom of speech, freedom of the press, freedom of religion, democracy, and civil rights. The freedoms of religion, thought, and expression form the core of liberal beliefs.[6] By extension, modern political liberalism, which began with Franklin Delano Roosevelt's policies of the New Deal, emphasized caring about the welfare of the people and working toward equality for all.[7] (Liberalism can also, of course, veer into an embrace of the free market with an emphasis on individual choices within the free market economy, also known as "neoliberalism"; this rhetoric has infused ideas of "choice" and "agency" with hyperindividualistic notions of consumerism.) As Michael Walzer wrote when critiquing liberalism, "Each individual imagines [herself] absolutely free, unencumbered, and on [her] own—and enters society, accepting its obligations, only in order to minimize [her] risks."[8]

This rhetoric of political liberalism then extended into the core foundations of liberal feminism, which, unlike radical feminism, often focuses on individual "empowerment" without looking at the bigger social structures that systematically restrict and subjugate women. Mary Becker wrote, "Part of the problem is the failure of feminists, particularly feminists working for legal change, to look at the big picture: a social structure that is male-centered, male-identified, male-dominated, and which valorizes qualities narrowly defined as masculine."[9] While many groups of feminists took seriously the struggles of working-class women (particularly socialist feminists, anti-imperialist feminists, and postcolonial feminists), most liberal feminism emphasized, particularly at the outset, the plight of more formally affluent women, as bell hooks has aptly critiqued: "From the very onset of the women's liberation movement these women [working-class and poor women] were suspicious of feminism because they recognized the limitations inherent in its definition. They recognized the possibility that feminism defined as social inequality with men might easily become a movement that would primarily affect the social standing of white middle- and upper-class groups while affecting only in a very marginal way the social status of working-class and poor women."[10]

Liberal feminists emphasized the role of equality between men and women and "within-system" social change, while radical feminism emphasized structural inequalities and targeted the entire sociopolitical system that enabled women's oppression. For liberal feminists, incremental changes to norms and attitudes aimed at repairing gender biases—such as achieving pay equity, promoting women in workforces, breaking glass ceilings, getting more women into positions of power (governmental and corporate), and fighting back against hostile forms of sexism—constituted central goals. The National Organization for Women (NOW), which once included numerous radical feminists in its ranks (and even in its presidency), now promotes a largely liberal feminist agenda rather than a radical feminist one; its radical demands have largely been forgotten and ignored. NOW also focuses much of its resources on making electoral changes in the government, and mostly does not challenge the basic premises and foundations of gender inequalities. When it was founded, NOW sought to end job discrimination and fight for equal pay alongside health care, child care, and pregnancy leave. Its goals remain similar today—within-system change is at the fore, though its scope has expanded to include issues that affect a wider range of women, including disability rights, global feminisms, and antiracism.[11]

To push the metaphor a bit further, liberal feminists seek to repair the existing house without tearing down or examining its foundational structures, while radical feminists want to look at the root of the problems in the foundations of the house. If the house is built on shaky foundations, they may even want to burn the house to the ground and rebuild it altogether. Liberal feminists resist such dramatic gestures and thus often serve as the voices of moderate social change (and are remarkably fickle when it comes to political struggle). Liberals tend to follow the lead of mass public sentiment (for example, neither Barack Obama nor Hillary Clinton explicitly and unequivocally supported same-sex marriage until years after the 2008 election, when it became more fashionable, and they never explicitly talked about it as *right* or *moral* prior to 2012).[12] Radicals, on the other hand, often revel in unfashionable ideas long before they become normalized or mainstreamed; they do not mind offending people and will strongly call out injustices that people do not want to publicly address or rectify. Their commitment to understanding the roots of patriarchy means that they typically address difficult or painful subjects without the luxury of having mainstream audiences already in agreement with them. The claim made by the Industrial Workers of the World (an early twentieth-century union, also known as the Wobblies, that wanted unions for the entire working class and preferred direct action over electoral techniques) that "Humanity advances over a path blazed by radicals and stained with their blood" is true both literally and metaphorically.

Radical feminists focus on the broader structures of power that underlie, constrict, and inform women's oppressed social status. As second-wave radical feminist Ellen Willis wrote, "We argued that male supremacy was in itself a systemic form of domination—a set of material, institutionalized relations, not just bad attitudes. Men had power and privilege and like any other ruling class would defend their interests; challenging that power required a revolutionary movement of women. And since the male-dominated left would inevitably resist understanding or opposing male power, the radical feminist movement must be autonomous, create its own theory and set its own priorities."[13] She went on to write, "We will never organize the mass of women by subordinating their concrete interests to a 'higher' ideology. To believe that concentrating on women's issues is not really revolutionary is self-depreciation. Our demand for freedom involves not only the overthrow of capitalism but the destruction of the patriarchal family system."[14]

This complex description of radical feminism and its differences from liberal feminism raises an even more important question: What is at stake in radical feminist *activism*? This book gives details about the lives of four radical feminist women and the seriousness of their work and legacies, but it also showcases the costs of that work. Several of them were imprisoned for their activism and lost jobs because of it. They often lived without the financial safety net of a long-term partner (a price they pay now more than ever as they rely on Social Security incomes that disadvantage older unmarried women). They paid the price for their work in time (all of them devoted years of their lives to activism and organizing), including time away from their children, or not having children at all.

Attacking the foundational principles of American society—greed, individualism, patriarchy, media, family, church, et cetera—required enormous energy and commitment, including personal and reputational risk. These women were belittled in mainstream news media—*Time* ran a piece that argued "Many of the new feminists are surprisingly violent in mood and seem to be trying, in fact, to repel other women rather than attract them . . . 'Watch out! You may meet a real castrating female,'"[15] while the *New York Times* said of Ti-Grace, "Miss Atkinson is 29, unmarried, good-looking (in The Times, she has been described as 'softly sexy,' which is not *necessarily* a compliment to a feminist)"[16]—or, more painfully, put down by fellow feminists of their time. Still more, they continue to be trashed by many contemporary feminists, often enduring accusations of being out of touch, trans-exclusionary, moody, or irrelevant (see chapter 5, "Women as a Social and Political Class," for more details about this).

Perhaps most dangerously, as feminism has become more institutionalized—in the form of women's studies/gender studies programs and departments, more women in government, and more corporate leaders (and the deeply problematic "Lean In" movement[17])—feminism has become more invested in notions of *respectability* (and, by association, patience and likability). This may signal a death knell to radical whistle-blowing, rambunctious public activism, and the politics and ethics of troublemaking. Feminism began as a social movement based on collective activism, but has arguably morphed in recent years further into discourses about neoliberal individual "choice" (e.g., feminism enables the choice to wear makeup, engage in BDSM, get married in a red dress, or shave pubic hair), thus obscuring the radical edge of feminism with the thick goo of "girl power" and "women's empowerment."[18] (I have often written about the crushing pressures on women to remove their body hair, and women's overwhelming compliance with this norm, as one such example of how norms of respectability get imposed onto women.[19]) Within academia, feminists must engage in the same sorts of rhetorics, politics, and priorities as other university professors, seeking "respectability" through highly individualistic publications, conference presentations, and (too often) a distancing from radical social activism. As Roxanne Dunbar-Ortiz said in a public plenary talk she gave with Dana Densmore and me, "We all three here are activist-scholars, militant feminists, trying to embody all of those things together without breaking them down separately, which hasn't been great for a successful career in academia."[20] And yet, if we are true to the foundational principles of feminism itself, ones that value concrete social change and an unraveling of assumptions about gender and power, we would understand that activism, scholarship, and militant politics *must* go hand in hand; stripping any of those aspects away, or distancing from feminist praxis, would insult and undermine the core values of feminism itself.

We need radicalism—its difficulty, its provocations, its challenges to notions of respectability and politeness, its wildness, its insistence that we keep on digging—more today than ever before. And, more specifically, we need radical *feminists* in this particular social and political moment, with the ascendancy of xenophobia, sexism, racism, white supremacy, and patriarchy saturating the landscape of American politics. We need persistent complainers, incessant troublemakers, and a threat of disruption to the status quo. Without the presence of radical feminists, gender norms stay static, economics create greater gender gaps in salaries, and few feminist laws are passed.[21] Without knowing some of these histories of our feminist foremothers, we risk losing their knowledge—or seeing second-wave feminism as Gloria Steinem and Betty Friedan, rather than as Florynce Kennedy and Valerie Solanas. We need edges and roughness, controversy and contradiction, arguments and rage, persistence and guts. We must refute cowardice and simplicity, politeness and popularity, respectability and self-promotion. Ultimately, as these women's narratives show, we need to fight against discourses of patience and moderation, insulation and unity, seeing these as outgrowths of those unwilling to take risks and too willing to hide behind the shifting tides of political sentiment without trying to *change* those sentiments. Instead, we need firebrand feminism—troublemaking, agitating, revolutionary, and hotheaded.

WHY FIREBRAND FEMINISM?

This book features the politics, lives, and works of four radical feminist women—Ti-Grace Atkinson, Kathie Sarachild, Roxanne Dunbar-Ortiz, and Dana Densmore—whose activism, leadership, organizing, and political theories changed the trajectory of early US feminist politics by pushing the women's movement into a more radical posture. Together, we look back at the histories of second-wave radical feminism while also looking forward to contemporary feminist conversations and the relevance of early second-wave radical feminism to those conversations. Their "take no prisoners" stance about everything from academia to liberalism, "girl power" to trans studies, indigenous struggles to the brainwashing of women, weaves together the core of this book. In this sense, this book is far more than a story *about* these women—although much of their bravery, ferocity, intelligence, and personality are clearly on display here—as our conversations serve as a backdrop for an extended conversation about the impact of early radical feminism on contemporary feminist thought. Ultimately, this book showcases their provocative and "still ahead of their time" thoughts alongside the pressing challenges of creating oral histories of radical feminism.

The question of why this book, and why *now*, also haunts the dialogues showcased in these subsequent chapters. Surprisingly few texts have meaningfully documented the history of radical feminism in the United States, and those that do exist focus primarily on anthologizing classic radical feminist writings or recounting events rather than framing radical feminism as something with clear connections to contemporary (third-wave and beyond) feminisms. Few scholars have spoken at length with radical feminist women. Even more, the history of feminism has clearly prioritized the histories and lived experiences of liberal (that is, incremental, organization-based, institutional) feminisms rather than their more radical counterparts. The continued, celebrated success of people like Gloria Steinem[22] and Robin Morgan often serves to smooth out the edges of radical feminism and to, as Ti-Grace Atkinson would say, "defang" the movement.[23] Second-wave radical feminists today are often remembered (if they are remembered at all) through a lens of dismissal (e.g., "transphobic"), rejection (e.g., "too white"), condescension (e.g., "silly" or "too narrow"), bafflement (e.g., "Why karate?"), and uncertainty (e.g., "What's the difference?"). I am interested in rejecting these overly simplistic mischaracterizations of radical feminism by instead highlighting some of its edges, complicating existing narratives of feminism and radical feminism, threading new memories into our existing stories of radical feminism, and carving out space for more contentious or difficult stories of the late 1960s feminist movement.

The oral histories presented here showcase the determination of early radical feminists to shape the conversation about a variety of subjects that would eventually come to define third-wave feminisms: sexuality, making an archive, body politics, indigenous rights, trans rights, refusals, intersectionality, and the importance of feminist rage. These four women still have much to say about the directions (past and present) of feminism and the movements aligned with it. And, though they all consider themselves colleagues and allies, they differ from each other in meaningful and productive ways. These points of contention and overlap inject the book with a spirited, controversial, and sometimes combative flair, as the activists not only explore their differences with each other, but also work toward refuting the premises of liberal feminism in its entirety. They also skewer traditions of conservatism, reminding us that the forces of fascism (which often arrive with a happy, friendly face) and oppression are never totally out of reach. Further, these women embody the assertion that women must *act collectively and boldly* in times of great social stress. Together, we examine women who resisted (and how they resisted) in order to think about, study, and understand the *contributions* of radical feminism. They reflect on, and fire back about, the conditions of late-1960s feminism as it speaks to today's world.

Firebrand Feminism showcases the stories and reflections of four women who have led, by all accounts, extraordinary lives. We travel widely in these conversations: through "red-diaper" childhoods, adventures with Sandinistas, protests, sit-ins, freedom rides, marches on the Pentagon, separatist communes, the halls of academia, and militant coalition-building. In doing so, we see that these women, along with their feminist comrades, inhabited and transformed the history of women's rights, sexuality, love, friendship, science, and politics, and they did so largely without the recognition they deserve. In essence, this book addresses the trials and tribulations of being a radical feminist over a fifty-year cycle of ebbs and flows of feminist mobilizations. It is meant as a way to promote dialogue and discourse, provoke responses and discussions, and challenge oversimplified constructions of radical feminism.

This book explores six key themes: Feminist Rage (chapter 1); Radicalism and Refusal (chapter 2); Tactics (chapter 3); Sex, Love, and Bodies (chapter 4); Women as a Social and Political Class (chapter 5); and Intergenerational Dialogues and the Future of Radical Feminism (chapter 6). I chose these chapters based not only on these four feminists' written works but also on the issues that they spoke about with the most frequency and passion—for example, they worked more on reproductive rights than on prison reform, and they thought more about sex and love than they did about interpersonal violence. Within these six themes, these women ask (and answer) difficult questions about identity politics and tactical interventions, critique our obsession with sexuality and the body as the canvas upon which we examine social inequalities, and reframe the importance of seeing women as a collective force. As the women fuse together activism and theory and fill in crucial blind spots in radical feminist history, this book calls to task liberal feminists, critical body scholars, historians, queer theorists, and social movement scholars, asking them all to think more deeply about the impact of radical feminism and its role in inciting social change. Drawing upon their narratives, I craft an argument for the sustained relevance and importance of radical feminist thought, and for the crucial work yet to be done that must draw from and rely upon their stories. Ultimately, *Firebrand Feminism* looks carefully at the future of radical feminist thought and the ways that these ongoing conversations invite us to carefully assess our history before we can adequately move forward into a more radical future of feminism.

INTRODUCING THE FIREBRAND FEMINISTS

As I introduce each of the radical feminists included in this book, I showcase not only their accomplishments but also their own narratives about their lives. Wherever possible, I have included an assortment of details about them that give a window into their childhoods, early feminist coming-of-age stories, relationship and children statuses, major written accomplishments, engagement with radical feminism, activist endeavors, careers, and current activities. I weave together in this next section the biographical stories of their lives with some of their own words to fill out these details more fully and vividly and to contextualize how their personal biographies relate to their feminist activism.

Ti-Grace Atkinson

One of the founding foremothers of second-wave radical feminism, Ti-Grace Atkinson was born on November 9, 1938, in Baton Rouge, Louisiana. Named by her grandmother to reflect the Cajun roots of her childhood—with "Ti" coming from the French word *petite* and "Grace" for her grandmother, Grace Sydmir Broadus—Ti-Grace grew up the youngest of five girls in the family. Her sisters also each had two names: Robin Louise, Mary-Wynne, Frances Gay ("Frani-Gay"), Thelma Byrd ("Temi-Be"). Her two older brothers, John and Richard ("Dickie"), both died quite young; John drowned in a swimming pool at age eight, and Dickie died of double spinal meningitis at one year of age.

On her name, Ti-Grace said, "I kept the 'Ti,' which is Cajun, and I kept it because I knew I was going to live in the North and I did not want to forget or let anybody else forget that that was part of my heritage." Her father, Francis Decker Atkinson, a chemical engineer, moved the family around after he left Standard Oil to work for the Atomic Energy Commission in Hanford: "I changed schools many, many times before I graduated from high school, so it's sort of more of a modern story in that way. It's so odd because each of us thinks that our childhood is more or less what everybody else's is, even though you know it isn't."[24] Ti-Grace watched her father navigate the oil business and its corruption from a very early age.

Ti-Grace's mother, Thelma Broadus Atkinson, grew up in Virginia with traditional Southern values that distinguished between Dixie and non-Dixie states: "Both sides of my family, they were warring sides, so that also confused things. My grandmother never referred to my father in any way but 'That Yankee.' 'Francis, for a Yankee, you're not that bad.' He tried to please her for years, and she'd thank him, but he was a Yankee." Ti-Grace describes growing up in a family of all women after her grandfather died: "The idea that women were inferior in any way was just something I'd never heard. It gives you a little different attitude about things." Still, she described her mother as "very traditional, like with a vengeance. Her variation was 'Southern Belle.' Everything would put her in a swoon. She was tough as nails, but she was delicate—very unhappy, very talented, brilliant." When Ti-Grace once asked her why she bothered with graduate school, her mother burst into tears. "She was born in 1899, so she came of age just when women got the vote and the idea that you could do anything—but not much had changed. So you went to school thinking you could do anything, but then there were no real jobs or careers."[25]

She remembered her childhood as full of secrets, even about health issues: "In my family, you weren't supposed to speak up. You weren't supposed to talk back. When we had been at Hanford, there were all of these nuclear waste leaks and I was diagnosed with leukemia and it was all hush-hushed. I'd been really sick when we went up to Alaska the summer I was fifteen. There was a lot of lying going on."[26] She later found out that the radiation effects of uranium had made her and others sick.

The teenage years presented some difficult challenges for Ti-Grace. Her mother had married her father, then divorced him, and then again remarried him, which resulted in moving around frequently to chase his various new jobs. Ti-Grace admits that she felt unhappy with this arrangement, so she eventually ran away from home to live with her older sister, Robin, in San Francisco: "They hired detectives to find me, but because my first name is so difficult, the detectives kept getting lost. Nobody would ever put it down right, thank God. So, then they found me, and my mother was furious because I had embarrassed the whole family, so she said, 'How would you like to get married?' This was when I was only sixteen, seventeen. So I said, 'To whom?' The only person I'd gone out with was a very (like seventh!) distant cousin, so we got married and that was that. My grandmother was furious. She wouldn't come to the wedding."[27]

Marriage had disastrous consequences for Ti-Grace. "I was pretty catatonic," she recalled.

> I was very depressed. I didn't realize it. I mean, I was just in a deep, deep depression. I didn't recognize how odd it was until, if Charley [her husband] would leave for a long period, I'd jump up and I'd be racing around and running to New York. "What's going on here? I have all this energy!" I was resentful, and I was also trying to fit into this role. He claims that he knew I was

inching toward the door when we got married, but I wasn't really conscious of that, primarily because I didn't know how I could survive. I think I have an inclination toward depression, but I think that I'm able to keep it under control. I couldn't keep it under control with the marriage. I can't keep it under control if I'm really going against myself. Then it overwhelms me and becomes about survival.

With the help of her grandmother, she left the marriage. Her grandmother said to her, "'That's enough of this. I've been thinking about this and you have character. You don't need him. You can survive. You are not going to necessarily live in luxury, but you can manage.' So I went home and filed for divorce."[28]

At the time of the divorce, Ti-Grace had enrolled in a five-year BFA program at the University of Pennsylvania and at the Pennsylvania Academy of the Fine Arts. After her divorce she needed an income to support herself, and she subsequently met people in New York who suggested that she try her hand at art criticism: "They would pay for my trips to New York, and I got into writing criticism." This also led her to feminism. She recalled that she was first drawn to feminist ideas through French feminist philosopher Simone de Beauvoir's *Second Sex*:[29]

In the summer of 1962, a sculptor friend of mine was reading *The Second Sex*. He said to me, "You've got to read this book!" So here I am: I'm a painter and living down in SoHo, going to Elaine de Kooning's for showers because I had no hot water, and I started reading *The Second Sex*. I realized what had turned me off about marriage was something about the structure. When my ex-husband and I went to get my divorce there wasn't "no-fault" yet. My husband said, "I can get you for desertion," and I said, "You were the one who moved." Well, that's when I found out about the law—that two people become one and the law is determined by wherever the husband lives. *Whoa.* I had lost my freedom of movement when I got married. I was trying to remember what I signed when I got married, and all I could remember was some little piece of paper with hearts or flowers or birds near the place we would sign. It's the only contract of its kind where the terms aren't listed.[30]

Ending the marriage, Ti-Grace said, proved quite difficult in an age that predated "no-fault" divorce. "The judge said, 'There's no reason for this divorce here.' I said, 'We don't like each other.' 'So what does that have to do with anything?' I said, 'We have nothing in common.' He said, 'What, does he beat you?' I said no. 'Well, you have to have some reason.' I said, 'Sometimes he drinks a little.' 'Oh, he's a drunk, okay.' I knew I'd never get married again. Why do women keep getting married? It's conceivable somebody could be happy *despite* being married but never *because* they were married." The divorce gave Ti-Grace newfound freedom to read and explore politics:

> I started reading all these books about the women's movement. This must have been 1962, 1963. I had a lot of anger, and *The Second Sex* just goes on and on and on and on and on and on. It's like, *drip, drip, drip*; you know, it really affected me. In 1965, I wrote Simone de Beauvoir. It was a long letter and was really quite radical. I knew the Church was a main enemy. I knew you've got to get rid of this, this, this, this, and we need to organize something to do it. Beauvoir wrote me back. She said that all women were discriminated against, but the form it took varied, so it didn't make sense to organize outside of national boundaries. She gave me Betty [Friedan]'s name and said she was pulling together this organization.[31] I finally called Betty in 1966. I had never had any political experience. I had had political exposure, I realize now, but not in terms of doing things. I wasn't a red-diaper baby.[32] I wasn't any of these things.[33]

After writing for *ARTnews* with plans to pursue a life as an art critic, Ti-Grace changed plans quite dramatically. She joined NOW when it first began in 1966, eventually becoming the president of the tristate region for New York, New Jersey, and Connecticut in 1967. An ardent critic of marriage, she wrote: "As women become freer, more independent, more self-sufficient, their interest in (i.e., their need for) men decreases, and their desire for the construct of marriage which properly entails children (i.e., a family) decreases proportionate to the increase in their self-sufficiency."[34]

In 1968, she split off from NOW forcefully and publicly when the organization decided to maintain its organizational hierarchical structure (for example, insisting on a single long-term president rather than mutual governance or rotating monthly leadership among the women) and when it refused to address systemic issues surrounding abortion and sexuality. NOW also refused to support Valerie Solanas after she shot Andy Warhol on June 3, 1968. Shortly thereafter, Ti-Grace founded the October 17th Movement,[35] which a year later evolved into The Feminists, a radical feminist group that remained active from 1968 to 1973 (though Ti-Grace's personal involvement with the group ended in April 1970). Ti-Grace said of this split with NOW, "Everybody in NOW said they wanted a revolution. Everybody wanted a revolution. I didn't know anybody who didn't want a revolution and I couldn't understand why every time it came to an action, we would have big fights even though we all said we wanted the same thing." In particular, Ti-Grace wanted to go after marriage as a target for feminist criticism: "They weren't going to go after that. They'd say, 'Oh yeah,' and sort of agree with you on the surface, but when you talked about doing something about it, there was no way."[36] With The Feminists, Ti-Grace could thrive as an activist and public speaker, unchained by the constraints of NOW and its liberal "within-system" goals.

Throughout the late 1960s and early 1970s, Ti-Grace self-published several pamphlets and gave numerous activist speeches on college campuses and community forums in US, Canadian, French, and German cities. Most notably, Ti-Grace made history by arguing publicly against the Catholic Church (and being physically assaulted during a speech at Catholic University), crusading against marriage as a form of spiritual and physical oppression, advocating political lesbianism as a response to patriarchy, and claiming that vaginal orgasm represented, as she titled one speech, a "mass hysterical survival response."[37] She protested the anti-woman policies of the *Ladies' Home Journal*, battled the New York City marriage bureau, fought to reconfigure abortion politics away from "right to privacy" as its basis, aggressively protested the *New York Times*'s gender-segregated want ads (where women were relegated to secretaries and stewardesses and men got all of the intellectual jobs), publicly defended *SCUM Manifesto* author Valerie Solanas after she shot Andy Warhol by saying that some woman had finally *done something* about the oppression they experienced, and was recognized by the *New York Times Magazine* as feminism's "haute thinker."[38]

During this time, she also forged an alliance with Simone de Beauvoir, befriending her and visiting Paris, where she gave speeches on women's rights, female nationalism, sexual violence against women, and abortion organizing. She supported herself by "living on the edge." In the early 1970s, she was asked by Links Books to compile an assortment of her highly controversial speeches and writings into a collection called *Amazon Odyssey: The First Collection of Writings by the Political Pioneer of the Women's Movement*, which was published in 1974. She also pursued philosophy as an academic discipline and specifically focused on political philosophy and the philosophy of logic. Ti-Grace has spent much of her life teaching in different universities, including the University of Washington, Columbia University, Case Western Reserve, Harvard University, and Tufts University.

These accomplishments, impressive as they are, still do not fully convey Ti-Grace's role as a nucleus of radical feminism. She stayed active in the women's movement from the mid-1960s until the mid-1990s, working tirelessly for women's rights. Perhaps what is most significant is the sustained personal contact that Ti-Grace had with a multitude of her famous contemporaries: famed Black Panther lawyer Florynce Kennedy, feminist writer and theorist Simone de Beauvoir, first-wave pioneer Alice Paul, *Feminine Mystique* writer Betty Friedan, iconoclast and would-be assassin Valerie Solanas, radical antipornography crusader Andrea Dworkin, *Dialectic of Sex* writer Shulamith Firestone, *Sexual Politics* writer Kate Millett, radical feminists Anne Koedt and Ellen Willis, famed critic of psychiatry Phyllis Chesler, photographer-of-the-bizarre Diane Arbus, and Warhol superstar Edie Sedgwick (among others).

Since 2007, she has been pulling together her personal papers and general archive, covering some fifty-plus years, and trying to make sense of these decades. Most of her papers now reside at Harvard University's Schlesinger Library, though some are owned by the Dobkin Collection, and some are still in her possession.[39] She has worked to remain self-sufficient; in

2015, she organized the tenants in her building to fight against mandatory eviction from the city of Cambridge, Massachusetts, saying, defiantly, "They messed with the wrong bitch."[40]

Kathie Sarachild

Kathie Sarachild (born Kathie Amatniek on July 8, 1943) was a founding organizer of the women's liberation movement of the 1960s, with a lifetime commitment to "freedom organizing," a phrase she learned as a volunteer with the Student Nonviolent Coordinating Committee (SNCC)[41] in the Mississippi civil rights movement in 1964 and 1965.[42] Growing up as a red-diaper baby, she learned very early on about struggles for justice and the importance of fighting against inequality. In the seventh grade, she campaigned with her mother to allow girls to take shop classes and boys to take home economics classes. In college, she helped defeat the curfew and sign-out restrictions on women's dormitories and later opposed the Vietnam War as the only woman on the editorial board of the *Harvard Crimson*.[43]

While doing activist work with SNCC, she spent thirteen days in jail; the house of a family she stayed with was teargas-bombed and shot into. She helped to register voters during Freedom Summer in Batesville, Mississippi.[44] Guided by the SNCC organizers to "fight your own oppressors," Kathie has been working primarily in the women's liberation branch of the freedom movement since 1967, and has also been active in the labor movement. In 1968, she crafted slogans like "Sisterhood Is Powerful"—first used in a flyer she wrote for the keynote speech she gave for New York Radical Women's first public action at the convocation of the Jeannette Rankin Brigade[45]—and developed strategies that fueled the wildfire-like spread of feminism.

Kathie designed a program for "consciousness-raising," a tool used by women's liberation groups to analyze women's experiences. Two friends and colleagues, Shulamith ("Shulie") Firestone and Anne Koedt, called Kathie "the originator of consciousness-raising."[46] Kathie first presented her paper "A Program for Feminist 'Consciousness-Raising'" at the First National Women's Liberation Conference outside of Chicago on November 27, 1968. It was later published in *Notes from the Second Year* in 1970; the collection included articles on women's experiences, theories of radical feminism, and the founding of radical feminism, along with a series of pieces on consciousness-raising and organizing. Kathie later wrote "Consciousness-Raising: A Radical Weapon," a paper presented to the First National Conference of Stewardesses for Women's Rights in 1973 in New York City.[47]

The concept of consciousness-raising—and of much of radical feminism—argues that people must use their own lives as a basis for political activism, bringing in seemingly minute or trivial aspects of life (love, sex, the body, domesticity, and so on) into the fight against patriarchal oppression.[48] Kathie wrote, in "A Program for Feminist 'Consciousness-Raising,'" "In our groups let's share our feelings and pool them. Let's let ourselves go and see where our feelings lead us. Our feelings will lead us to ideas and then to actions. Our feelings will lead us to our theory, our theory to our action, our feelings about that action to new theory and then to new action."[49]

Involved in some of the dramatic actions that made the "women's liberation movement" a household term, she was one of four young women at the 1968 protest of the Miss America pageant who hung the women's liberation banner inside the convention hall in Atlantic City. The protests drew over four hundred feminists to the city; they famously threw symbols of women's oppression into a "Freedom Trash Can," including tampons, false eyelashes, mops, bras, and kitchenware.[50] Kathie famously shouted "Women's liberation!" and "No more Miss America!" as the new Miss America was being crowned.[51]

In 1969, Kathie led the new radical feminist group Redstockings in the disruption of a New York State abortion reform hearing where legislators were listening to a so-called "expert" panel consisting of twelve men and a nun. Redstockings interrupted the hearing to demand that women testify as the real experts on abortion and to demand a repeal of all abortion prohibitions.[52] This led, soon afterward, to the first "abortion speak-out" of the women's liberation movement: a public hearing where women discussed their experiences with the then-illegal procedure. This was the first use of the term "speak-out" by Women's Liberation. Kathie also wrote the Redstockings' "Principles"[53] and was editor of the anthology

Feminist Revolution, published by Redstockings in 1975 and by Random House in 1978.[54] She also served as the founding coeditor of *Woman's World* newspaper in 1971.

Kathie grew up with her mother, Sara Amatniek, and her sister, Joan Amatniek. Sara was an award-winning artist and printmaker and an active member of the National Association of Women Artists; she was a member of NOW and participated in Redstockings alongside her daughter.[55] In 1968, Kathie began using the matrilineal last name "Sarachild" to honor her mother and to protest the expectation that children would always take their father's or husband's last name.[56]

Kathie married Daniel Harmeling,[57] a fellow civil rights activist, in Gainesville, Florida, in January of 1995, and has four stepchildren. For many years Kathie supported herself and her movement work with earnings as a union-affiliated motion picture editor in New York City. Today she is analyzing, organizing, and mobilizing for women's liberation as director of the Redstockings Archives for Action project and the Redstockings Women's Liberation Archives.[58]

Roxanne Dunbar-Ortiz

Roxanne Dunbar-Ortiz was born on September 10, 1938 in San Antonio, Texas, where she lived only a short time before relocating permanently to a rural part of central Oklahoma. The daughter of a landless farmer, Moyer Haywood Pettibone Scarberry Dunbar, and a half–Native American mother, Louise Edna Curry Dunbar, Roxanne grew up poor and suffered from disabling bronchial asthma as a child. She had three older siblings—two brothers and a sister. Her paternal grandfather, Emmett Victor Dunbar, a white settler, farmer, and veterinarian, was a labor activist and Socialist in Oklahoma with the Industrial Workers of the World (IWW, or "the Wobblies") from the early 1900s to 1920. The Wobblies worked to abolish interest and profits and advocated for "public ownership of everything, no military draft, no military, no police, and the equality of women and all races."[59] Roxanne believes that the stories of her grandfather inspired her to lifelong social justice activism.[60] Her father was born in 1907, two years after the IWW, and he was named after three of the organization's founders: William Moyer, Big Bill Haywood, and George Pettibone.[61] A prominent union activist, he organized sharecroppers, tenants, cotton pickers, and wheat thrashers throughout the area and, as a consequence, was beaten by the KKK, which left him with brain damage; he eventually moved the family to Texas because the KKK ran him and fellow Wobblies off. Roxanne recounted that her father always said that the rich wheat farmers bankrolled the Klan: "They swelled up like a tick—night riding, killing stock, burning barns and crops, lynching, burning crosses. Good Christians they were."[62]

Roxanne's mother, Louise, fiercely religious and a stark contrast to Roxanne's father's staunch atheism, had a difficult childhood of her own. Roxanne said, "She grew up harsh, you know—a little 'half-breed' on the streets, an orphan. She got saved by the Baptist church and she became a very rigid antidrinking person. Her dad was an alcoholic and she probably drank until she got saved, even as a kid. Her brother was a lifelong alcoholic. She became a fanatic about it. We were really poor and she was okay until she started drinking again and then the demons came out of her. She was really violent."[63] Roxanne was thirteen years old when Louise began drinking again; she noticed that her mother drank in secret, with bottles falling out of her purse or car. Drinking alcohol was illegal in Oklahoma at the time. "She was arrested a lot," Roxanne said, "but people would just say she had a mental illness and she was crazy."[64] Prior to that, Roxanne had forged an identity she admired: "I finished school that year on top of the world: I had managed, despite asthma and vitiligo, to find my niche in the community at the top. I was a good Baptist girl, a Rainbow Girl, the smartest girl and the best typist. I had arrived and felt confident. Now I would be in high school and read Shakespeare, act in school plays, perhaps even make the baseball team, because I was growing out of my asthma. But the ominous summer that followed my graduation foreshadowed a bad time ahead."[65]

During Roxanne's high school years, Louise continued to escalate her drinking but also became more independent of her husband, taking a job as an assistant at a newspaper. Louise beat Roxanne and repeatedly tried to get boys to marry her (against Roxanne's will). When her mother's drinking escalated even further, Roxanne decided she needed to leave: "I felt trapped alone with my parents, and scared for my life. Nighttime was filled with terror that kept me awake and trembling. Mama and Daddy would fight all night after he stumbled in drunk, and she screamed accusations about his carousing."[66] Roxanne left Piedmont, Oklahoma, at age sixteen, to live first with her brother and then with her sister. She got a job working at the second-largest bank in Oklahoma City, and she started trade school.[67]

During that time, she met a boy, Dan Callarman, whom she married once she turned eighteen. Roxanne wrote, "Marriage was my way out of my class and into the middle class."[68] For a time, Roxanne worked at the bank while supporting her husband through school; she remembered this time as "alienated labor" in which she was overworked, broke, and lonely until she eventually got fired for suggesting that the bank workers needed a union. She got work at a minimum-wage job shortly thereafter and experienced intensifying symptoms of insomnia, night terrors, menstrual cramps, migraines, and asthma attacks. In 1960, immediately after her husband finished school, they left Oklahoma together for San Francisco, California, where Roxanne would live for most of her life. She never saw her mother again; Louise died in 1968.[69]

On the drive to California, Roxanne had an epiphany that she would need to leave her husband and forge ahead alone: "I acknowledged that my destiny would not be with [Dan]. I would have to find my way alone somehow, someday, without family or protection. I found myself headed for the Promised Land, without God, without a history, born again in a sense, in search of freedom."[70] After arriving in San Francisco, she stayed married for a short time longer and immediately enrolled at San Francisco State College, taking classes in history while slogging through the domestic hell of marriage: "I did the marketing and cooked the meals, afterward washing the dishes. Weekly, I hauled the dirty laundry to the Laundromat and I ironed, swept, vacuumed, and scrubbed. I managed all of our expenses."[71] In the midst of taking extra classes and managing the household, she got pregnant with her daughter, Michelle Callarman, who was born on October 20, 1962. Roxanne divorced Michelle's father two years later. Though Dan eventually secured full custody of Michelle due to "desertion" (after Roxanne went to Mexico City for the summer with her boyfriend and future husband, Jean-Louis), she and her daughter stayed quite close.

In 1963, Roxanne graduated from San Francisco State College, a largely working-class university that focused on undergraduate education, with a major in history. Following graduation, she left her life in San Francisco to join activists in Cuba; later, she worked with the American Indian Movement (AIM) and the women's movement. From 1967 to 1972, she was a full-time activist, living in a variety of places within the United States and traveling to Europe, Mexico, and Cuba.

During this time, she began her doctoral studies at the University of California, Berkeley, to work on her PhD in history; partway through, she transferred to UCLA to complete her degree. Here, she became involved in organizing: "I was so pissed off at everyone—my boyfriend and everyone—just reacting to everything. I can't do this all alone. I'm going to go crazy." She eventually quit UCLA "in this sort of fury" and returned to Berkeley to learn how to better organize people. She had been a leader on the UCLA campus, but there was not much of a movement there back then. She felt stifled by this:

> I can't learn anything here because everyone is looking to me
> all the time for the answers. . . . I didn't know the answers
> and I didn't know anything. So I moved to Berkeley in December
> 1967 . . . this was coming on '68, when everything went crazy
> and the Black Panthers dominated everything, all the politics.
> That's really why I came up. I wanted to learn from the Black
> Panthers, but it was the time when Huey Newton was in prison
> and everything was around "Free Huey." It was just constant. I
> would go to the Black Panther office and it was always just chaos
> and they were just like, "Go to this rally," or "Go raise some
> money for the Panthers." It seemed like a mess. Over here in San
> Francisco, it was right after the Summer of Love. There were like
> ten million drugged-out kids in the street. It was a little more
> interesting because I did some work giving out food and politiciz
> ing hippies, but that's not really what I wanted to do either . . .
> then Martin Luther King was shot.[72]

Having spent time working with Martin Luther King Jr. and various Black Panthers, Roxanne felt increasingly distant from peaceful strategies of social change. Shortly thereafter, sitting in a café in Mexico City, she read about the "super-woman-power advocate"[73] who had shot Andy

Warhol and decided to leave Mexico immediately, eager to be a part of "that delicious moment, that exciting, formative time."[74] When she heard about Valerie Solanas shooting Warhol, she felt that someone had finally stood up to patriarchy and she began fantasizing about Solanas as a symbol of women's rage: "I would go to the United States to launch this revolution with this superwoman ideology, and also find Valerie. Because I had come out of four years of graduate study in history, I thought Boston was symbolically and historically a perfect place. I started calling everyone I knew. We would organize to defend Valerie, and we would take the whole 'Free Huey' movement as a model to create this 'Free Valerie' movement. Everyone was always copying everyone, so it's hard to get a new idea. I was tired of playing the 'Who's more oppressed?' games in the South and wanted a change."[75] Roxanne became concerned with who would represent Valerie legally, knowing how pivotal legal representation could be in times of social crisis.

Rushing back to the United States, Roxanne believed that the women's revolution was imminent and that Valerie should be defended and supported at all costs. She said:

> It seemed to me like the most obvious thing in the world that
> we would defend Valerie Solanas. After all, she wrote her mani-
> festo and had made points we just couldn't ignore. It's maybe
> not what we would have chosen, but you don't get to choose
> everything that happens when an issue bursts forth. It would
> be like rejecting Malcolm X because he was too radical or he
> was a Muslim or he's about "by any means necessary" ideology.
> I thought Valerie could really be an amazing "reader" of things,
> or a person who would speak out more radically than anyone else
> because now that she shot Warhol, she couldn't go back on her
> radicalism.[76]

Roxanne had arrived in Boston to form, or find, a female liberation movement. Inspired by Valerie Solanas, Roxanne cofounded the radical feminist group Cell 16, a militant feminist organization that advocated separatism, self-defense, celibacy, karate, and radical resistances to patriarchy. They read the *SCUM Manifesto* as "sacred text" while laughing hilariously at Valerie's wicked satire. This group emulated Valerie by writing and selling their propaganda on the streets of Cambridge and Boston, even charging men for conversation, as Valerie had done. They picketed the new Playboy Club, studied martial arts, and roamed the streets of Boston in groups, daring men to be offensive.[77]

Local women's liberation groups had started to form in Chicago, New York, and Washington, DC. After linking up with several of these groups, Roxanne and fellow Cell 16 cofounder Dana Densmore arrived uninvited to an invitation-only three-day planning meeting for the National Women's Liberation Conference in Sandy Springs, Maryland, in August 1968. The women at the meeting, though all self-described militants, "cowered at the thought that their feminism might make them be perceived as 'man-haters.'"[78] Roxanne and Dana decided, "Those groovy women needed a little consciousness-raising so we filibustered, disrupting their rigid agenda and calm discussions with select readings from *SCUM Manifesto*."[79] They caused a big controversy when, as feminist Charlotte Bunch recalled, they read aloud excerpts from *SCUM Manifesto* and called it "the essence of feminism." In fact, Roxanne believed Valerie Solanas's contribution to feminism was so substantial that she and Cell 16 read aloud from *SCUM Manifesto* as the group's "first order of business."[80] With Ti-Grace calling *SCUM* the "most important feminist statement written to date in the English language,"[81] the publication had become a kind of required reading among radical feminists within months of the shooting.

Roxanne's activism continued through the next several years. In May 1970, she helped to organize a conference in Jackson, Mississippi, right before the Cambodian strikes ordered by President Nixon. She remembers this as a catalyst for her to leave the country:

> I just felt so alienated at my own conference. I was pretty well known by then. People came, women came, from all over and kind of changed the nature of the conference. Not many women talked. I went around listening to different presentations and panels, and people were talking, and I thought, *No one is actually talking about separation in the world and what can women do to change the United States? I can't do this.* So I went to Cuba and joined the Revolutionary Communist Party, which was then the RU

[Revolutionary Union], and that was a big mistake. It was going in this other direction, and it went underground and stuff.[82]

Roxanne returned to San Francisco during the height of consciousness-raising and objected to the political priorities of local cultural feminists: "I didn't know what to make of it. Some of the women were very active in things. Sometimes their feminism, especially their Berkeley-style PC [politically correct] feminism, was difficult. What you eat, what you drink, what you wear, every little detail of life and how you raise children. God, I wouldn't want to be their children, you know? But Berkeley was a bit extreme."[83]

Though Roxanne maintained deep distrust for academia, she nevertheless finished her dissertation at the urging of a mentor who convinced her that her involvement with Native American politics would be helped by her credentials having a PhD: "At the law school of Santa Clara, I got recruited by the American Indian Movement to get involved in the Wounded Knee cases. I took my life in a different direction. There were very few Native scholars at the time. They needed expert witnesses to have credentials, and there were only two or three Native American lawyers, and only one was really dedicated to the movement."[84] She wrote her dissertation on a case in Lumberton, New Mexico, and graduated from UCLA with a PhD in history in 1974.

Following graduation from her PhD program, she continued her involvement with AIM and the International Indian Treaty Council, beginning a lifelong commitment to international human rights. Roxanne had joined the Wounded Knee standoff in 1973 (where members of AIM occupied Wounded Knee for seventy-one days to protest conditions on the reservation) and was among those called to testify during the December 1974 hearing on whether the United States government had jurisdiction over actions committed on Sioux land. She said of this hearing: "It was packed in the courtroom. There wasn't a jury, so we filled the jury box with elders. There was an encampment outside the courthouse with at least four thousand people. I was surrounded by Vine Deloria [Jr.] and Lakota elders who told me I'd have the 'privilege' of converting the court transcripts into a book."[85] The account of these hearings appeared in her first book, *The Great Sioux Nation*.[86]

Following her years on the road, Roxanne took a position in the very small Native American studies program at California State University, East Bay (formerly Cal State Hayward; nine thousand students attended at the time, "all working class"). The university tried to fire her after the first year because they wanted to eliminate the program, but she organized with students to block the program's dismantlement and the university changed its decision: "I never have been in any way beholden to the institution, so it's hard for me. Prestige doesn't matter when you're a leftist."[87] While there, she helped to found the women's studies and ethnic studies departments.

Roxanne maintained her position at Cal State East Bay for thirty-four years, teaching for only seventeen of those because she took extended unpaid leaves of absence to do other sorts of activist work. On being a radical in academia, she said, "I really saw [my primary role] as teaching in the classroom, and I always got along with all of my colleagues because I never got on any committees to judge them. I was never the chair, so I was never the competition. I never taught summer school. That's always the thing they're killing each other over. I never got spoiled on 'We get paid half as much as the UC system.' I never got spoiled on having a high salary."[88]

In 1981, she was asked to visit Sandinista Nicaragua to appraise the land tenure situation of the Miskito Indians in the northeastern region of the country. (The Sandinistas were Marxist rebels who overthrew the US-backed Somoza family dictatorship/dynasty that ruled Nicaragua from 1936 to 1979.) The two trips she took there that year "coincided with the beginning of the United States government's sponsorship of a proxy war to overthrow the Sandinistas, with the northeastern region on the border with Honduras becoming a war zone and the basis for extensive propaganda carried out by the Reagan administration against the Sandinistas."[89] Active also in monitoring the Contra War, she took over a hundred trips to Nicaragua and Honduras during the 1980s and fought actively against the Reagan administration's corrupt efforts to illegally back the contras.

Roxanne maintains a close relationship with her daughter, Michelle, who she describes with affection: "My daughter is great. She and I are really great friends. I feel so lucky that she didn't reject me completely. She is really my hero. She really embodies this real respect for other women's trust. She tends sometimes toward what I call 'letting men off the hook' by thinking they are total imbeciles. She's a great artist too and, though she lives a pretty lean lifestyle, gets by fairly well."[90] Michelle wrote of her mother, "My mother is my hero. . . . I am not comfortable out on a limb; I would much rather hug the trunk. My mother dances on that limb and shakes the leaves down on her critics' heads."[91]

A prolific and impactful writer, Roxanne is the author of numerous books: *Red Dirt: Growing Up Okie* (1997, 2006); *Outlaw Woman: A Memoir of the War Years, 1960–1975* (2002, 2014); *Blood on the Border: A Memoir of the Contra War* (2005); *Roots of Resistance: A History of Land Tenure in New Mexico* (2007); *An Indigenous Peoples' History of the United States* (2014); and, most recently (with Dina Gilio-Whitaker), *"All the Real Indians Died Off": And 20 Other Myths about Native Americans* (2016). Her first published book, *The Great Sioux Nation: An Oral History of the Sioux Nation and Its Struggle for Sovereignty*, was published in 1977, and was presented as the fundamental document at the first international conference on Indians of the Americas, held at UN headquarters in Geneva, Switzerland.[92] A new edition, *The Great Sioux Nation: Sitting in Judgment on America*, was published in 2013. Roxanne continues to spend much of her time writing about feminism, indigenous rights, and radical activism, frequently giving book readings based on her latest works.

Dana Densmore

Dana Densmore—the daughter of Donna Allen, a founder of Women Strike for Peace[93] and an activist on the board of the Women's International League for Peace and Freedom, born March 27, 1945—grew up working in the peace movement. She said of her childhood, "The feminist consciousness was always there through my mother, and the activism was always there. I was active in a lot of other levels of social activism. I had already been involved in the core sit-ins in the South and was arrested and had a case that went to the Supreme Court."[94] Dana described her mother as perpetually impatient with the gender roles and limitations of her time, saying that her mother had worked at Arlington with various code breakers during World War II and that others had said "she was by far the smartest one there, and also beautiful, and everybody was in love with her." Dana recalled her mother's discontent: "She said that gender roles were like being suffocated under sour cream or something—like she just couldn't breathe. The weight of contempt and dismissal and just being so taken for granted, and the arrogance, ignorance, presumption—even the slightest stepping out got stomped on so heavily. There was so much pent up for my mother about that."[95]

Dana said that her father, Russell Wykoff, was at times intimidated by her mother: "She was an amazing character. He respected it, and sometimes he felt unhappy—a little intimidated by the way she could be so formidable in argumentation. It's not that she was actually more intelligent, but he didn't have quite the drive and command that she did."[96] Dana grew up in Chicago, where her parents had lived while they were in graduate school. Her next two siblings were born in Chicago, after which they moved to upstate New York, where her father's first job was, followed by a move to Washington, DC, when she was twelve years old. Her father worked as the education director for the Association of Western Pulp and Paper Workers (AWPPW)[97] union located in Albany, New York, and then became the education director of the AFL-CIO in the Industrial Union Department.[98] Dana has three siblings and describes being close to two of them; she claims no child was the favorite in the family, but that they were highly influenced by their parents: "They were very interesting people."[99]

As a teenager, Dana fought against nuclear testing with the National Committee for a Sane Nuclear Policy[100] alongside her mother, whom she also joined for numerous peace demonstrations. She also advocated for the draft resistance movement by doing draft counseling,[101] which she cites as the moment she knew that the peace movement was ready for women's liberation. She attributes Betty Friedan's *Feminine Mystique* and Simone de Beauvoir's *Second Sex*[102] as foundational texts, though her activism also inspired her about the potential of the women's movement: "There was something more that was needed—at least for it to turn into the movement that it did. The movement that it turned into was relying on the energy of the New Left activists.[103] I was moved by those books, but they needed activism, and the movement needed activism, and it needed people that were willing to toss all the conventions and all the rewards."[104]

Within the New Left, Dana realized that women were being mistreated and taken for granted. "The people that were really countercultural, that did not have any investment in the systems of rewards and social approval and deprivation, were essentially the people in the New Left movement," she said. "And meanwhile, they—that is to say, we, the women that were involved—were getting an incredible education in the tension between what we were working for, what we were putting our lives on the line for, and how we were being treated by those very organizations and the men of those organizations."[105] She attributed bad treatment by men on the left as a key catalyst for the women's movement and for her personal involvement in the women's movement.

The need for a radical feminist intervention became ever more pressing to Dana. She and a few others started thinking in radical terms about women's status and roles, a move which came with immense risk: "The people that were willing to go out—they were largely alone. But then, as there got to be more and more, it was more safe, or the word could spread. But it was really frightening for the earliest ones."[106] Specifically, Dana credits Bernardine Dohrn,[107] a member of the Weather Underground, as the catalyst for her recognizing the full need for a radical feminist movement. She said:

> [Dohrn] had talked about it, and she was saying, "We women
> of the New Left aren't going to put up with this anymore." So
> my involvement, or really anybody's involvement in this radical
> wing, was coming directly from Bernardine Dohrn. That was very
> much connected. I got to know other women that came to it from
> other parts of the country—women that came out of social justice organizations in the South, and various other parts of the
> New Left. And it was always the same kind of story, and they
> liked to quote stuff like Stokely Carmichael's comment about the
> "position" of women,[108] and they talked about the flagrancy of
> the disrespect. It wasn't just that women had to do all the typing
> and the cooking.[109]

(She is referring to SNCC leader Stokely Carmichael's alleged quote that "The only position for women in SNCC is prone"—which, according to historian Ruth Rosen, was said initially as a joke, but later became a point of contention when women addressed the serious sexism of SNCC and the civil rights movement.[110])

In 1968, Dana cofounded the Boston radical feminist group Cell 16 with Roxanne Dunbar-Ortiz. She said, "That spring, Roxanne Dunbar came to town, and that's when things really took off."[111] A lifelong scientist and one of the pioneers of radical feminist science studies, Dana helped to found *No More Fun and Games*, a radical feminist journal for which she wrote numerous essays and commentaries. She has written about topics as controversial as celibacy, the "hang-up" of sexuality for women, and the need for sexual independence from men; as a scientist, she has written about Newton, gravitational pull, and elliptical orbits.

Thinking back on the early days of writing for *No More Fun and Games* and working with other women in Cell 16, Dana recalled the vicious backlash they faced from men: "The rage, a pride in the real violence of the men that were confronted at the beginning, or threatened. When I say 'confronted,' I don't even necessarily mean face-to-face holding them accountable, but just the refusal to go along with the prescribed categories, was so threatening, and the reaction so violent, that there was even some physical violence." Dana later wrote about men as "the enemy" in order to provoke a reflection about masculinity and privilege, saying, "You are making us the enemy. We weren't necessarily saying that you are doing physical violence to us. And the implication of that is, 'We will fight back as if our testicles were on the line.'" Dana also prized the idea that she could have objections to sexual objectification—particularly at her workplace—and that those objections were understood explicitly as a rejection of all sex: "That someone can be all for sex, and still not find being objectified sexy, was hard for them to understand."[112]

Dana described her romantic and family relationships as complicated: "I always just knew what I thought, knew what I wanted, and whoever I was with had to be good with that, had to like that." She had two children (she did not use their names) who she described as independent and autonomous: "I mean, one's a boy, and so he does whatever he does, but I'm sure he's very careful about things. And the girl, yeah, she's definitely her own person. And there's a granddaughter who's definitely her own person!" Dana says that she finds it deeply pleasurable to see her children stand up for things they believe in: "I don't say there aren't issues or problems or patterns that they still get into, but they can imagine standing up—in fact, to the extent where they cannot understand how things were at the time [in the 1960s and 1970s]. They say, 'What? That happened? I would not have put up with that!' Anything from how you need to dress or how you need to behave or you can't play guitar because you're a girl, you know." Thinking back on the major contribution of feminism to her children's generation, she said, "What [my children] don't hear is, 'Put that thing away—you're embarrassing me.' Or 'Don't speak up,' or 'You should be in the kitchen. We don't want you in this conversation. Don't cut your hair short.' And they say this is not about feminism. And guess what? It isn't. It was made possible by feminism, but what it is is just being a self-respecting human being. And that's a victory, because that's what we wanted. Just to be able to be a self-respecting human being, being who you are."[113]

THE CIRCUITOUS PATH OF RADICAL SOCIAL CHANGE

Taking stock of the history of radical feminism—alive in these following six chapters as we move through their ideas about rage, radicalism and refusal, sex and love, tactics of activism, women as a social and political class, and intergenerational dialogues—allows for a reconsideration of the value of radical feminist politics both historically and today. As their brief biographies show, each of these women has led an extraordinary life, and each was ahead of her time in thinking, activism, politics, and theory. Roxanne, Dana, and Kathie each came from families that had strong connections to labor history and justice movements, showing how social movements are not distinct entities, but instead are infectious, overlapping, and building upon each other.[114] Each of these four women had extraordinary childhoods—some born into families where leftist politics and women's power were assumed, some born into families where they had to leave in order to thrive—just as they had extraordinary adulthoods, filled with the challenges inherent to living through times of great social upheaval.

Listening to them reflect on their lives and actions has been one of the great pleasures of my life, as it has enriched my understanding of the circuitous path of radical social change. That Ti-Grace Atkinson knew and corresponded with Alice Paul and Simone de Beauvoir is but one example of this path; if we are wise, we learn from each other, listening across gaps in time and space, sharing stories in hopes that these will have a lasting impact on the future. We keep an ear out for the radical voices buried beneath the cacophony of liberal, moderate, and, most dangerously, conservative ones. We remain vigilant about the destructive qualities of cowardice, moderation, and passivity. We try to dig out a history of those who may have been too busy with social actions (or too villainized by those actions) to effectively document those actions. We take pause at sweeping dismissals of "certain types of women" from the feminist canon, and we recognize both the value (optimism, energy) of youth and the foolishness of being too narrow and short-sighted to see that others have come before and laid the foundations for our very lives and livelihoods. We watch closely and feel intently for the rumbles of change, the tremors beneath the surface, and the fault lines about to break, waiting to crack open.

| 1

Feminist Rage

> Anger stirs and wakes in her; it opens its mouth, and like a hot-
> mouthed puppy, laps up the dredges of her shame. Anger is better.
> There is a sense of being in anger. A reality and presence. An aware-
> ness of worth. It is a lovely surging.
>
> —TONI MORRISON, *The Bluest Eye*

THE SPECTER OF ANGER HAUNTS FEMINISM (AND FEMINISTS) in powerful ways, as it symbolizes the force of change, the pain and trauma of living as women, and the backlash of dismissive and reductive stereotypes that ignore women's legitimate complaints. Feminist rage is everywhere—from the quieter corners of the Internet to the full-throttled protests harnessed by the Black Lives Matter movement and the Women's March—inviting attention, demanding to be taken seriously. Drawing distinctions between anger as a source of ideological disagreement—that is, provocative debates or intellectual banter—and the actual *affective* and emotional experience of anger, radical feminism has contributed much to our understanding of the potential utility of anger and the value of feminist rage. Can anger serve as a way of *living* or *being*? Can feminists feel anger without destroying themselves or feeling buried beneath its intensities? What does rage *do*, and how can feminists reckon with the potentially transformative and destructive qualities of rage?

This chapter looks at feminist rage, or the utility of anger (collective, individual, directed at the self, directed at a common "Other" or enemy) to feminist politics. Radical feminists have historically embraced rage far more than their liberal counterparts, seeing it not as an obstacle but rather as a conduit for social change and as a necessity for a radical reenvisioning of the social world. As such, the question of how to best direct feminist rage—and the potential pitfalls of transforming rage into actual violence—infuses much of the contemporary debate about women's anger. This chapter begins with a consideration of anger and rage in the early women's movement, followed by a conversation about the role of violence in feminist politics and the various forces that have attempted to contain and control women's violence. I then trace radical feminism's tenuous relationship to Valerie Solanas, author of *SCUM Manifesto* (1967) and would-be assassin of Andy Warhol, to explore the role of rage through textual and material violence. The chapter concludes with a discussion of anger and violence in language alongside an imagining of the future of feminist rage, particularly in light of the legacy feminists have inherited from late 1960s and early 1970s radical feminism. We move through discussions of how to express rage, the histories of collective anger, debates about the value of martial arts, and the power of words and actions as expressions of women's outrage.

LET IT RIP: THE ROLE OF ANGER IN THE WOMEN'S MOVEMENT

Roxanne Dunbar-Ortiz and Dana Densmore have decades-long ties as activists, allies, collaborators, and friends. Both worked within Cell 16, the Boston-based radical feminist group that formed in 1968 and prized collective decision-making, martial arts, women protecting other women, and political celibacy. The group earned a reputation for rambunctious and even outrageous social actions, drawing upon women's collective rage to fuel their efforts.

Roxanne was living in Boston in 1968 when she met Dana at the Boston Draft Resistance Group. Dana introduced Roxanne to the term "women's liberation," and they started to discuss political meetings and texts, particularly Valerie Solanas's *SCUM Manifesto*. In order to find like-minded women, they put an ad in the local free weekly announcing "formation of the Female Liberation Front for Human Liberation. Goals are personal-social, surely inseparable. To question: All phallic social structures in existence. The historic-psychological role of females. The ability of any human to be half a person. To demand: Free abortion and birth control on request. Communal raising of children by both sexes and by people of all ages. The end of men's exploitation of human, animal, and natural resources. For females no longer or have never been able To Breathe! (Men are invited to contribute money, materials)."[1]

They rapidly recruited like-minded women to the group. Betsy Luthuli (later Betsy Warrior) answered the ad and attended the first meeting with a woman named Stella. In Roxanne's memoir of these years, she remembered that she persuaded her neighbor, Ellen, to attend, and another woman named Marilyn joined, along with a graduate student named Maureen, who later became Roxanne's roommate.[2] There were many early discussions about each person's various beliefs and how these worked into the group: "We tried to think of a name for our group, but were reluctant to define it at that early stage. None of us wanted the emerging movement to be called women's liberation, however thrilled we each had been when we first heard the term."[3]

In its early days the group was called Female Liberation (or Female Liberation Front); it later morphed into Cell 16. After the first meeting, they decided to publish a journal. The first issue had no name; the second was called *No More Fun and Games: A Journal of Female Liberation*. Their profile grew as Roxanne and Dana attended meetings of similar groups and Roxanne clashed with Betty Friedan at a TV station interview. Still, Roxanne said, "We did not yet even regard ourselves as a 'group,' and certainly not an organization."[4] The group, which had recently recruited Helen Kritzler and Abby Rockefeller, talked for a time about merging with a larger one to support a national organization, but decided to stay autonomous and focus on the journal instead; they considered the journal a weapon that they would use to attack patriarchy. They also decided they needed a name before someone else came up with one for them. New member Jeanne Lafferty said she felt like a member of a cell, which Dana latched on to. Roxanne noted their address as being 16 Lexington and proposed Cell 16 as the name. Abby liked it, and the name stuck: Cell 16.[5]

I interviewed Roxanne and Dana together in conversation during the Revolutionary Moment women's liberation conference in Boston in

March 2014. When I spoke to Roxanne and Dana about women's rage and the role of anger in the women's movement, they vehemently disagreed about the utility of anger. Dana argued that anger had some value: "It's important not to be afraid of it, not to be silenced by that accusation of anger. I think Roxanne is much more appreciative of the value and power of using rage and accessing that rage. My perspective is much more that the best thinking comes when you can make some detachment from anger, that if you can recognize the evils and see it clearly, you're going to get the best results. Now, that doesn't mean that you always have to express it in an urbane way! Or a ladylike way. Spit on that!"[6]

Dana's concerns about feminist rage centered on women tearing each other apart instead of directing their anger toward a common enemy or a common target that actually oppressed women. She worried that too often women direct anger only toward themselves or each other. "But I am also very aware of the damage that is done when people indulge themselves in raging against people who disagree with them," Dana said, "and it doesn't help people working together for common goals if they're at each other's throats over those differences. That's where the problem comes in. When we're unjustly treated, there's a certain discharging of frustration and resentment and of self-protection."[7] Emphasizing the importance of directing rage toward the actual source of oppression, Dana reflected on the pain of watching women see each other as the enemy instead of recognizing the *actual* structural enemies of patriarchy, racism, and classism: "We saw that a lot in the early women's movement. People did not rage out against the real enemy because the real enemy was way too powerful, so they would rage out against people on their level and sometimes even below."[8]

Thinking creatively about how to best channel rage and anger, Cell 16 had as one of its central goals the practice of martial arts. This arose from an incident when Roxanne was walking at night in Boston with Abby Rockefeller and other members of the group and they were accosted by some men in a car. Roxanne yelled at them, and the driver tried to hit her with a tire iron but was stopped by Abby's tae kwon do block. Roxanne recounted, "Women defending women was new and wonderful to us, and for me, being defended by a woman was one of the most satisfying moments of my life up to that point."[9] The clear need for feminist self-defense inspired Cell 16 to think about how best to take matters into their own hands.

As a starting point for implementing a self-defense program, Cell 16 started a women's class at the tae kwon do studio where Abby had studied, inspiring Roxanne to feel that it should be a part of a women's revolution. "I began thinking of Tae Kwon Do as a metaphor for revolution," Roxanne wrote. "The philosophy behind the practice was beautiful: self-defense to win. I believed we had to mobilize a social force to operate in that manner. I wanted our group to go out into every corner of the country and tell women the truth, recruit local people, poor and working-class people, to build a new society. . . . If women gained consciousness of their own oppression and learned the techniques of self-defense, revolution would follow."[10]

Roxanne believed that this emphasis on martial arts helped women to channel their anger to an external target rather than themselves, something sorely needed given that women were socialized to blame themselves for their own oppression. "Our turn to martial arts was related to how to channel rage and how to, only in self-defense, ever use force," Roxanne said.

> At least for me—and reading my letters to my different friends who had given me my letters from that time back, I realize how important that was to me, in that we mainly talked about the physical. Having been an asthmatic and a sickly person all my childhood, that was important to me too. But more important was the mental, because when you grow up in a violent atmosphere, violence is normalized. And, of course, a lot of very poor people, they do just that, you know? They cannot attack the power sources, not even their bosses, because it's too much of a risk. Losing a job, or being put in jail or a mental institution, becomes risky. And so the rage gets expressed in one way or another, as alcoholism or drug use—which don't really control it because it actually increases the violence.[11]

Admitting to having a bad temper, Roxanne described martial arts as a way to channel her anger away from self-inflicted violence: "My bad temper is counterproductive. It was never really useful. It scared a lot of people away, and I had to make a lot of apologies, sometimes just not speaking to people for a year or so." She characterized martial arts as a way of directing rage appropriately:

> Martial arts is extremely important for me and [that] is one
> of the reasons I wanted to see it spread. You don't even really
> have to include the feminist politics in it for it to have that effect.
> It's sort of like what Neil deGrasse Tyson, that astronomer, says:
> "What's great about science is you don't even have to believe
> in it for it to be true!" I think with Cell 16, if we had been more
> conscious of that transference and actually promoted it that way,
> I think we could have done some things with women's anger at
> the time.[12]

The release of anger, and the potential power of directing anger toward something other than oneself, constituted a major focus of early radical feminism. Anger directed toward the self resulted in body hatred, alcoholism, drug use, depression, lethargy, apathy, self-harm, self-loathing, and lack of political activism. On the other hand, anger directed toward a target—toward a common enemy, a common goal—allowed rage to flourish in a healthy way that emphasized women's agency and power. Roxanne encouraged others to express their anger: "Anger coming out was better than not, just because it had been suppressed so much in women. We always heard, 'That's inappropriate. Don't get angry.' If I suppress anger, I get migraine headaches or I have an outburst. It's counterproductive."[13] Roxanne believed that anger constituted a way to care for the self, to understand one's relationship to the social world, and to feel the intensity of oppression. Ti-Grace Atkinson also believed this, wholly endorsing the prospect of women's anger: "Let it rip. Just let it rip."[14]

THE WAITING KNIFE: FROM ANGER TO VIOLENCE

Postcolonial theorist Frantz Fanon and many other radicals over the last five decades have implied or directly stated that violence constitutes a critical component to all radical resistance movements. According to

Fanon, oppressed people must always be in a position to strike back, to threaten violence upon the oppressor, to *become* violent when necessity demands it. Other social science studies concur with this assessment, arguing that changes in welfare policies, rape laws, and affirmative action have arisen from feminist groups using, or threatening to use, disruptive and sometimes violent tactics.[15]

Ti-Grace Atkinson, musing on Fanon's teachings, expressed surprise that women have not been more angry and more overtly violent during the last fifty years: "Fanon was dealing with the colonized who had been physically and violently oppressed and tormented, tortured, and how they regain any sense of self is by, in a sense, taking their souls back by striking out. I think it's remarkable that women, given their circumstances, have not been more violent." [16]

Thinking about women taking out violence on the wrong targets, Ti-Grace said:

> Women are often violent to their children out of frustration, and women are human beings, so if they are really circumscribed and in despair, it's going to go someplace, that energy. My own theory and experience is that women turn this rage on in safe places, which means [toward] those who are less powerful, and inward to themselves. They also have depression and other ways of becoming dysfunctional, so we must ask: *Where is that rage going?* It's got to be there. Sometimes it can be expressed through extreme religiosity; sometimes it becomes a feeling of self-hatred. It's got to go someplace.[17]

Taking into account the history of Russian Communist politics, Ti-Grace added that women's anger can sometimes have revolutionary implications as long as it remains self-interested. She said, "I was reading this correspondence between Lenin and [Russian feminist] Alexandra Kollontai and other Bolsheviks. . . . Lenin was asked why he bothered with the woman question, and he responded, 'Because women and kulaks [small landowners], they were the most reactionary forces of society because they were fighting for themselves. That's really the best basis of coalitions—self-interest.'"[18] Revolutionary anger, then, is an anger based on self-interest and self-preservation, something women have too often been stripped of throughout history.

Looking back on the history of violence in the women's movement and in key moments throughout history for women, Kathie Sarachild said that there was a certain mythology around peaceful protest that needed to be rectified in the histories of women that circulate in the United States:

> There's a myth that great advances for women have been done peacefully in a certain way. It comes up in the feminist movement that we haven't ever benefited from violence in our progress. I think it's kind of how you look at it, because violence—for instance, taking the vote, winning the vote in the United States—there's a big question about how that happened. If you read suffrage history, the original sources, the National Woman's Party, it turns out they kept trying to get President Wilson to introduce it to Congress. In 1919, they were getting very close to passage, and at that point World War I was raging—violence galore—and revolutions were breaking out in Europe that were giving women the right to vote.[19]

Kathie added that violent action was necessary to secure the right to vote. "Suffragists were going on hunger strikes and being jailed. It was quite wild what was going on in the United States," she said. "Wilson decided that he would, after all, introduce the Suffrage Amendment into Congress, and he would introduce it as a war measure. Now, that had a lot of resonance back then. It was almost like an exact parallel with the Emancipation Proclamation, which was also introduced as a war measure. It wasn't just to help win the Civil War that Lincoln finally [signed the Emancipation Proclamation]. By making it a war measure, that was how he was able to get everybody to agree to it." Kathie went on to say, "I think that basically our winning the vote had a lot to do with the world politics of the time, and there were these violent revolutions all over the world that were giving women the vote. I mean, we were in competition. Our establishment was in competition with all of that going on. In a certain sense, women in the United States did win the vote because of revolution and armed struggle. We benefited from that. It might not have been totally direct, but it was there."[20]

The history of feminism and its relationship to violence was, and continues to be, a tenuous one. (Some feminists dislike violence as a tactic because, they argue, it replicates the practices of hegemonic masculinity and the police state.) While the vast majority of historical cases of women being violent toward men typically involve self-defense during domestic violence assaults, there have been a few high-profile cases of women committing murder, or engaging in violence during political struggles. Mostly, though, women's violence is often seen as trivial, or about "crimes of passion," rather than about organized, collective political resistance. And, as the previous story suggests, when women draw from violence around the world, or use their bodies to physically struggle for their rights, those stories often get erased altogether in favor of portraying women as polite and reasonable.

Some celebrated leaders of feminism, for example, had episodes of violence, a curious omission from the overall story of feminism. Ti-Grace remembered that the author of *The Feminine Mystique* had attempted violence against her husband during their divorce:

> Betty Friedan, earlier, had told me she was going through a divorce, and when I was not a threat to her yet, she would be very supportive and confiding and so on. I remember she was really in a fix, because she had a place somewhere on Fire Island with her husband, and they had a big fight, and she chased him down the beach with a butcher knife, screaming that she was going to cut it off. Betty said lots of people saw her, and her husband was going to bring this up in the divorce proceedings, and what was she going to do? I said, "Well, there were witnesses, so what can you do? You got to brazen it out. Just say, 'I'm a passionate woman, what do you want from me?'" I remembered that, and I thought it was good advice.[21]

With regard to the tension between collective violence enacted through a social movement and individual violence perpetrated by one woman against someone else, Kathie in particular expressed serious reservations about the utility of individual women's violence: "I don't think individual action of any kind really gets women much at all. Maybe you could get a little improvement in your life. If you use violence to defend yourself against someone who is going to kill you and you successfully do it, it definitely does help you. You save yourself. I think we have to look at the situation." Kathie went on to argue that context matters and that no feminist movement should make an absolute sweeping statement about the utility of using physical violence (or not) against another person: "The only rule, I think, is that we shouldn't rule out anything. It would depend on the conditions, time, and place."[22]

THE PROBLEM OF VALERIE SOLANAS

During the early days of the feminist movement, shortly after the 1966 founding of NOW, conversations about anger were abundant. Women started to understand that their oppression connected to other women's oppressions, and that topics like housework, sex, rape, abortion, and violence had political implications. That said, high-profile cases of women being violent toward others—particularly for reasons other than "crimes of passion"—were incredibly rare at the time. In 1968, the year that violence and feminism would most intersect, anger and outrage permeated public consciousness, yet women's particular violences (those they endured and those they perpetrated) remained largely invisible. Women felt rage without an outlet to express that rage; they felt anger without a symbol of their anger.

Valerie Solanas, a smart, ambitious, frustrated writer who had recently penned an outrageously funny play called *Up Your Ass* (1965) and a vitriolic, perhaps satirical (perhaps not) manifesto advocating the elimination of all men called *SCUM Manifesto* (1967), in many ways beautifully embodied the contradictions of women's anger and rage at the time. With an IQ in the ninety-eighth percentile, she had entered graduate school in psychology only to discover that opportunities for women to advance were limited by assumptions that women would marry and therefore did not need graduate funding. After dropping out of graduate school, Valerie moved to New York City (and eventually to bohemian Greenwich Village) to pursue her writing and to seek out publishers and producers for her manifesto and her play. She had met Andy Warhol in 1967 at the Factory and had believed Warhol had agreed to produce her play; when he did not deliver (and when he lost her copy of *Up Your Ass*), Valerie retaliated in the most violent of ways.[23]

On June 3, 1968, Valerie rode the elevator up to the Factory with Andy Warhol and, after a brief conversation, shot him, along with art critic Mario Amaya. She exited the building and turned herself in to a traffic cop in Times Square, declaring, "The police are looking for me. They want me. He had too much control over my life."[24] News of the shooting spread instantly (curbed sharply by the subsequent shooting of then-presidential-candidate Bobby Kennedy two days later in the kitchen corridor of the Ambassador Hotel in Los Angeles). It immediately provoked divisions among feminists about whether Valerie deserved feminist legal representation and protection or whether she should be disregarded as an idiosyncratic, violent, and mentally ill woman.[25]

Valerie Solanas shooting Andy Warhol represented a major turning point in the history of feminism. The episode provoked consequential disagreements within NOW: One camp (liberal feminists) believed that Valerie's action had nothing to do with feminism and that attention should instead focus on issues like equal pay and abortion, while another camp (radical feminists) believed that Valerie Solanas shooting Andy Warhol symbolized something meaningful about women's rage and that feminists should work to defend her (or at least protect her from a worse fate in prison or a mental institution). Following ongoing disagreements about Valerie Solanas, Ti-Grace Atkinson resigned from NOW and started the radical feminist group The Feminists. Anger, she believed, should have a major role in feminist politics, and violent women who fought back should not be disregarded as irrelevant. For radical feminists, Valerie Solanas, with her combination of angry and vitriolic writings alongside actual violence against men, represented a compelling, perhaps heroic, way of feeling and expressing rage.[26]

Unwittingly, Valerie Solanas fractured NOW and spurred the formation of new radical feminist groups: New York Radical Women (1967–1969), The Feminists (1968–1973), Cell 16 (1968–1973), New York Radical Feminists (1969), Redstockings (1969–present), Chicago Women's Liberation Union (1969–1977), the National Black Feminist Organization (1973–1976), and the Combahee River Collective (1974–1980).[27] Ti-Grace remembered the controversies that Valerie sparked by shooting Andy Warhol: "We kept having these awful fights, and Valerie Solanas was one of the fights. Are we or aren't we for women? What's going on? So, seeing so much violence, you kept noticing, you kept hearing things about how many women got killed. Battering was starting to come up. It was being talked about. Women were just victims everyplace, and if you didn't want to be a victim but you saw all of this, it was just overwhelming. Real, real rage. So, Valerie was sort of in another world."[28]

Ti-Grace remembered her reaction to first hearing about the Warhol shooting:

When I saw that this woman had shot Warhol—well, first I should tell you—I first heard of her from this woman she lived with. She said she was afraid of Valerie. This woman felt Valerie was violent toward her, and she didn't want any contact. [Valerie had a tendency to throw acid in people's faces and often threatened violence against people.] That was all I'd heard, and I was getting a zillion calls a day, so this didn't stand out. When I heard that Valerie had shot Warhol, and she had said something like, "He had too much control of my life," the first thing I thought was, *Warhol is not exactly the exemplar you'd choose for male supremacy.* I knew he was asexual, so it wasn't some personal relationship, and the *New York Times* presented it as if it was somehow connected with feminism. This was right after a big piece on feminism, so everybody was aware of this anger building. All I saw was she had shot Warhol, and I knew he was exploitative. Some woman had done something appropriate to the feelings we were all having. She was fighting back. That's what it felt like. The paper said when she would be in court, so I just naturally went down. I raced down, and who do I see coming up the steps in criminal court? Flo [Kennedy]! So Flo and I by then have the same instincts, and her feeling was, like any black person she saw going into the judicial system, they're going to be in trouble. They needed help. She was on her way. We were both on our way.[29]

Like many angry women, Valerie had a particularly difficult tempera-
ment. Ti-Grace visited Valerie in prison and—alongside Flo Kennedy, a
notoriously outrageous and brilliant civil rights attorney who had worked
on high-profile cases for numerous Black Panthers and artists like Billie
Holiday, Charlie Parker, H. Rap Brown, and Assata Shakur—did what she
could to help her.[30] Their efforts only met with Valerie's rage in return,
though Ti-Grace believed Valerie's case had compelling contrasts to most
cases of women's violence against men: "If you cared about her at all, she
became really abusive. I was trying to help her and she became abusive
with Flo, too, and Flo just—well, she abused Flo once and Flo was done."
Ti-Grace continued:

> Another lawyer in NOW made a good point. She thought the
> Solanas case was interesting in that almost all the cases of vio-
> lence where women were involved, the victim was either a father
> or a lover; there was a sexual connection. But, from the news-
> papers, Valerie seemed to have an economic motive—this meant
> she must be "crazy." The fact that her actions would not fall into
> the usual category of sex-related crime, but an economic one,
> made her crazy. While men killed each other all the time for eco-
> nomic reasons without being 'crazy,' this was, from that vantage
> point, a sex discrimination case on its face that had to be looked
> into. I thought that was really a rather cool assessment. I was
> coming from another place, you know—all my rage and so on
> and so forth.[31]

In light of Valerie's violent actions and disavowal of feminism as a
social movement, the question of whether to consider Valerie a feminist
(or include her in feminist history as part of the movement) conflicted
Ti-Grace:

> No. No. . . . She's a part of my archive, but I don't think of her
> as part of my feminist archive. She was a glitch, a mistake. The
> fact that she keeps coming up—you could say that means we as
> women, as feminists, yearn for some violence, or somebody to
> fight back, and she looked like she was fighting back. Is there a

hunger for that? Is it an expression of somehow the woman not being the victim all the time? But the feelings are mixed. It's fantasy, too. It can be a kind of flight. Certainly, she met some fantasy of mine.[32]

Remembering her complicated feelings about Valerie's anger, Ti-Grace said:

At first I was gaga. I felt she was a martyr; my heart was all over everything, but it took me a couple of months before the ice water hit. I think a lot of people had this impulse of being moved by her story somehow—wanting to give her a chance in some way, at least hear her side—but if you've got any proximity to her, you can see the confusion. . . . She's a very, very tricky figure. I knew her, and I don't speak with much confidence, and that's a sign of somebody who knew her! Later, I kept seeing people who were interested in Valerie and who responded with a kind of excitement. I asked this one woman, "Why does she attract you?" because I realized she wasn't interested in deep feminist questions. She said, "Well, she seems to have some panache, some style about it; you know, she shot somebody." In a way, I have to say that was probably what attracted me, too. I was filled with rage, and I thought it was somehow appropriate to "just shoot them all!" It certainly seemed deserved, but it was a misreading of what was going on.[33]

Dana Densmore believed that Valerie played a key role in smashing and destroying previously held notions about women's "ladylike" roles, and that she made a major contribution to thinking about feminist rage. Dana described Valerie's work as transformative in its destructiveness:

Well, the first thing that occurs to me to think about in what you're saying is this role of the idoloclast, a breaking of idols. That was what *SCUM Manifesto* did at that stage of the emerging women's movement. If you have *Feminine Mystique* on the one hand and *SCUM Manifesto* on the other, we see there was still the heavy weight of these idols of the patriarchy. What *SCUM Manifesto* did, in a way, was just come in and break things, smashed them, and in doing that, it changed the consciousness and allowed for something new, something that was cleared away, to emerge. When you come in with a sledgehammer, somebody has to come along and get the nuances because some of those nuances do matter. There was a need at that time for somebody like Valerie to say those kinds of things in that language. That uncompromising language demonstrated that one need not be ladylike. One need not even be fair. To some extent, I think we do not now need her the way we did at that time, yet I think it is always good to be on the lookout for times when new idols are coalescing and to be ready to come in and smash them.[34]

In addition to the more cerebral contributions she made to feminist rage, Valerie also made a personal imprint on early radical feminism.[35] Roxanne considered her early exposure to Valerie's anger to be tremendously impactful: "For me, it was very emotional, the identification with Valerie. It was the spark that really made me come to Boston. I was in Mexico City, and I was going to Cuba, and she shot Andy Warhol. I read about it and thought, *I have to go back. The revolution has started.*"[36]

Thinking about Valerie's destructive energy and the importance of violent anger, Roxanne drew inspiration from *SCUM Manifesto* and the Warhol shootings: "Valerie influenced Cell 16. We knew that we had to rebuild everything. We had to deconstruct and rebuild all of it. We had to burn everything down. Thinking back on her, I am so grateful for Valerie Solanas."[37] As Roxanne wrote in a July 5, 1968 letter to her then-boyfriend: "Valerie's is a voice in the wilderness shouting her rebellion, saying she will accept no arguments to the contrary, allow no loopholes or fancy devices that could be used to counter her argument. She is EVERY-WOMAN in some basic sense. She is my mother and other broken and destroyed women, a martyr for all women everywhere. In that way she is not so different from Che. Read her manifesto closely. She wants us to see, not a new man, but a new human being created, and now."[38]

Roxanne described the writer's anger as effective and influential: "What I liked about Valerie is she didn't just go off the handle. She actually had good aim. She managed her anger. She's kind of unique in that way. I had never met anyone who used anger and words so effectively. Had she not shot Andy Warhol, things would have been different for Valerie. The shooting becomes an excuse for everyone looking at her to see that as the definition of who she is, rather than her use of words as swords. Her words were much more effective than that act of shooting Warhol. That act really inspired me." (Roxanne rightly suggested that *SCUM Manifesto* would have had more rhetorical power *without* the shooting, though it would not likely have been published through official channels.) Thinking about how the women's movement is remembered now, Roxanne added, "I couldn't just go down into the narrative that is told now about the women's liberation movement, and all the nostalgia. I am not a nostalgic person. I hate the nostalgic. It's counterproductive and kind of sick. It's *very* hard to be nostalgic if Valerie Solanas is in the picture."[39]

Roxanne also connected her feelings about Valerie's anger to her feelings about other oppressed people: "I think a lot about the 'damned' people—the people who are damned. That was my mother, you know: part Indian in a white community, alcoholic, violent. I saw it. I was a victim of her violence and terrified of her. That was my mother, if she could have just expressed herself. She wouldn't have had to be destructive in a really negative way. So, I had this deep affinity about it, and for all the damned and left out." Roxanne felt especially inspired because Valerie did not come from a place of privilege: "I could know immediately, just based on the little description in the paper, that she was a street person—maybe a prostitute, maybe a lesbian, living on the street, a kind of hanger-on. I thought, *This is one of the damned. And the damned has acted. And not as a symbol.* There was, as Fanon would say, a kind of cleansing through violence."[40]

Dana countered Roxanne's appreciation of Valerie's violence by expressing her feelings about violence more cautiously:

> I think one can say, categorically, that suppression of anger,
> let alone repression, is bad, and that anger is better than that.
> Feeling, experiencing, and expressing anger is—unless the expression of it puts you in danger, of course—categorically superior to

suppressing it. However, I think that is something better than either of those options. Anger is a response of feeling like a victim, and there is another perspective, which is to *look with clear sight at the situation, however bad it is.* There are situations that are very hard to look at with clear sight. They're so offensive to one's personal state, offensive to any sense of justice and humanity. But, to look at it with clear sight, and instead of saying, "I am the victim of being in this world," to say, "What am I gonna do about it?" To take a perspective of "Yes, in objective reality, horrible things are happening, and there may be horrible things happening directed at me." But to still be able to say, "What am I gonna do about this? What action am I gonna take to improve the situation?"

To this statement, Roxanne replied, "What is really dangerous about angry women? Words are the thing that have the most power." Dana laughed and said, "Men would rather you shoot them!"[41]

THE DIFFICULT LANGUAGE OF ANGER

The notion that words can redeem anger, or save it from its worst qualities, has a long history in radical social movements and resistance movements. Angry genres like manifestos, as well as personal narratives embedded in autobiography and memoir, have given voice to, and have legitimized, women's anger.[42] Further, complicated histories of the dissemination of hate speech have woven with resistance movements and their aims for centuries.[43] The difficult language of anger—how to express it creatively, forcefully, impactfully—stands in stark contrast to the more careful and cautious use of words in some feminist circles; indeed, tensions between politeness, humor, and rage abound in feminist uses of anger.[44] How to use language to represent anger is an ongoing challenge for radical feminists.

Roxanne expressed dislike for the ways that highly academic language often strips words of their power and impact, rendering them obscure, distant, abstract, and useless: "Postmodernism, deconstructionism, and poststructural language—using Lacan and Judith Butler and others—they have kind of taken the power out of words by dissecting meanings, turning language into codes. There's not much passion there. The closest example that I can think of for someone who unites passionate language and postmodernist codes is Slavoj Žižek. You can understand about one-third of what he has to say, but there are jewels in there. I mean, he reminds me of Valerie! He's got spit flying out of his mouth when he talks!"[45]

Roxanne, Dana, and I discussed how the problems of postmodernism and the relative lack of rage found in postmodern thought relate to its connection to philosophy. As a consequence, most people doing serious feminist work in postmodernism come out of the incredibly sexist discipline of philosophy (where women are discarded altogether, or expected to perform incredible reverence for sexist male philosophers). Roxanne agreed, reminding me, "Judith Butler has never been able to get a job in her field. She teaches women's rhetoric and the classics at Berkeley because philosophy doesn't hire people like her."[46] Dana added, "Some of the women in philosophy departments are starting to make a revolution. They're starting to get together, in a way." In academia, the culture of paying homage to what people have previously written or thought has a long and well-documented history; hence, the manifesto genre, devoid of footnotes and citations, inspires particular anxiety for those within the academy. Dana described the manifesto as a genre with emphasis on the realness of living: "It's as if the ideas are real and the ideas themselves are alive. The scholarly perspective is more anxious about ideas, believing that an idea isn't real unless you can say that six people thought it before! With dates! And page numbers!"[47]

Reacting to the perceived need for down-to-earth, ambitious, far-reaching work on radical feminist issues, Roxanne and Dana described the contents of their radical feminist journal, *No More Fun and Games*. Begun in 1968, the journal included a variety of pieces on a range of topics: political celibacy, domesticity, orgasm, Marxism, science, maternity, sisterhood, being single, art, and politics.[48] Looking back on the experience of writing for the journal, Dana argued that it became a way to channel rage and to express the power of words: "I think naturally if you're not ruined by academic training, you can understand the relationship between words and power. I mean, all the people that were writing in the journal had some kind of academic training, but the rest of us were talking ideas."[49] Roxanne added:

I had real ideas *despite* my academic training, not because of it. But it was kind of on the same level. My idea was that everyone can write, they have language, and if they have the gift of literacy, they have language. Language isn't born. Everyone can write, and it's really true, all those women, they've never written anything before, but they could write and express so it was all the same. Language can, in some circles, become so rarified that people think they don't have language. They think they don't have anything to say, because they can't manage it in this sophisticated way. It's a weakness.[50]

Dana found that when she went to graduate school to receive formal training in academic work and writing, no one seemed to really care about original ideas:

You come in and you learn scholarship by shadowing current scholars, so that's why in a dissertation it has to be focused on "Who said?" and "Who said?" and "Who said?" with all the citations. But *you* can't. It's not about your ideas. That was made very clear to me: "No one cares about your ideas." And maybe that's one thing when you're twenty-two, but it's quite a different story when you see senior scholars still afraid to have their own ideas—writing articles and books with the same dense thing, six levels of citations, footnote after footnote. We should be getting *new ideas. What do you think?* Why do I have to wade through all these other people who got it wrong? I want to know your fresh perspective on this![51]

To understand anger, to manage it or contain it or express it, Roxanne and Dana both believe, people have to value the expression of new ideas and inspired ways of thinking, writing, and working. Roxanne fondly looked back on Cell 16 as alive with fresh ideas:

We sat around thinking about and talking about ideas. It was very exciting, because all of my graduate peers and all of my professors, from my first year of college to my PhD program, were all male. I never had a female professor. I was mostly the only woman student, too. There were five women out of six hundred history graduate students. It was exhilarating to sit and talk with two women who were my best friends, these two historians. We just talked about ideas all the time. It was so thrilling. One of them died that next year in a plane crash, and I lost the other to cancer a year later. And so I was literally left without an intellectual community. I still had all these men, and my partner was into all this French literature stuff, which I'm glad I learned about, but then I found women through a newspaper ad and they joined Cell 16. Just from an ad! They showed up. These brilliant women and these conversations we had together. It was just so thrilling.[52]

THE FUTURE OF FEMINIST RAGE

As these narratives show, if mainstream feminist politics moved women's rage from a marginalized or sidelined aspect of the movement to a central place in feminist identity ("I am feminist and I am enraged"), this shift could move feminism in new and compelling directions. As Dana argued, rage should play a central role in feminist politics: "It is extremely important to be willing to not be afraid of the feminist rage, but to assert its legitimacy, and, furthermore, its appropriateness in the face of the injustices that exist in the real human suffering of women in this war on women. Certain discernment has to be made, because you can rage yourself into paralysis, but I think it's important not to be silenced by the accusations of stridency like 'Oh, you're a hater,' or 'You're just angry,' or 'You're upset.' Rage is sensible and appropriate, necessary."[53]

Rage is a part of the radical feminist legacy. Looking back on the histories of anger in the beginnings of radical feminism, and the importance of Valerie Solanas, I might argue that feminists should also frame rage and madness as necessarily overlapping. In other words, part of the work of radical feminism is not only to integrate rage into our self-understanding—a sense of righteous anger that arises from conditions of oppression—but also to accept that madness haunts the edges of rage. Madness and rage are closely associated, both discursively and literally—angry women are often labeled "crazy" no matter what they do, just as rage can evoke feelings of madness, loss of control, and "losing it."

In a panel discussion I did in 2014 with feminist philosopher Avital Ronell, performance artist Karen Finley, and sociologist Lisa Duggan, I argued for an acceptance of the relationship between madness and rage, not only as inevitable, but as a productive site of feminist knowledge-making:

> Women are haunted by madness in a different sort of way than
> men are. Madness follows us around; we will be accused of it
> at some point, called names of madness, and are constantly sub-
> jected to having to suppress and manage the various moments
> that madness is launched at us and hurled at us. Valerie has
> always helped me to think about why it's a terrible project to dis-
> tance ourselves from our own madness, or to suppress it or not
> have those things follow us around. In the academy, feminists are
> engaged in various kinds of PR campaigns about what kind of
> feminist we want to be, and how much madness we're really will-
> ing to take on. I get asked a lot about whether Valerie is a defen-
> sible person—whatever that means—and I really hate that sort
> of question for that exact reason, because Valerie invites thinking
> about how we push away the radical or the destructive—the
> madness impulses, perhaps—and that's a really bad idea. We
> have to collect those impulses and carry them with us as people
> moving through the world. As feminists, we must embrace
> being haunted by madness.[54]

We need, in short, a feminist politics willing to take rage and madness *into* its political core.

Rage and madness have transformational potential, and as such, should not be disregarded within a movement like feminism. Roxanne once conceptualized Valerie Solanas as a "destroyer" by saying: "Perhaps destroyers like her can never transform their energy, but only inspire others."[55] By this she means that anger, violence, and madness work in tandem with destructive impulses, allowing for an "unworking" and sabotage of the existing system (Valerie's priority), encouraging a rebuilding from the ground up. Radical feminists teach us that anger and its associated forms of destruction might make way for more productive strategies for building a less sexist world, imagining new roles for women, seeing their complaints and their oppressions not only as legitimate but deeply valuable and even generative. In this chapter, these radical feminists took as a starting point that women's anger was valid, important, and worthy of taking seriously. Anger allows us to say unsayable things, see in new ways, and find new tactics for negotiating the deep complexities of madness, sisterhood, loneliness, community, social movements, collective injustice, and transformational social change.

| 2

Radicalism and Refusal

> A civilization is not destroyed by wicked people; it is not necessary
> that people be wicked but only that they be spineless.
>
> —JAMES BALDWIN, *The Fire Next Time*

THE QUESTION OF WHAT MAKES FEMINISM RADICAL, OR HOW
radicalism can inform the core of feminist thought, underlies much of
contemporary conversations about the utility of a more radical approach
to gender politics. What does it mean to identify as a radical feminist,
and how has such an identity shifted and changed since the late 1960s?
Can feminist politics have revolutionary intentions? Can the mundane
aspects of women's lives radicalize them? These questions inform this
chapter as we move from the origins of radicalism through the tactics and
practices of refusal.

This chapter examines the complementary and overlapping projects
of understanding radicalism—particularly as it contrasts with liberalism
and liberal feminism—while also exploring why refusals (the "no") represent a crucial part of radical feminist politics. I begin by exploring the
specific meanings of the word *radical,* and how the language of radicalism
has been misused and appropriated in ways that have distorted the actual
meaning of the word. I then trace the boundary lines between liberal
feminism and radical feminism, showcasing why such a distinction is not
only productive and exciting but also politically necessary. In the second
half of this chapter, I examine refusal as a useful tactic of radical feminism, both historically and today. I then specifically look at how refusing

institutions like marriage symbolizes a key moment where radical feminist politics diverge from liberal feminism.

THE ORIGINS OF THE WORD *RADICAL*

The origins of the word *radical*—digging into the roots of something—have not been explicitly taught to most scholars and activists born after the late 1960s. *Radical* as a political term was likely first used by British politician Charles James Fox, calling for "radical reform" to establish universal manhood suffrage; it then morphed into a term used to describe anyone who pushed for parliamentary reform.[1] It was also frequently used to connote leftist politics by the Industrial Workers of the World ("the Wobblies") as they worked for "one big union." The Wobblies argued, in a published pamphlet from 1957, "It is well to note that from radicalism has flowed all that makes life better today than yesterday. It is now, as in the past, the only force capable of leading the world out of its night of hunger, hatred and fear. Humanity advances over a path blazed by radicals and stained with their blood. So long as there is injustice there will be radicals. The name itself is the proudest title of free men and women."[2] In subsequent years, this version of *radicalism* was used by feminists coming up through the second wave of the late 1960s and early 1970s.

This absence of learning about the origins of radicalism, particularly for young feminists, has led to a consciousness gap about the work of radicals and what they do. Most specifically, *radicalism* means that one is doing the work of undoing, unworking, digging deeper and deeper into something until its origin story is clearer and more defined. It requires an interrogation of the root structure of something and its story. In this sense, radical feminists engaged in the task of trying to dig into the root structure of patriarchy in order to uncover its origins and intents.

In a conversation with Dana Densmore and Roxanne Dunbar-Ortiz, Dana described this lack of awareness around the origins of radicalism as a major problem: "Well, if you don't go to the roots, you're not going to know how to fix something. You don't know where it comes from. You *have to* go to the roots, even if it's not polite and turns up ugly things; then, you name the ugly things. That's going to the roots."[3] Roxanne added, "That's why *radical* is so misused when people say 'the radical right'—because they're not radical. They're going to a made-up past, not to the root."[4] Dana continued, "The reason why young people don't know what *radical* means is because they pick it up by context, as we learn language generally, and in that context it's just used as name-calling."[5]

When I asked them if *radical* has been appropriated as a kind of identity disconnected from the actual word—people calling themselves radicals without understanding what *radical* means—Dana said, "The original people that were using it—the people calling themselves 'radical'—knew what it meant, but now it just means 'extremist' and therefore is not sensible."[6] Roxanne also framed this as a way to disparage people across party lines: "It's a name-calling thing against the right and against the left. They say, 'Oh, the radical left and the radical right,' and it's Hillary Clinton as the radical left, and then Rush Limbaugh as the radical right. I mean, those aren't even balanced, first of all—but neither one of them is really true to that word, of going to the source."[7] Dana added, "And neither one of them is calling themselves that! It's just name-calling, and the people that use it as name-calling don't know what it means. They aren't thinking. They just mean it as saying something nasty about someone."[8] Roxanne said, "But sometimes it's a compliment from the anarchists!"[9]

Dana addressed the difference between radical and liberal feminists:

> The way I think of it is, to what extent are you invested in social approbation? To what extent do you let that affect your sense and your assertion of who you are? Are you afraid to speak up? You might choose not to speak up. I think of *liberal* as more working within the system. People should do what they can do, and if people can't go all the way, that's wonderful they're doing what they can do. And they can make a difference, and they have. I'm for authenticity and integrity. People need to do what feels right to them. It's not always going to be what I would do.

Thinking about the early days of Cell 16, Dana said she felt drawn toward the more radical women compared to the liberal women: "When Cell 16 was in its heyday, I found that the people more interested in the status quo and not ruffling anybody's feathers too much, we found them uninteresting, boring. They're not going anywhere, so we didn't pay that much attention to them. We didn't really have that much in common. If we met them we treated them like comrades and were very positive, but that's not where we wanted to put our energy."[10]

Thinking about the power of early feminist texts that dug into the root structures of women's oppression, Roxanne returned to *The Second Sex*. Published in 1949, the wide-reaching, sweeping critique of gender relations, the condition of womanhood, and the historical oppression of women served as an inspirational text for much of early radical feminism. Simone de Beauvoir was born in 1908 and had lived in a middle-class family in Paris; she went on to publish twenty-five books, and *The Second Sex* is often heralded as the beginning of second-wave feminism.[11]

Roxanne admired de Beauvoir's way of doing radical work: "It really gave me newfound respect for Simone de Beauvoir's *The Second Sex*. She had all of this research known to humankind by then, and she wrote it during the late 1940s! All that was known of biology, she wrote down, and nothing in there really has been disproven. She worked in the tradition of Marx and Engels and really went to the roots to create such a piece of knowledge. It was a model of how to do that, how to make that kind of analysis. There was no other text at that time with that much usefulness to it."[12]

In my conversation with Roxanne, she talked at length about the misuse of the words *radical* and *radicalism*, along with the dangers of young activists not understanding what *radical* means. Thinking back on her own trajectory of radicalization, Roxanne said:

> In the '60s, when we were using [the term], we were really trying to get to the bottom of things, to the truth. But now, calling myself a radical has been discredited, like a lot of other words— like *militant*. *Militant* used to be a perfectly standard term for a labor activist . . . and now it's ISIS! It's al-Qaeda! "Militants did this; militants are beheading people," and you call them militants! That's something else entirely. But we used to use *radical* and *militant* interchangeably with *revolutionary*. *Revolutionary* sounds like you're bragging, saying "I'm a revolutionary," but it's very

overt or aspirational. *Radical* is the term that doesn't sound like you're bragging so much, claiming to be Che Guevara.[13]

The right-wing appropriation of words used by the left presents a major challenge to both historicizing and understanding the contemporary manifestations of radicalism.[14] Kathie Sarachild felt troubled by the appropriation of the word *radical* by conservative forces: "We are shining a spotlight on a word that has been hijacked to mean 'right-wing' and radical, when the opposite is the truth: The word *radical* has been stripped of its political history and political position on the left, not the right—on the side of the historical revolutionary fight for radical principles. A specter is stalking the political conversation in the means of mass communication: the specter of real radicalism."[15]

In terms of how to respond to such appropriations, Kathie emphasized the importance of turning negatives into positives, of moving language to suit the movement: "Turning it into its opposite would mean to make a bad connotation into a good one—turn something that people have been ashamed of into something to be proud of. . . . I am learning over the years that there's almost nothing that's really new. It started with the civil rights movement as it evolved into the black liberation movement. It retrieved black history and launched black power, black consciousness, black pride, black is beautiful."[16] Drawing from her history with SNCC, Kathie recalled how white feminists drew from the history, experiences, and expertise of the black power movement for inspiration:

> Those of us white folks who were working with organizers and the Student Nonviolent Coordinating Committee or SNCC— the new SNCC program was for white folks to fight racism by bringing liberation programs into the white community. White women's liberation organizers immediately began to adopt the same "turn it into its opposite" tactic to women's liberation organizing with women's history like black history, women's studies like black studies, women power like black power. The slogan "Sisterhood Is Powerful" came out of my efforts to apply the thought-provoking and thought-changing political tactics that

I was picking up from the black movement. In fact, the names of the activist organizations—WITCH [Women's International Terrorist Conspiracy from Hell], B.I.T.C.H., Redstockings—were all examples of turning derogatory terms into their opposites, restoring truth in obliterated history and sources to the terms.[17]

Speaking of her childhood and how she came to understand the word *radical* and the importance of radical thought, Kathie said:

I grew up in a family that considered itself radical. The term was actually used in a positive way in my family. They weren't rich, like the FBI tries to portray radicals and reds—far from it. Until I was five years old, my mother was a divorced single mom teaching English as a second language in an adult night school while trying to get a master's in art education for teaching high school. My grandfather took care of me during the day, because my grandmother was the breadwinner of that family, due to my grandfather having lost his business during the Great Depression. My grandmother managed to go to one of the early free tuition universities—City College of New York—where she got a BA degree in the 1920s, and they all lived in a rent-controlled fourth-floor walk-up apartment in various places in New York City. Even my adopted father—when my mother and he got married—they were, I guess you could say, "New York bohemians." Their loves were art and science.[18]

Kathie went on to describe how she learned early on about solidarity and the importance of sticking together through struggle:

Even when it was a struggle to get work in those areas, they all considered themselves radicals of various stripes. My father also volunteered for his union. I remember him explaining to me simple but important concepts that I also applied to "Sisterhood Is Powerful," like "In union, there is strength." Because of all of this, I learned at an early age that the term *radical* came from the Latin word for *root*, and it was explained to me that *radical* from the Latin word *root* doesn't mean extreme. It means getting to the root of the problems in society and finding the root of the problem—finding the root solution in theory and action. There was a lot of talk about the problems in society, and there was a lot of singing and listening to the records of Pete Seeger, the Weavers, Paul Robeson, and Odetta[19] . . . Somewhere along the line I also got the impression—probably from my new father, who along with his radical politics was also into engineering and loved science—that the word *radical* also had something to do with being scientific, with a scientific approach, and science meant, after all, that you not only look for a theory of why things were the way they were, but you also had to put your theories to the test in practice.[20]

With vehement insistence that there is no such thing as the "radical right," Kathie argued that the concept of radicalism has been grossly distorted and appropriated by people who want to characterize themselves as "respectable" moderates:

I don't think there is a radical right. I guess you could say there's a far right, but I wouldn't say "the radical right." That's a phrase that has been planted by the establishment to ruin the word *radical* and make it unusable by people, and to make it less politically meaningful. Radicals have disappeared completely from the vocabulary. *Radical* in the true sense—the left sense—was gone, because you had two opposing groups: the liberals and the "radical right." No one would even talk about the radical left! It was always the "radical right" and liberals. It's sort of like the way they talk about the middle class. We're supposedly not a classed society, but the term "middle class" gets used. How can there be a middle class when we don't talk about the other classes and we don't really hear about them?[21]

As with many aspects of history, people often forget that words and phrases connected to social movements have origin stories, too. Kathie reflected on the early radical feminist movement and the origins of the phrases "women's liberationists" and "radical women":

When I first got involved, we were calling ourselves radical
women. There were all these debates about whether we should
call ourselves "women's liberationists" or "radical women."
Shulamith Firestone[22] was very strong on our using the term
"radical women" and I—being a red-diaper baby—thought it
would get us in trouble to use the word "radical women," and
that radical was one of those terms that would scare people,
so why use the term *radical*? Anyway, she won the argument,
and so we used the word "radical women," and I'll never forget
that one of the members, Ros Baxandall[23], went on the David
Susskind show with three NOW women. Ros said, "We've got
this journal, *New York Radical Women*," and gave the address
several times, and we got tons of mail from it—the kinds of
things that Gloria Steinem claims only she got when she started
Ms. magazine. People weren't afraid to write to us when we
were called "radical women"—they would say that they had been
waiting for this all their lives. We got letters from all over the
country. I think that when you have real things to say, and you
speak to people's lives and aren't scared of things, people will
come to you.[24]

In conversation with Kathie Sarachild, Ti-Grace Atkinson also expressed infuriation at the appropriation of terms and words associated
with liberation. She felt especially appalled by corporate appropriation
and co-optation of liberatory words: "So much is co-opted! It's hard not
to confuse co-optation with influence. The heart of the ideas that radicals
have carved out is gone. I remember after the late '60s that General Motors
would say they had just brought out a revolutionary new car. It just made
the word cheap, meaningless. It almost made a joke of it, depowering the
concept of revolution. We have to work really hard to keep the original
meanings behind words."[25]

RADICALISM MEETS FEMINISM

While first-wave feminism clearly influenced second-wave thinking about
feminist politics and priorities, the phrase "radical feminism" did not gain

recognition until the period of 1967–1969, with the development of three radical feminist groups. First, New York Radical Women, a socialist feminist group in New York City, united anticapitalists (who saw capitalism as the source of women's oppression) and feminists (who saw male supremacy as the source of women's oppression) together as "politico-feminists." When New York Radical Women fell apart in early 1969, the feminist side of the split referred to itself as "radical feminists" and eventually led to the founding of Redstockings, a militant radical feminist group that coined many of the most well-known feminist colloquialisms ("Sisterhood Is Powerful"; "consciousness-raising") and held some of the most historically recognizable protests (such as the Miss America protests).[26]

At the same time, women from another New York City–based group, The Feminists, founded by Ti-Grace Atkinson following her split from the National Organization for Women, also used the phrase "radical feminist" to describe themselves. Shortly thereafter, in late 1969, Shulamith Firestone, who left Redstockings, joined with Anne Koedt to form New York Radical Feminists, the first organization to use "radical feminist" in their name.[27]

Given this relatively recent history of thinking about *radical* and *feminist* as clearly connected, I asked Roxanne how she saw radicalism and feminism overlapping. She responded, "When radicalism got introduced to feminism, what became defined as radical wasn't the old left and right arc; it was more about sexuality. Radical feminists were often separatist—not necessarily just lesbian separatist, but *separatist*—but also there was a term of 'radical lesbianism.'"[28] (Radical lesbianism, according to Monique Wittig, argued that heterosexuality was a "political regime" built on the "submission and the appropriation of women," and that women should refute heterosexuality for political purposes.[29])

Roxanne differentiated *radical* from its historical use, during the late 1960s, to its current use:

> *Radical* just came to mean a kind of extreme—that you were
> on the extreme fringe of whatever it was, like in women's libera-
> tion. These terms are so difficult in the United States, because
> the media uses them in different ways than we do, so it's self-
> identifying. I probably wouldn't say I'm a radical feminist now,

but I did then, and I didn't mean it as separatist. I mean it as the right to be, to meet, separately—the necessity that shouldn't be denied, that allowed me autonomy—and that's very different from what it meant in left and right circles.[30]

Positioned against liberal feminism—which advocated for within-system change, pay equity, and women having equal access to the resources men already had access to—radical feminism took up a different set of priorities. In contrast to liberal feminist interest in, as Martha Nussbaum writes, the "equal worth of human beings" and "antifeudal" opposition to the "political ascendancy of hierarchies of rank, caste, and birth,"[31] radical feminism was more interested in far-reaching revolution than incremental reform. While liberal feminists emphasized legal equality between men and women,[32] radical feminists wanted to dig deeper into the source of those inequities, including inequities that played out in the minutiae of everyday life. In terms of how radicalism and feminism *do not* overlap, Roxanne argued against the possibility of a radical equality-based feminism: "I think the brand of feminism which is the equity feminism, mostly having to do with economics—I don't think that would overlap with feminism, where there could be a radical and a nonradical version of that, because it's already circumscribed within the capitalist system. Unless feminists specify, 'I'm talking about socialism and equal distribution,' the assumption is that you're talking about equity *within the system as it is*, so there's almost no way that that can be radical. Preserving the status quo is not radical, and neither is changing it slightly."[33]

When I asked her what she saw as the key differences between radical and liberal feminism, Roxanne elaborated on this claim about economic equality:

Liberal feminism is really about economics. It's not all bad, if you support decent wages and stuff like that, but so much of the time liberal feminism is more about giving lip service to working-class women or welfare or the rights of families, child support, and so forth, but it's basically about being equal on top. For example, liberal feminism wants a proportion of women in higher places in Congress. This is more about counting the different nations that have women heads of state—quite a few, now—and you notice it really doesn't make that much difference, so it becomes a kind of individualistic effort.

In her most scathing critique of liberal feminism, Roxanne framed liberal feminism as only for elites: "In the end, liberal feminism isn't really dedicated to bringing everyone along. It's sort of like making all boats float by you floating to the top, and that will help the rest of us down here, and that's the definition of liberalism. Radicalism *has to benefit all women,* or it's not feminism. It's not exclusive to one class."[34]

Ti-Grace also expanded on this conceptualization of radical feminism by emphasizing the difference between the way radical feminism started and how it got co-opted:

> The concept of radical feminism started one way and it got co-opted very quickly. Initially, it was a distinction between mainstream feminism and radical feminism; we were much more identified with changing the whole society and seeing the problem of sexism as universal in the society. It would require major, major changes, not nibbling around the edges. This led us to dig deeper and deeper and deeper. After the late '60s and early '70s, it got much more into the essence of womanhood, and it became a phrase that meant nothing. Radical feminism, in terms of a *movement*, was only a very few years. I think partly it was much harder than we acknowledged to ourselves.[35]

Recognizing that there are different risks and emotional investments in radical change (looking at underlying institutions and frameworks) and liberal change (sticking within the system), Ti-Grace returned to the emotional toll of early radical feminism:

> I think emotionally we didn't talk enough to each other about how scary it was. I mean, just to strip away so many beliefs that we'd all just never questioned before, and the future was more and more vague. We didn't know what the alternative was. First

of all, you had to get the garbage out, and you sort of started thinking about alternatives, as far as what happens with the children and things. It was scary. I think we didn't talk about that very much. The future felt tentative. There's this mountain, and the mountain gets bigger and bigger that you're going to have to pull down. You think it's just a little hill, and then you hear other women and what they've come up against, and you add that and you add it and you add it, and it just grows and grows and grows and grows. It strung people out. And you have to *live* at the same time, which, for the most part, you neglected; we were barely hanging on. That can't last. You have to have something more stable.[36]

Another key objection that Ti-Grace had toward liberal and academic feminism was the insistence on postmodern theories—that is, theories that argued for no objective truth, a shifting sense of meaning-making, no grand narratives or ideologies, and a lack of coherent reality; theories advanced by intellectuals like Jacques Derrida, Martin Heidegger, and Jean Baudrillard—to understand women's social problems, rather than material inequalities. When reflecting on the differences between radical and liberal feminism and the problem of postmodernism, Ti-Grace said:

One is trying to get at the causes, and the other is dealing with the symptoms of it, individual instances of it. Radical feminism digs at the bases of gender inequity. It's not at all postmodern. The whole emphasis on language, as opposed to material change, was important. Radical feminism cares about the material conditions of your life in terms of how you can afford to think and feel. I think these things go around and around and around. I'm sure there will be a generation where they reinvent it. There were women raising really basic questions in the so-called "first wave," too, like Victoria Woodhull.[37] When they were first exploring things, they had more radical voices. I think you try to get more and more women involved, which is good, but the hazard is that you don't want to offend, so you ask for less and less and less.[38]

Looking ahead to the future of radical feminism, Roxanne outlined the key differences she sees between today's radical feminists and radical feminists of the late 1960s:

> There are a lot of young women who call themselves radical feminists who are, I think, almost neoliberal. It's lifestyle, appearance, a kind of in-your-face challenging of power. Back in the '60s, we wanted to not fall into obeying the norms, so we refused to dress up every day as a kind of rebellion because dressing up was the norm. That's how I think a lot of young women who call themselves "radical feminists" are rebelling against the old feminism, or how they perceive it. They don't want to be the straight-laced and dour, overly serious and no sense of humor sort of stereotype, so they have made themselves bright and shiny— but in some ways, this just means that they're jumping back into old stereotypes about women! It's a funny circle—very strange.[39]

On a more hopeful note, envisioning future directions for radical feminism, Roxanne emphasized the intersectional work of radical feminist activists:

> A lot of those young women are applying what they interpret as a feminist approach to all kinds of things, like prison organizing, incarceration studies—and there are so many women involved with that that are very radical, committed feminists. They are working to abolish the whole prison system, and I find them to be really useful, really great. It's a great application of radical feminist work. It made me feel really good to know about it, because at some point radical feminist theories had to be applied to things, or it just sort of spins into only consciousness-raising or whatever. I like watching women work on immigration issues, watching Asian and Latina women who are very radical feminists, applying this to their work.

Assessing the impact of early radical feminism on these new approaches to diverse feminist activism, Roxanne said, "It's nice to see some of those seeds that we planted of the rhetoric getting used in this way. They wouldn't give that genealogy about where those ideas came from, but we're the ones that put those ideas in the air, put it into the mix, and they reached for it. I like it better when people can trace and give credit to where things came from, but they don't always do that. I didn't either, when I was young! I mean, later, I would say, 'Oh, they were already doing this back in the '50s. We didn't invent this from scratch.'"[40]

Imagining her future vision for radical feminism and the need to think and envision the role of radicalism differently, Roxanne described the hazards of liberal/equality feminism:

> Radical feminism has to go about trying to change the system structurally, paying great attention to center the women in it, because if the women benefit, then men automatically will, too. It's like the Equal Rights Amendment—the men could have benefited if we'd done it right, because the fear was that giving women in the trade unions any "special privileges" would be a problem. At my university, they wanted women during their periods or during pregnancy to have a place to rest. Why not give that to men, too? I mean, they get stressed and sometimes need to rest. Instead, what they did was close down all the women's spaces at my university in order to protect men's equal rights! This is when the rhetoric of equality becomes dangerous—we take away from everyone, instead of benefiting everyone. That kind of "equality" is what you get when you go through legal mechanisms; it has consequences you didn't predict. That's why we need radicalism—to challenge the roots of it all.[41]

ANARCHY MEETS RADICAL FEMINISM: REFUSAL AND THE "FREEDOM FROM"

Within the framework of anarchist principles of positive and negative liberty—that is, the "freedom to" do what we want to do, and the "freedom from" having to do what we do *not* want to do—the question of women's so-called "freedom" looms large. In my previous work, I have taken up the question of what constitutes these competing ways to be free: the "freedom to" do things we want to do and the "freedom from" doing things we do not want to do with regard to women's sexuality.[42] For example, if women have the freedom to run for political office, wear whatever clothes they like, and assert their desires for more equitable housework, does this also mean that they can *refuse* certain aspects of their gender roles as well? Can they say no to sex, refuse to work, go on strike in their own homes, not buy into certain political viewpoints, not engage in emotional labor at their jobs, and have the freedom from constant childcare? What kinds of freedoms are easily imagined and prioritized, and which are more difficult and evasive? Radical feminist views on refusals reveal much about women's (lack of) "freedom from" having to do things they do not want to do, particularly as radical feminists pay attention to the root causes of women's oppression and look at the relatively mundane aspects of women's lives (e.g., the body, sexuality, reproduction, domestic labor, and emotions and affect).

Many early radical feminist groups had a near-constant preoccupation with refusals, seeing the rejection of traditional expectations of women as a tactic in attacking patriarchy and making visible the material and lived conditions of women's lives. When I asked Roxanne Dunbar-Ortiz about the importance of refusal as a feminist tactic, she described the precariousness of the late 1960s as the context in which refusal emerged:

> We really did think we were on the edge of catastrophe then,
> with the atomic bomb—and we *were*. It's just amazing that the
> Soviet Union was restrained enough, because I don't think the
> US really was. They used the bomb to control. That's why they
> dropped the bombs. They didn't need to make Japan surrender.
> They did it to show the world: "This is what." And it worked. We
> were so scared. But then we got unscared and said, "Well, we're
> doing to die anyway, so let's dismantle this place and rebuild it.
> The worst thing that can happen is we die, and that's probably
> going to happen if we don't do something." It's very much like
> the climate change that I see now—in young people saying,
> "There's *not going to be a future* unless we do something." I think
> the audacity of refusal comes out of that.[43]

She added that she saw that rhetoric and rationale for refusal as a parallel to the audacity she saw in Native American communities who, as a tactic for survival, refused the intrusions of the US government: "My admiration for the indigenous resistance is immense. They're against all odds, but when it's about survival, something happens to human beings. Sometimes it can be paralyzing, or you find a way to live with it, but more often we're seeing women emerging as activists, fighting back, refusing to die."[44]

When speaking of refusal as a tactic of radical feminism, Roxanne celebrated its potential: "A lot of refusal is rhetoric. But rhetoric shouldn't be dismissed as 'just rhetoric,' because we're about language. I think that the powers that be try to convince us that you have to *do things* so people get busy with projects and tasks, with this and that project—but *they're not thinking*. They're not reading. They're not conversing. They're not studying. They're not putting their minds to work about things. Everyone's capable of it. They don't have to have a higher education, but people think that's true, so all the energy gets dispersed."

Remembering her actions with Wounded Knee and Alcatraz in the American Indian Movement, Roxanne discussed the virtues of uniting activism and the rhetoric of refusal: "In the '60s we made refusal a rhetoric, but it was productive to have Occupy Wounded Knee[45] for two and a half months, or Occupy Alcatraz[46] for eighteen months, or the women that went and occupied the *Ladies' Home Journal* offices.[47] You could call it a publicity stunt or agitprop, but it's actually an action that matches the rhetoric. I think we've lost confidence, to some extent, in that style. We think we have to tone it down."[48] Adding that she works with Native people to stop white men from inhabiting their lands, she said:

I think to empower the Native people, you have to believe in
the power of really loudly refusing. A lot of indigenous activists
believe they have to find a way to "tone it down," and I think
that's a tendency that's troubling. Really good people who want
to do the right thing, who want to establish trust, who don't
want to turn off or scare off people, they feel a real responsibility
to the Native community. They don't want to just go and barge in.
But I think if the Native people are in the leadership and they're

out there demonstrating, I think they *shouldn't* tone that rhetoric down. They should create platforms to speak even more loudly, with a megaphone.[49]

REFUSING INSTITUTIONS

Refusal can also extend into how women imagine their relationships to institutions like marriage, religion, prisons, the military, education, and even the adoption of social roles. Even *among* radicals, the powerful trappings of institutions remain difficult to disentangle from, revealing the powerful ways that institutions perpetuate inequalities even among those who fight against such inequalities in other ways. Imagining ways to refuse institutions, then, applies not just to those outside of social movements, but also within them. Radical feminists often spent time figuring out *why* they wanted to be a part of certain social institutions at all, and what drove them toward (or away from) different life choices.

Thinking about her childhood, Kathie learned early about the hypocrisies and hazards of forging new ground with gender roles in the home:

My parents also taught me that there should be equality between men and women, but that the wider world had a long way to go in catching up with that idea or making it a reality. I learned the term 'male chauvinism' from them. My mother worked all the time, growing up, and my father did a lot of housework. Friends of mine later told me that until they met my family, they had never encountered a family where a man did the housework. Instead of gossiping about men who did the housework, my family would gossip about families of their radical friends whose men did *not* do the housework! Or they would say things like, "They didn't like working for women." I got the strong impression from them that people who considered themselves radicals weren't supposed to have attitudes like that, but that many of them still did, and this was one of the problems in the world. These were still reigning ideas, even among people who call themselves radical or progressive.[50]

Kathie talked about the importance of refusal and the ways that her mother worked to instill in her the right to refuse: "The issue of the treatment of women, and inequalities women faced, was always the one closest to my mother's heart. My mother wanted to try to help protect me, or at least prepare me as much as possible to deal with the things that might stand in the way of my happiness and freedom. She would tell me things like, 'Don't fall for the free love line from men who call themselves radical.' Things aren't yet equal, and men benefit from their greater freedom at women's expense."[51]

Ti-Grace discussed the refusal of institutions by weighing whether the institution was salvageable or whether the institution was beyond reform. She said:

> Radical feminism—the division between radical feminism and what had gone before—was the distinction between an institutional approach to a scattershot, or the symptoms of sexism versus the causes or ideology. There are all sorts of terrible things that happen to women which are the product of how we're seen and the institutions which define us, and each woman who joined radical feminism had a different experience, all of them terrible. They were illuminating, but they were endless. We have limited resources when thinking about our strategies and interventions. Sometimes I've used the image of bowling and ninepin—you really want to get something that's going to knock out as much as possible. And, by approaching the primary institutions which have defined women historically, it's going to get you further because one symptom can be replaced by another (you can just shift those around), so what you want to go after are the things that are *fundamental*.[52]

When thinking about which institutions fundamentally informed and governed women's oppression, Ti-Grace took aim at kinship structures in this country: "In that sense, marriage and the family are fundamental. Marriage, because it's a legal institution, you can get at it in terms of defining it." Ti-Grace took particular issue with what she called "double-role institutions," or institutions that are defined by the roles within them.[53] She said:

> What is still devastatingly remarkable to me is how skillfully the second wave of the women's movement has avoided drawing the obvious analogy between the role of slavery as the institutional basis for racism and marriage/family as the institutional basis for sexism. Both slavery and marriage/family are defined as double-role institutions. These roles are complementary and hierarchical in nature: master-slave; man-wife. In the law— FOREVER—these institutions have been/are distinguished by the guiding (intellectually superior) necessity of the dominant participant and the primary physical function (fieldwork, child-bearing and -rearing, and domestic labor) for the submissive "partner." If these roles are "equalized," neither institution exists any longer as unique.

She continued, "It's true that my analysis depends upon the law and social practice, going back to the first written records and up to the present time. But women's 'beliefs' about what marriage and the family might signify is quite different. For women, they believe that somehow 'love' is what a marriage contract means. This would be a bit like a slave being flattered that a master wanted to buy him/her for their physical beauty as opposed to how much work could be wrung out of that body."[54]

She went on to explain:

> I saw this first used sociologically about slavery as an institution. Slavery is defined by the double role of master and slave. If you get rid of the inequity involved in this hierarchy, the institution of slavery is dissolved. I used this similarly for marriage: man and wife. It's an institution that is defined by these two roles. There is no 'equalizing' these roles. If that were possible, the institution of marriage would be dissolved. There is nothing else in law which distinguishes marriage as a contract except for the "complementarity" of these two roles. Women, especially, imagine

that "love" is somehow stipulated in the marriage contract. Of course, it isn't. Nor, I believe, could it be. You can't make a feeling mandatory. Can you?[55]

In light of the recent passage of the marriage equality legislation (the 2015 Supreme Court decision *Obergefell v. Hodges,* which found that the fundamental right to marry is guaranteed to same-sex couples by both the due process clause and the equal protection clause of the Fourteenth Amendment), the question of whether marriage as an institution is problematic at its core has taken on new meaning. Does the recognition of same-sex marriage fundamentally alter the heterosexist, patriarchal underpinnings of the institution? Does it change the structural disadvantages that women have faced for hundreds of years? Can same-sex marriage laws queer the meaning of marriage?

Many radical queer scholars and activists have maintained, both pre– and post–the 2015 Supreme Court decision, that marriage is a morally bankrupt social institution that cannot be reformed, even with the addition of same-sex couples to the institution.[56] Scholar and activist Mattilda Bernstein Sycamore has argued that assimilation is a kind of violence and that queer people should never aspire to be married:

I would say "the violence of assimilation" to describe the ways in which gay people have become obsessed with accessing straight privilege at any cost; it's almost like cultural erasure is the goal. Marriage and military service and adoption and ordination into priesthood are suddenly "gay issues," whereas things like housing, health care, police brutality, gentrification . . . those? As if to say, "Oh no, we can't be concerned with any of that! We're just so excited about gay cops, because if we have gay cops gunning down unarmed people of color, then we have arrived!" It's the nightmare of identity politics where gay becomes an end point, a rationalization for celebrating the worst aspects of dominant-culture straight identity: nationalism, racism, classism, patriotism, consumerism, militarism, patriarchy, imperialism, misogyny; every other form of systemic violence becomes a hot accessory.[57]

In line with many of the radical queer opponents to marriage equality legislation (and to same-sex marriage altogether), Ti-Grace, too, argued that people cannot reform or work from within the system to change double-role institutions because the institution itself creates violence and inequality that cannot be merely reformed: "At that time [the late 1960s], people were critiquing slavery as a double-role institution, [stating] that you couldn't really reform it. I mean, you could—and people did make modifications so that slaves were treated somewhat better, and so on and so on. And it's not that that had no value. But there's really no way to reform it so that slaves are treated as human beings. You've got to abolish it."[58]

Conceptualizing marriage as a double-role institution, Ti-Grace explained the danger of leaving the institution in place at all: "With marriage, you literally have a double-role institution. There is no purpose for it other than the two roles. So, if you get rid of all of the role aspects, you've abolished the institution." Ti-Grace expressed urgency about the abolition of marriage and the necessity for women to refuse marriage as an institution:

> When it comes to refusal, I say this: If you see something that is bad for you and your kind, why would you advise people to participate in it? There is a lot we know on the surface about how marriage is bad. There are other layers where it's harder to say for sure what would survive, what wouldn't survive, how it would be transformed. On the other hand, you could say that, in fact, marriage has been undermined since the 1960s. Fewer people do it, but a lot of the reason for that, I think, is that there's less advantage for women in getting married, economically, and that has to do more with the economic conditions happening today. Religion is also an institution, but I think I agree with Marx that it's the "opiate of the masses." It just puts you to sleep.[59]

When thinking about how early radical feminists laid the groundwork for thinking more critically about marriage, Ti-Grace expressed hope that marriage will continue to devolve in importance and relevance for women:

Liberating women is not a one-generation thing. [In the late 1960s], when anything seemed possible, the momentum was such that much more could be achieved. Given that it is going to be multigenerational, even going at the highest speed, then you can say, "Well, does an institution like marriage offer any protection to women?" in this long process. For example, if a woman is married, when her husband dies, she gets his Social Security. So, the impoverishment of elderly women is usually because they only have their own income to depend upon. That's the result of sexism. Once you acknowledge a multigenerational effort, you can argue for a strategy of gradual abolishment that factors in these things. I think that the more you see and understand, the more you don't want to participate in certain things.[60]

Ti-Grace went on to give direct advice to young women about how (and why) to refuse institutions like marriage:

I think trying to be independent and trying to not marry, for example, and trying to get your head around the idea that you're going to support yourself, and that that's going to be primary, and that relationships are going to be secondary, are all crucial. Women's survival has primarily depended upon their relationships, so relationships become primary. That's a major switch, to think about yourself first. I would also say that they should keep informed, but information is basically brainwashing nowadays. It's difficult to get. Sometimes I just refuse to listen to the news because it's going to be lies. Figuring out what is and what isn't a lie can be crazy.[61]

In agreement with Ti-Grace, Roxanne, too, considered marriage especially dangerous for women. She said that it disproportionately impacted women in a negative way and that, like many institutions, women could not see clearly the constraints marriage placed on them. She also disagreed with Kathie's emphasis on marriage as positive: "Kathie Sarachild really pushed the marriage contract, believing men had to be made responsible. She had a whole argument, and I think she was partly right, but it's usually the women who are the losers in marriage, especially if there's a child or something. There's no contract, there's no child support, because there's no legal responsibility. She was definitely in the minority on her views of marriage. I think most of us were against marriage, against institutionalized control of sexuality, and marriage had never really been in the interest of women. It was always patriarchal in its inception."[62]

Roxanne went on to say that radical feminist critiques of marriage, building on the momentum of the women's movement and women's discontentments with patriarchal institutions, had long-lasting impacts: "It made a big impression. The divorce rate went up tremendously, and the number of people living alone and living together, experimenting with whether they could live together before getting married, went up. People would live together for seven and eight years, and then they'd decide if they would get married for practical reasons. Still, relationships often fell apart, because something about the institution does change you—how people regard you—so it's different. And usually there's a heavier burden on women—the role she should be playing."[63]

Understanding the burdens placed upon women to uphold certain institutions, and the profound impact of refusing to participate in those institutions, became important to locating the value of early radical feminist thought. Assessing the origins of radicalism and the initial union between radicalism and feminism allows for greater understanding of the high stakes of radical social change. At the heart of these conversations lie painful and difficult decisions about how to define radical feminism (often with ideological splits, even among allies) and how to imagine a new set of priorities for radical feminist activists and organizations. Refusal is at the heart of such conversations. (The second-wave insistence on refusal also contrasts sharply with third-wave constructions of women's freedom as the *freedom to* do what they want, rather than the *freedom from* having to do what they do not want to do.) Refusal, then, became a crucial lens through which radical feminists saw opportunities for symbolic and literal rebellion, as they pushed back against practices and institutions that oppressed women.

3 |

Tactics

The test of one's humanity is to stand with the truth as best one
can make it out, even if totally alone, and to fight *for* that truth. This
is the measure of liberation.

—TI-GRACE ATKINSON, *Amazon Odyssey*

THE WOMEN'S MOVEMENT, PARTICULARLY ITS RADICAL EDGES,
transformed the conditions of women's lives and laid the groundwork
for much of the important work that followed over the next five decades.
Ti-Grace Atkinson, Roxanne Dunbar-Ortiz, Kathie Sarachild, and Dana
Densmore were masterful tacticians, putting forth their activist impulses
as a priority over other aspects of their intellectual and personal lives.
Thinking together with other women in their circles, they imagined a
variety of tactics that had far-reaching consequences for women's lives
today. They strategized about abortion and how best to frame women's
right to abortion. They raised consciousness and elevated the discussion
of naming and language. They worked to organize women from a variety
of racial, class, and sexuality backgrounds. And, of course, they imagined
a world in which women had their own archives and institutional memory. Most of all, they embodied the slogan "Deeds, not words."

This chapter interrogates the specific, unique tactics utilized during
early second-wave radical feminist activism, first by exploring how these
women helped to start the women's liberation movement (particularly its
more radical wing) and then by imagining the individual and collective

value of having shared grievances in the form of consciousness-raising groups. I then examine their feelings about Flo Kennedy, famed civil rights attorney and radical feminist leader. The women discuss how radical feminists fought together for abortion rights, and explore the radical roots of that organizing. The chapter concludes with a discussion of naming and language, tactics of self-defense, and the value of committing to feminist activism instead of engaging only in thinking and theorizing about oppression.

STARTING THE WOMEN'S LIBERATION MOVEMENT

The bumpy road toward creating a social movement held many obstacles and roadblocks in its early years. Kathie Sarachild recounted the process of envisioning an entirely new way of seeing women's roles, relationships, values, and priorities:

> From the beginning, even before the women I was working with adopted the description 'radical feminists,' we were very much acting on the assumption that what we were doing was a learning process, as we embarked on trying to start a mass women's liberation movement. We would have a lot of learning to do, and there would be a lot of trial and error—a lot of experimenting as we went along. We assumed that we would all need to be critiquing our results and those of others. The phrase "science of liberation" appeared, along with the phrase "criticism and self-criticism." . . . We learned that we would not win unless we constantly improved our aim, our firepower, and our understanding through experimentation and reflection.[1]

The women's liberation movement arose from women's struggle to find voice in a world intent upon trivializing and silencing women's lives. In June 1967, radical feminist Jo Freeman attended a "free school" course on women at the University of Chicago, led by Heather Booth and Naomi Weisstein,[2] after which the three women organized a women's workshop at the National Conference for New Politics in September 1967.[3] At the conference, a women's caucus was formed—led by Jo Freeman and Shulie Firestone—that presented its demands during a plenary session. Their efforts met with condescension by National Conference for New Politics director William F. Pepper, who physically patted Firestone on the head and said, "Move on, little girl; we have more important issues to talk about here than women's liberation." Following this meeting, Freeman began a newsletter called *Voice of the Women's Liberation Movement* and helped to form the Westside Group, the first second-wave Chicago women's liberation group. Freeman's newsletter gave the women's liberation movement its name.[4]

The strategists and leaders of the movement drew upon many other social movements and their histories when devising goals, tactics, and targets.[5] Kathie recalled some of the movement's early influences:

> There's a beautiful saying, so emblematic of what we radical feminists were trying to say about the need for an independent women's liberation movement: "Who would be free must strike the blow." A classic motto of virtually all nineteenth- and early-twentieth-century liberal movements, picked up from a line in one of Byron's[6] revolutionary poems: "All oppressed people must unite and act as an independent force in order to be free." The motto was part of the introduction to African American antislavery leader Frederick Douglass's autobiography,[7] and the English militant suffragists inscribed it on their banners. Marxism implied the same classic principle in revolutionary heritage to the rising new working class—the wage workers of the capitalist economy.[8]

Kathie emphasized that the late 1960s fomented revolution and gave the women's liberation movement momentum:

> The idea of feminist revolution arose in a revolutionary time. Freedom and revolution were in the air, over the airwaves and the in-print media coverage, in the civil rights movement at home and revolution abroad. . . . The civil rights movement and the racially integrated buses and freedom riders and them being bombarded; separate white and colored restrooms and

drinking fountains; police dogs and fire hoses used against peaceful demonstrators; the killing of black and white voter registration workers—all certainly called into question how free our country was when it came to race, but this was spurring public questioning about the state of US freedoms on other fronts, too.[9]

Kathie recounted the importance of starting a movement based on certain foundational beliefs: "In 1968, in 'A Program for Feminist "Consciousness Raising,"' I wrote, 'Our feelings will lead to our theory. Our theory will lead to action. Analyzing our theory will lead to new action and new theory and so forth.'"[10] Deeply devoted to the concept of making an archive and writing down the grievances and experiences women shared in their consciousness-raising circles, Kathie noted that they wanted to move beyond mere conversation:

> We began pretty much right away to demonstrate how serious we were by taking the time not only to sit around doing postmortems and evaluations of our actions, but to write them up. You can see this in the journal, *Notes from the First Year*, of New York Radical Women[11] in June 1968. There were also postmortems on the Jeanette Rankin Brigade[12] action in the brand new national newsletter out of Chicago called the *Voice of the Women's Liberation Movement*,[13] along with commitment to self-criticism to become more effective. We wasted little time at getting into criticism of other feminists' work and analysis or taking on divisions and how to proceed with them.

Kathie also described how radical feminists developed principles with connection to other historical social movements: "Many of radical feminism's principles—unbeknownst to us in any solid chapter-and-verse way, and mainly only sensed by some instinctive freedom-struggle savvy— were actually basic principles of a general radical heritage and part of a lost revolutionary consciousness, far better known and widespread in the United States in the nineteenth century and early part of the twentieth century than they were to the radical activists of the 1960s."[14]

In addition to these more distant histories, Kathie also believed that Betty Friedan's *Feminine Mystique* laid the groundwork for questioning why women in the "world's most 'liberated' country" were doing so poorly:

> Betty Friedan suggested early on that women could learn from the freedom riders. Three years later, she led the organization for women whose acronym, NOW, was borrowed from the civil rights movement slogan "Freedom Now." Much has been said about the civil rights movement inspiring and guiding the organizers of the women's liberation upswell in the United States in the 1960s, and this was certainly true for me. The civil rights movement—particularly the work in the movement sparked and organized by the youth group SNCC, was the most powerful influence on me. NOW was the first new feminist organization in almost fifty years, as Jo Freeman put it.[15]

Kathie forcefully reiterated the core ideas critical to the success of building the women's liberation movement:

> Number one: It pays to fight. I knew from the history of union movement struggles that it pays to organize, but it took me longer to learn that generally, if not always, it pays to fight, although people do better when they fight better, and they fight better collectively. You can study ways of fighting better. You can talk to people. You can read. But there is one absolutely necessary ingredient element in getting better at fighting, and that is to *begin* to fight. As the lyric from the freedom song "Keep Your Eyes on the Prize" goes, from the civil rights movement: "I know the one thing we did right was the day we started to fight. Keep your eyes on the prize, hold on, hold on." Which leads me to my next point. Number two: Join an organization. The importance of this was driven home for me when I saw Stokely Carmichael,[16] who I had admired as one of the SNCC freedom organizers and worked with occasionally in Mississippi. I heard him speak in 1996 during

Black History Month at the University of Florida, and the main message he had that day was for all students to join an organization. He urged people to join an organization. Women need to go on building the feminist union, the women's liberation union, or women won't be free. Nothing has happened yet to change my mind about that conclusion.[17]

Kathie continued her list of advice:

Three: I urge you to act. Even in the area of learning to get better and better at being scientists of women's liberation, and scientists of revolution, you have to act. This is probably an impossible piece of advice to believe before you put it to the test, but to be able to use history—to be able to get something from it and put it to practical use as a scientist of women's liberation—you have to begin to try to change history. There's a quote from SNCC that says, "Before reading a freedom fighting history book, make a freedom fight." When I read that, it really helped me understand how history had become so much more available for me to use after I had become really engaged with a movement, on a level of getting in there and trying to figure out what to do and trying it and acting. Suddenly I could evaluate the history I read, to see, "Is this useful? Is that useful?" because you're in charge of the history you read. Don't ever follow someone who says, "You've got to follow. You've got to do this because history tells you to." The reader is in charge of which history seems useful and which is not, and then it becomes a fantastic resource of ideas from what to do because you're picking them and you're applying it to the present. Finally: I urge you to work on building the independent women's liberation power base and making it stronger locally, nationally, and internationally.[18]

TACTICS OF ORGANIZING

Women working as a collective force—believing in and supporting each other, working tactically to achieve common goals, and imagining a future that benefits all women—became a centerpiece of early radical feminism. Ti-Grace Atkinson has long been a highly vocal advocate for women to work together as a collective:

> Obviously, obviously, obviously, moving as a group makes the most change. It's just an element of force—you know, *protest*. If it's one person, if you're a member of an oppressed group, you're weak. But if a lot of these weak links get together, it counterbalances and you can make change. You have to agree, in some ways, about what the goals are, because that's where your actions are going to be. A lot of progress happened through sex, sex discrimination cases, different demonstrations—but when you look at the overall change, it's not as much as some people thought it was or would be. So, in a way, whatever brings women together, mainly around some sort of theme or goal, that's important.[19]

For Ti-Grace, the crux of feminist organizing centered on moving women away from thinking of themselves as victims, and moving instead toward broader, deeper analyses of the roots of their own oppression:

> I think the reason why we got into a kind of "victim movement" was around rape and our rape organizing. It's important—but if you look at the pattern, it's almost all about that. It seeps into women's consciousness. You're defined as a victim, and you really can't do that much about it. You're not really thinking strategically, because you don't think you're capable of it, and you don't have the power to do anything to change these things. In retrospect, I realize that we didn't talk enough about what must have been bothering all of us—that is, we didn't have an *analysis*. It was ongoing. Where we put our energies, what to hit, was a moving target in itself.[20]

When thinking about tactics for how to improve conditions for women as broadly as possible, Ti-Grace (much like Roxanne believed) said liberal feminism *did not* work because it did not elevate *all* women's conditions:

They had an analysis. It was just wrong. They wanted to get women into the mainstream of American society. We're 50 percent of the population. There's no way you can sneak 50 percent of the population past the vertical structure, so, logically, only a few can get by. Even though some women got improved situations, I think as long as you don't attack how women are defined, that it puts a limit on even those women. For example, I was looking at the Bureau of Labor Statistics—one of the few groups that kept tabs on black women, black men, white women—and what I found over decades was that these groups were just moved around like a shell game. But their relationship, as a whole, to people who had the power didn't change. In other words, we were sort of pitted against each other.[21]

This problem—illuminated later by Kimberlé Crenshaw in her work on intersectionality—highlighted the ways that white women and black men, for example, were promoted in order to protect employers from claims of sex and race discrimination, while women of color were largely forgotten and ignored.[22]

Ti-Grace went on, "There were shifts, but not in the basic structure. That's an unintended consequence of this fight. And I'm not saying women shouldn't fight for equal pay. Of course they should! But you've got to go after the structure and the basic principles of the structure. Otherwise, you're not really getting anyplace. That's what NOW didn't want to do, and that's why Valerie [Solanas] was such a big challenge. She was basically saying, 'Fuck you,' to the system, and she was doing it in a very transgressive way. That was really a challenge."[23]

FLORYNCE KENNEDY:
THE MASTER OF TACTICAL INTERVENTION

Florynce ("Flo") Kennedy, who mentored Ti-Grace, was a well-known civil rights lawyer, organizer, and feminist activist who represented high-profile cases including Billie Holliday, Charlie Parker, H. Rap Brown, and twenty-one members of the Black Panther Party.[24] In 1968, she sued the Catholic Church for interfering with women's abortion rights.

In 1974, *People* magazine called her "the biggest, loudest and, indisputably, the rudest mouth on the battleground where feminist activists and radical politics join in mostly common cause."[25] Born in 1916 and one of the first black women admitted to Columbia Law School (she threatened a discrimination suit to gain admission), Flo worked alongside the Panthers and helped to found the National Women's Political Caucus. (She famously helped to organize a mass women's urination protest at Harvard to dispute the lack of women's restrooms on campus.) She was also active in the National Organization for Women, the National Black Feminist Organization, and Black Women United for Political Action during the late 1960s. Flo critiqued the black power movement for placing women in a more auxiliary role and for having a sexist division of labor. She was committed to outrageous social actions; flamboyant and in-your-face mannerisms, speech, and dress; and numerous forms of activist interventions.[26] For example, when she toured with Gloria Steinem giving speeches on feminism, men in the audience would sometimes stand up and demand, "Are you lesbians?" Flo would respond—using an old phrase Ti-Grace often used—that it depended. "Are you my alternative?" she would wryly ask.[27]

Flo helped Ti-Grace solidify her understanding of how to organize and motivate people to work for social change. Ti-Grace described Flo's personality as ideal for bringing coalitions of people together: "Flo was brilliant. The young women especially gravitated toward her. People like myself were like her children in that she was very supportive, but, boy, if you got above yourself in some way, or if you were saying, 'Oh, well, that person's just so undeveloped,' she just cracked down a whip and cut you down to size. I remember Betty [Friedan] was very abusive to me, but she wouldn't go near Flo, because Flo would say, 'You racist bitch!' Flo would lay her out fast."[28]

Ti-Grace remembered Flo as the epicenter of activism during the late 1960s:

Flo was not typical. Everybody knew, no matter where in the world you came from, you were supposed to go to 8 East 48th Street, Apartment 3C. That was Florynce Kennedy. You'd meet everybody in the world there. Everybody had their flyers, or else, once Flo got finished, she made sure you'd have a flyer, and they were all in her briefcase. Everybody who came in got everyone else's flyer. She was a one-woman coalition builder. She had two telephones, three telephone lines. She had two or three TVs going, all news, all the time. Everybody who walked through the door, when she heard your voice, she'd say, "Oh, darling, sweetheart, come in. Ti-Grace, come in. Whoever, Joanie, come on. Oh, darling, I'm so glad to *see* you." She just made you feel great, and you'd go in there and you'd look at these other people and you'd think, *What are they doing here?!* Everybody's looking at everybody else. It was great, and it was very important—very important.[29]

Recalling her first meeting with Flo, Ti-Grace remembered her as dynamic, well-connected, and always in motion:

I joined national NOW in the fall of 1966. There were no meetings of anything. New York NOW had its first actual meeting in February 1967. I met Flo Kennedy at that meeting. . . . The first time I saw her, I was fascinated by her. She seemed incredibly elegant and so contained. She kept putting up her hand and making suggestions that just sounded like she was from Mars to me, but the way she handled herself, the way she would propose things as a motion, the way she seemed to take it so well if it didn't pass and she just kept doing what she thought should be done—she didn't let anybody step on her. I thought, *Wow*.

Ti-Grace went on:

She and [Simone de] Beauvoir were my two main mentors. Beauvoir taught me about women, and Flo taught me about everything else. She would urge you to come here, come there, so I went to black power conferences. I went to New Politics [a Democratic Party movement supporting Eugene McCarthy and Robert F. Kennedy]. I went to hear about everything, and my eyes were just bugging out. I'd never done a demonstration, and Flo takes me to the Pentagon. She took me over to the Vietnam Veterans Against the War[30] and she said, "This is Ti-Grace. Now, you take care of her." So I'm arm-in-arm with these guys, right? They lock arms, and I find myself at the steps of the Pentagon. They're attacking the actual Pentagon! Of course, we all got gassed and the rest of it, but they took care of me. That was really baptism by fire.[31]

As Flo Kennedy was heavily involved in both the women's movement and the civil rights movement, Ti-Grace learned much from Flo about the two: "I once asked Flo about the comparison between the black movement and the women's movement, because she had been active for a long time, and she said, well, she was curious to see if the women's movement could learn from the black movement so that they could maybe miss one mistake that the black movement had made. I said, 'What have you found?' She said, 'Not missed a one!'" Thinking about the wider recruitment of black women and other women of color to radical feminism more than liberal feminism, Ti-Grace believed coalition-building required understanding the root issues: "Get the issues right and then women will come—and the women you want will come, if you get it right. The problem with NOW was that they were really interested only in promoting a few women, whatever color—so it wasn't racist in intent, but in the end, it fell out that way. You also had successful women like Flo, who is going to be very conscious, and she's going to bring other things to the table. It will cut wider."[32]

Flo had a clear sense of how to bring people together from across social identities, cultural boundaries, and a variety of self-interests to coalesce around common goals. Ti-Grace recalled the lessons she learned about organizing from Flo:

It seemed clear to me that she was brilliant and knew an awful lot of things that I didn't know. She had incredible style. In terms of how to live and how to be political, it was obvious that she was a star. She was somebody that you would want to follow around and figure out. . . . I still think Flo was a really incredible, incredible figure, and I think about her a lot. She used to talk about the pathology of oppression. She meant the pathology of the oppressed.

She developed these ideas from watching the black movement. With women it's really clear, simply because of our numbers: We have to be cooperating—there are too many of us—so we have to internalize this identity of the oppressed and we have to collaborate for sex-based oppression to work. That means that our whole identity is built to facilitate and oil the wheels of oppression. So, since it's in our interest to change things, we have to change our identities and peel these parts away. That's very painful, because you think it's what keeps you safe, because that's what the culture tells you. If you don't conform, you're in danger—but conformity means conforming to your oppression, and *that's* the pathology. It's a work that is never completed. Every time you think, *Wow, I didn't realize that I was doing this or that*, or *Wow, that was really against my interest*, you peel that away, and then you say, "Wow, that's it." Then you rest a little and there's a whole other layer.[33]

Flo's legacy for radical feminism cut across racial and class divides, bringing people together and leaving a long-lasting imprint on other feminist activists. Recalling Flo's funeral in 2000, Ti-Grace described how it felt to consider Flo's legacy:

When she died, we were all there, and we were glad to see each other. I remembered something, her great imagery. She did some divorce work. She was something in the courtroom, because she was so brilliant but so unorthodox. Anyway, I remember she was counseling this woman who had been beaten up, and the woman said, "Well, but afterwards he's so nice to me." "Well," she said, "I don't know about you. I'm sure you're right, and I'm sure he's very sweet, very nice. But this is how I see it. Do you see that bathroom over there? That toilet? Just imagine that there's this most beautiful, perfect red rose in the toilet bowl, but it's got stuffed up and everybody's been shitting in there, and it's full. Now remember, there's still that perfect red rose at the bottom. Now, to me, nothing's worth it to go through what I would have to go through to get that rose. But maybe it's worth it to you." It was just in the way—and she had her nails done—and she had a way of expressing it so it was just artistic. It was very powerful. And so I recounted that at her memorial. It was vintage Flo.[34]

TACTICS OF ABORTION RIGHTS

Women's right to abortion, a topic that galvanized many early radical feminists, became an urgent issue in the late 1960s and early 1970s. Building on the momentum from British organizers (led by Marie Stopes[35]) in the 1920s and 1930s, US women in the late 1960s decided it was time for American women to have abortion rights. Inspired by the work of Margaret Sanger,[36] US activists expressed outrage that abortion on demand (not only to protect the life of the mother) was not yet legal in all fifty states during that time. To end unwanted pregnancies, women often had to rely on shady, medically subpar "back-room" clinics and doctors.[37] Some estimates suggest that between two hundred and one thousand women per year died seeking abortions.[38]

Ti-Grace, who had a NOW telephone line in her apartment, recounted years of listening to women talk in desperate ways about unwanted pregnancies, an experience that radicalized her:

I was pretty clear that women's freedom depended on their having control over their persons. I was for repeal of all the abortion laws. You read all these horrible stories about women dying with botched abortions in backstreet alleys, mangled. Women are dying there. You realize, *Whoa*. In my marriage, I had known that if I got pregnant I'd never get away, so I got the connection between reproduction and death. I started speaking out before these commissions, and they'd all be saying, "Oh, I wonder how many abortions she's had." All of this really radicalized me. It made me mad. I thought, *This is really serious*, so I kept fighting within NOW that we had to come out on abortion. I said, "There are all kinds of groups coming out on abortion, and we're supposed to fight for women, and women are dying and we're not going to open our mouths? What's going on?" I really couldn't understand it. Nobody gave a shit about these women.

Ti-Grace went on:

> This wanting or needing an abortion—this could happen to any-
> body, and society must hate women to put them in such a posi-
> tion. No birth control was fail-safe, and yet everything pushed
> you to having sex. You *must* have sex. So you have the Sexual
> Revolution. You have all the complexity of the abortion move-
> ment, which is a problematic bag. Politically I think you have
> people who are in it for free sex—people who aren't feminist at
> all, except insofar as they want women to not have any reserva-
> tions about sexual activity, and, much less, preferences. People
> were coming to a peak of rage that was not shared by everyone. It
> depended on what you were working on, but this was especially
> true for people who worked on abortion. For myself, it was hav-
> ing that NOW telephone in my apartment and just hearing com-
> pletely unconnected instances of how women were discriminated
> against.[39]

The sense of shared rage and collective anger fueled the feeling of necessity about abortion activism; clearly, something had to change, as women's need for abortion was reaching a breaking point. Ti-Grace described the overall context of gender politics in 1968 as harrowing:

> Oh, someone went to a bar and they were thrown out because
> they were with a woman friend, and you have to have a man
> accompany you. It was all over, all over—just all over. A business-
> woman who had bought a first class ticket for the plane, but they
> wouldn't let her sit in business or first class, because only men
> could sit there. Trivial, but constant. Women couldn't open their
> own bank accounts without a male signature. I mean, just every
> place, every place, every place, every place—especially in our sys-
> tem, where no laws are ever taken off the books. So it was just
> like, *drip, drip, drip, drip, drip.*

Recalling how bad it was for women seeking to end pregnancies, Ti-Grace said, "With abortion, it was the humiliation. I felt humiliated that these women had to call a stranger, and they always had complications. They never had money. Many of the people doing the abortions were crazies. Some of the women got raped on the tables, and it was really, really, really sick, sick, sick, heavy, heavy, heavy. I mean, you have to understand how women were hated."[40]

Coalitions grew from the deep roots of this shared anger about abortion, though the ultimate tactical decisions on abortion were in some ways a disastrous miscalculation that ultimately split the movement and undercut its political leverage. Ti-Grace remembered that the coalitions for abortion rights stretched across identity lines:

I met radical women through abortion, primarily, and made
these connections, even though our backgrounds were different.
We were reaching across lines. We looked different; we dressed
differently; we lived in a different part of New York. These were
the women who seemed to be willing to think outside the box.
They didn't care. None of us cared where it took us. We wanted
this, and we were mad. I don't know exactly how others felt inside,
but I know I was really, really angry, and it was unacknowledged.
Even the only formal feminist organization wasn't doing anything—
or finally they came out for "reform" on abortion.

Ti-Grace had major reservations about basing abortion rights on the right to privacy: "I said, 'Don't do that. You're basing your position around the fetus, and you're leaving women vulnerable. You're leaving it wide open.' But people thought, *Oh, well, we can do it on privacy. We've got all this support now and we can become more radical later.* It doesn't work that way. This is your shot, and you have to take it. This is the time you've got to get it on the right ground. But they just didn't."[41]

These abortion rights battles helped Ti-Grace to understand the absolute necessity of *radical* feminism rather than liberal feminism:

So it's a lack of seriousness: I mean, what is it that makes a
radical feminist? What is the difference between people who
are satisfied with the mainstream and those who aren't? Part
of it is how we see ourselves, and I guess it's normal, in a sense,

that people simply want things fixed so that their lives are going to be better. Still, I think what I really got from *The Second Sex* was a conviction that women were a *class*—that regardless of differences, in terms of our parents' circumstances, that the nitty-gritty is the same. I was completely confused about why women wouldn't fight for other women, particularly on abortion, when they had no Catholic hang-ups. Why didn't they identify with our struggle? Would I have, if I hadn't had that telephone in my home? Would I have, if I hadn't grown up in a home primarily of women? I don't know. I just don't know.[42]

Thinking back on the question of abortion and revolution, Ti-Grace said, "We talked about defining what we meant by 'revolution.' We meant very different things—very different things—and as soon as you say that, well, *ciao*! I mean, we're not talking about the same thing at all. Very clarifying. It was sort of like, in many ways, radical feminism came to mean the opposite of what feminism started out as."[43]

When speaking with Kathie Sarachild and Ti-Grace Atkinson about abortion rights in a public forum, I quoted a 2013 article in which Supreme Court Justice Ruth Bader Ginsburg said that abortion rights had "moved too far, too fast, and left themselves open to attack from the right."[44] As a bit of history, the landmark Supreme Court decision *Roe v. Wade*, decided on January 22, 1973, ruled that bans on abortion were unconstitutional based on women's right to privacy. The case was built upon a 1970 Texas case ruling that banning abortion was unconstitutional; further, the decision was based on precedent set by *Griswold v. Connecticut,* which ruled that government interference in "adult consensual marital sexual relationships" was unconstitutional based on the protection of the due process clause of the Ninth Amendment. That case, which involved the arrest of the executive director of Planned Parenthood for distributing birth control illegally, was appealed all the way to the Supreme Court; it was the first case in which the Supreme Court recognized that there are behavioral matters into which the government may not intrude. Both of these cases centered on the right to privacy and articulated the idea that there are constitutional protections not explicitly listed in the Bill of Rights that must be protected.[45]

Reflecting on *Roe v. Wade* and the tactical decisions behind it, Ti-Grace and Kathie thought together about the tactical ways that they fought for abortion and the various regrets they had about how they approached the issue. Ti-Grace again reiterated her concern about basing abortion rights on the premise of the right to privacy instead of reproductive justice and women's fundamental right to control their bodies: "The grounds for *Roe v. Wade* were wrong. Basing abortion on the privacy argument was a mistake. Women have a right to control the persons and products in their bodies. I don't think *Roe v. Wade* was on the right grounds. It wasn't strong enough. Would it have stopped the attacks on it? Not altogether. They would get into the 'viability of the fetus' argument, which was a mistake—but we left ourselves open to that."[46]

The National Organization for Women, in particular, wanted abortion rights passed regardless of the premise upon which it passed, as long as it guaranteed women the right to safe and medically sound abortion procedures.[47] Between 1969 and 1973, they directed their efforts toward burdening the courts with numerous abortion cases, with the hopes that their collaborations with physicians and state prosecutors would ultimately force the Supreme Court to consider the legality of abortion.[48]

Recalling how feminists felt pressured to pass abortion rights quickly, even if on the wrong grounds or even if it made abortion more vulnerable to attack, Ti-Grace felt conflicted about taking more time to get it right: "I wasn't unhappy that a lot of these women could be helped sooner, because the situation when it's illegal is very difficult. It's hard to get good doctors to do difficult abortions on women further along, or women with multiple health problems, so you have to be really careful. You have to be in the hospital context. The women I knew seeking illegal abortions had no money. The guy was long gone. It was this constellation of bad circumstances, so I know there was urgency."[49]

Kathie expressed anger that the same opponents of abortion also opposed contraception, putting women in a double bind:

I guess I've come to feel that most of the so-called "opposition" to abortion—at least the money and the power behind it—also opposed contraception. A lot of it was strategic. It's not about religion, really. It's about population, and whether we are going to have a democratically controlled population with women giving input or not. There's already evidence of a birth strike that is going on in the United States. Whether it's because women actually don't want the bother of having children now that we've all got greater consciousness or because of economic reasons, there are none of the social supports that exist in Europe.

Kathie added that, in a capitalist society, the creation of a workforce becomes more important than women's rights, including their right to abortion:

Spending money on manufacturing things like contraception was more expensive, and we spend our money on the military, for defense. My point is that there is a fall in the birth rate even in the socialist and communist countries, where there were more social supports. There is a fall in the birth rate in Western Europe, now, where the social supports are great. I do think, with raised political consciousness and with fair compensation that women have special input into, there probably will be a birth rate replenishment—because after all, we need to replenish the workforce, we need to eat, we need to analyze. I like the slogan "reproductive justice" as opposed to "reproductive freedom," because it points to the fact that reproductive labor is the root of the problem and reproductive justice is the solution to the problem. Reproductive justice is not only the right to *not* have children, which is the right to contraception and abortion, but the right to be able to have children under good circumstances, which we don't have either, really.[50]

(Notably, the move toward the phrase "reproductive justice" and away from "reproductive rights" originated in the 1980s with the rise of groups like the National Black Women's Health Project and, later, SisterSong, both of which emphasized reproductive justice as a means to address the reproductive needs of women of color.[51])

Ultimately, abortion rights have remained constantly under attack since the 1973 *Roe v. Wade* Supreme Court decision, though the constitutionality of abortion remains in place (for now). Imagining a new context in which women have children under good circumstances—or where US parents have access to subsidized (or free) daycare, child care, maternity and paternity leave (paid, in particular), and schooling—continues to inform the core of radical feminist organizing and tactical interventions. Still, abortion is under constant attack, with nearly four hundred antiabortion laws introduced in 2015 alone (and this predates the Trump administration's vows to repeal *Roe v. Wade*).[52] As a message to all feminists, the radical feminist argument that *we must organize for rights on the most solid premise possible, as early as possible,* continues to haunt the uncertainties around abortion rights today.

TACTICS OF NAMING AND CONSCIOUSNESS-RAISING

The question of naming social movements and their ideas—and how names create identities, suggest political affiliations, and set a tone for different groups—also forms a major part of radical feminist history. From the phrase "radical feminist" to the names of various organizations and publications—the women's liberation movement, New York Radical Women, Redstockings, *No More Fun and Games*, Cell 16, and many more—naming establishes the identity of a group. Dana Densmore, in a 2014 talk entitled "Cell 16: Gender and Agency, with Digressions into Naming," said:

> We didn't want to call the movement "women's liberation,"
> because we didn't believe that "woman" was real. It was patriarchy's idol, a fantasy—an oppressive and alienating prescription
> whose intention and function was to force female people into a
> limited, subservient role for the service and convenience of the
> ruling class, the patriarchy, the ones who invented and enforced
> the definition and imposed it on female people (as they demarcated that class). Should one of us demur, or refuse the definition, or act outside its limitations, all the patriarchal voices
> joined ranks to assert that she 'wants to be a man' or even 'is
> a man' (by which, of course, they meant that she was a freak,
> not that she had entered into the privileged respected class). We
> resisted the prescriptions in many ways, personal and political.

We made theater of the cutting of one woman's long blond hair; we picketed the Playboy Club; we trained our bodies with martial arts and taught self-defense to other women. But we also found a very direct vehicle to deconstruct the gender idol.[53]

Dana situated the conversation around naming in the cultural upheavals of the time: "We were a strange, manic crew. . . . We didn't see an orderly future that would in turn become history and require documentation. Instead, we saw ourselves on the verge of a great upheaval."[54]

Kathie Sarachild also expressed a deep interest in naming, both as a key part of radical feminist identity and recognition and as a way to have connection to other social movements: "The question of names has been an important problem in both the black and women's liberation movements since their beginnings. There has been the revolutionary action of challenging the names of former slave masters given to blacks and the names of present husbands given to women (or the patriarchal tradition of automatically carrying the father's name)." She continued:

Oppressed people have had even their names taken from them, been made nameless or given the names of others. They have wanted their own names and have fought for them. Names are power. Names identify work and leadership that people can trace and link up with. Denying people names is denying them power, denying others information. There is power in knowing the source of things, power for the oppressed. When names are withheld without need, the people lose political knowledge, and knowledge of themselves. Withholding names can also be a way of denying accountability. Names are actually anti-mystique. The proper name reveals the source of an idea, clarifies and demystifies the process of politics and political thinking.[55]

Kathie became a particularly vocal proponent of women naming their experiences and sharing them aloud with other women—a tactic that came to be known as "consciousness-raising." The term first emerged at a 1967 meeting of New York Radical Women, when member Anne Forer said, "Would everybody please give me an example from their own life on how they experienced oppression as a woman? I need to hear it to raise my own consciousness." After this, Kathie started using the term "consciousness-raising" to describe the process of going around the room and talking about issues women faced in their lives.[56] Kathie said of the early design of consciousness-raising:

> The decision to emphasize our own feelings and experiences as women and to test all generalizations and reading we did by our own experience was actually the scientific method of research. We were in effect repeating the seventeenth-century challenge of science to scholasticism: "Study nature, not books," and put all theories to the test of living practice and action. It was also a method of radical organizing tested by other revolutions. We were applying to women and to ourselves as women's liberation organizers a practice a number of us had learned as organizers in the civil rights movement in the South in the early 1960s.[57]

Kathie added that consciousness-raising was designed to access the whole of women's oppression, rather than a mere few issues:

> Consciousness-raising—studying the whole gamut of women's lives, starting with the full reality of one's own—would also be a way of keeping the movement radical by preventing it from getting sidetracked into single issue reforms and single issue organizing. It would be a way of carrying theory about women further than it had ever been carried before, as the groundwork for achieving a radical solution for women as yet attained nowhere. It seemed clear that knowing how our own lives related to the general condition of women would make us better fighters on behalf of women as a whole. We felt that all women would have to see the fight of women as their own, not as something just to help 'other women,' that they would have to see this truth about their own lives before they would fight in a radical way for anyone.[58]

Consciousness-raising highlighted the interplay of women's emotions and lived experiences to generate solidarity between women.[59]

Speaking tactically of consciousness-raising, Kathie argued that consciousness-raising need not have only one form or goal but could be multiple and include many different methods:

> From the beginning of consciousness-raising—as you can see in the first program outlined in 1968—there has been no one method of raising consciousness. What really counts in consciousness-raising are not methods, but results. The only "methods" of consciousness-raising are essentially principles. They are the basic radical political principles of going to the original sources, both historic and personal, and going to the people—women themselves, and going to experience for theory and strategy. . . . It is striking how many people in the right circumstances can suddenly become experts by these standards! . . . Consciousness-raising, then, is neither an end in itself or a stage, a means to a different end, but a significant part of a very inclusive commitment to winning and guaranteeing radical changes for women in society[60]

Citing her surprise at the resistance she faced in encouraging women to adopt this tactic of consciousness-raising, Kathie described the radical roots of consciousness-raising: "There turned out to be tremendous resistance to women simply studying their situation, especially without men in the room. In the beginning we had set out to do our studying in order to take better action. We hadn't realized that just studying the subject and naming the problem and problems would be a radical action in itself, action so radical as to engender tremendous and persistent opposition from directions that still manage to flabbergast me."[61]

Kathie described how the labeling of certain forms of oppression as patriarchal in nature inspired backlash:

> The opposition took the form of misinterpretations and misrepresentations of what we were doing that no amount of explanation on our part seemed able to set straight. . . . Whole areas of women's lives were declared off limits to discussion. The topics we were talking about in our groups were dismissed as "petty"

and "not political." Often these were the key areas in terms of how women are oppressed as a particular group—like housework, childcare, and sex. Everybody from Republicans to Communists said that they agreed that equal pay for equal work was a valid issue and deserved support. But when women wanted to try to figure out why we weren't *getting* equal pay for equal work anywhere, and wanted to take a look in these areas, then what we were doing wasn't politics, economics or even study at all, but "therapy," something that women had to work out for themselves individually. When we began analyzing these problems in terms of male chauvinism, we were suddenly the living proof of how backward women are.[62]

Recounting the tremendous backlash that consciousness-raising groups faced, Kathie outlined many of the resistances that continue to haunt feminists today:

Some people said outright they thought what we were doing was dangerous. When we merely brought up the concrete examples in our lives of discrimination against women, or exploitation of women, we were accused of "man-hating" or "sour grapes." These were more efforts to keep the issues and ideas we were discussing out of the realm of subjects of genuine study and debate by defining them as psychological delusions. And when we attempted to describe the realities of our lives in certain ways, however logical—for instance, when we said that men oppressed women, or that all men were among the beneficiaries in the oppression of women—some people really got upset. "You can't say that men are the oppressors of women! Men are oppressed, too! And women discriminate against women!" Now it would seem to go without saying that if women have a secondary status in the society compared to men, and are treated as secondary creatures, then the beneficiaries would be those with the primary status. Our meetings were called coffee klatches, hen parties, or bitch sessions. We responded by saying, "Yes, bitch, sisters, bitch."[63]

DEEDS, NOT WORDS: TACTICS OF SELF-DEFENSE AND TAKING ACTION TOWARD SOCIAL CHANGE

In 1903, Emmeline Pankhurst, founder of the Women's Social and Political Union (WSPU), a British all-women suffrage advocacy organization, argued that it was "deeds, not words" that mattered for women's rights. WSPU members became known for physical confrontations, including smashing windows, assaulting police officers, staging hunger strikes, defacing public property, and committing arson. In 1918, British women secured the right to vote for women over age thirty, and in 1928, they secured the right to vote for all women.[64] This relentless early radical feminist emphasis on action—seen also in the work of the US suffragettes who followed shortly thereafter—signaled to second-wave feminists the importance of taking action, rather than merely giving lip service to social change.

For Cell 16, part of this strategy involved teaching women to challenge paternalistic notions that women needed men's protection. Notably, the history of the feminist self-defense movement points to the important mix of formal martial arts and informal street fighting, something Cell 16 (and specifically Dana) would become well known for. Prevention of women's victimization constituted a major goal of the early self-defense movement: Feminists argued that women needed to be able to prevent violence against themselves, and also prevent violence against other women. Tactics that aimed for practical self-defense skills ("street fighting") took precedence over some of the more formal modes of self-defense; women learned to fight the internalization of passivity and instead become assertive and loud, and to "make a scene" if attacked. Formal modes of self-defense and formal martial arts also offered women techniques typically reserved only for male students. This fusion of technical and psychological self-defense influenced decades of later developments in the feminist self-defense movement, including efforts spearheaded by Dana to connect networks of martial arts–trained women together.[65]

Dana described the reasons for prioritizing self-defense: "More central to our program was the equipping of ourselves and other women to defend ourselves from the violence used, then and now, to keep women in their place and punish women who stepped out of their place—such as walking down a public street, for example. But indeed, then and now, it wasn't even necessary to step out of place—because, for many men, hatred of women was so deeply experienced that just being female was enough in their view for just being punished by rape, sexual torture, and death." Dana emphasized the value of self-defense as psychological defense against the expectation that women should be fragile, defenseless, and afraid:

And it wasn't just the reality of the need to fight for one's life against actual attack. It was the feeling that one was vulnerable, the sense as one moved through the world that any pathetic creep could jump out and assault and our attempts to protect ourselves would be even more pathetic and ridiculous. How could we have any sense of dignity or privacy with that hanging over us? So at the very beginning we plunged into serious martial arts training ourselves and began self-defense classes for other women, leading after a few years to a formal martial arts school for women.[66]

Roxanne, meanwhile, recounted her experience learning to love the process of turning her own body into a weapon:

For Cell 16, tae kwon do—and its philosophy of being more than just self-defense, giving the body confidence, knowing you can use the body as a weapon—was important to us. You didn't need a gun; you didn't need a sword. In your own integral body—your elbow, your fingers—you can make every part of your body a weapon. That's a different kind of respect for the body. So rather than saying that women's shouldn't use their bodies like this, it introduces them to this practice that will automatically make them see their body differently, whatever shape or color it is. A self-confident body is created, even if they don't perfect the skill itself. I still have a lot of confidence in my body. It was a tactic and a practice of being able to defend yourself—a means to an end.

We saw something much bigger than that, too, specifically for women and little girls. Women could learn to use their bodies in ways that they hadn't used them before.[67]

Dana also felt that their commitment to martial arts represented a shift toward tactical action instead of rhetoric: "We were asserting that we can take initiative on our own, that we don't want to be attacked—we don't have to sit back and say, 'Oh, please don't attack us,' or 'Somebody please protect us!' You make it dangerous to attack you. It's not easy, and of course they say, 'It's not my fault when men want to attack me. Why should I?' It's a process of self-transformation." Dana went on to describe how the process of doing tae kwon do allowed her to transform her body physically and psychologically: "When we started, we thought we were getting that confidence, and it does a lot. It is possible to develop certain moves—even break boards or do some sort of sport sparring—and still have the same attitude of timidity and actually some image as a victim. So that grew into my really analyzing, 'What is the state of mind that stands against the reality of feeling like a victim? What is it when you feel powerful? How do you work with those things?' That became my very important contribution to feminism."[68]

Self-defense served a powerful role in changing the state of women's vulnerability, leading to, as scholar Jocelyn Hollander found, more comfortable interactions with strangers, acquaintances, and partners, increased self-confidence, and transformed beliefs about gender.[69] (Notably, the idea of teaching self-defense as a means to women's empowerment has again caught fire recently, as scholar Laura Kipnis has argued that women have overinternalized ideas about their own vulnerability at the expense of seeing themselves as powerful.[70]) Dana recounted how the feeling associated with becoming physically powerful was crucial to feminist politics:

It is impossible for a woman to have any sense of dignity or privacy if she's feeling like just about any man that jumps out of an alleyway could beat her up, kill her, rape her, whatever. How can you experience yourself as powerful in the world if that is hanging over you? There's no way to make yourself invulnerable.

Even a gun doesn't make you invulnerable. It's how you *feel*. If you feel that if something happened, you would conduct yourself credibly, in a way you could respect—that you didn't buckle, you didn't get paralyzed, you didn't do the ineffectual "Please don't hurt me"—you had already won.[71]

The emphasis on actions rather than mere words—whether self-defense or feminist activism—permeated my conversations with these radical feminists. When I asked Ti-Grace about the importance of words versus actions, she emphatically argued for actions:

Words are important for the revolution. I think you need both theory and practice. You don't know what the words mean until you see the action. If you think about it, throughout history women have been able to write, so they have this sort of mystical relationship with words and are frequently given to a lot of ver-bosity. It's very treacherous. People can say all kinds of the wild-est things, and it doesn't mean a damn thing. There should be a relationship between what you say and how you live your life. I think it's very hard for us to believe that we're important. That said, I reject the tendency in some French feminisms and in women's studies more generally to have words take the place of action.[72]

Like many other radical activists of her time, Ti-Grace put her physi-cal body on the line in the form of public protests, sit-ins, intrusions into spaces that excluded women, and direct actions to undermine power. For example, in March 1970, Ti-Grace and radical feminists Shulamith Fires-tone and Susan Brownmiller joined one hundred other women who went to the offices of the *Ladies' Home Journal* to demand that the magazine diver-sify its subjects, provide for its employees, and remove its sexist content. At the time, almost all of the editors of women's magazines in the United States with large circulations—*Ladies' Home Journal*, *Seventeen*, and *Good Housekeeping*, for example—had male editors. Few stories were written by women, and when women did write stories, they rarely talked about any-thing political.[73] As Ti-Grace recalled, the activists were fed up with how female journalists were handling women's rights: "All these women journalists, when it came down to it, were starting to really get sort of 'pukey,' settling for this or that or the other things. . . . It was disgusting to me, because we had all these demands, and then the journalists started backing down. This creep [the editor of the *Ladies' Home Journal*, John Mack Carter[74]] was sort of patting us on the head like we needed to be awakened."[75]

Ti-Grace and the other activists demanded to see John Mack Carter for a meeting. This meeting got off track. Carter belonged to an organization of journalists that excluded women, even though he ran a magazine that targeted twenty-eight million women; further, all but one editor was male, and the magazine had run only one article about black women in the preceding year. During the meeting, Ti-Grace and her colleagues demanded that the magazine hire a woman editor-in-chief, hire women of color at all levels of the managerial and writing staff, open an on-site daycare, stop publishing ads that degraded women, and stop promoting conservative ideas of "children, church, and kitchen" to women.[76] Ti-Grace told the story: "Shulie and I said, 'Let's get back to the demands.' The editor said something, and I said, 'Let's throw him out!' Whatever it was, I forget, but he said something inappropriate." Things started to escalate quickly: "Shulie started to climb on top of the desk, and of course Susan Brownmiller went, 'Oh my God!' Shulie was climbing over the desk, and I was behind her. I mean, we did this mainly to make him shut up." Ti-Grace threatened to raise the window and throw him out. "I was there," she said, "but it was not what I would call an action that encapsulated the heart of the problem, you know?"[77]

Later on, following her involvement in WARN (Women Against Richard Nixon), Ti-Grace joined Flo Kennedy for a 1972 "Kiss Off Nixon" demonstration in front of Nixon's campaign headquarters. They dressed in death masks and white shrouds to symbolize how Nixon was the "kiss of death" for women's rights issues like abortion. For their involvement in this protest, Ti-Grace, Flo Kennedy, and activists Merle Goldberg and Ellen Powell were all arrested.[78] The philosophy of valuing militant action over words also meant that Ti-Grace faced time in jail for this action.

This was not Ti-Grace's first arrest. In early 1970, Ti-Grace had left The Feminists and operated as an "independent." She wrote:

I went to lots of different demonstrations, etc. And I was doing a lot of speaking. At one of these demonstrations, I ran into Robin Morgan, who was trying to organize something around her having been fired from Grove Press for union organizing (at least this is what she told me at the time). What was being planned was a takeover of Grove Press, which would begin as a sit-in. I should have known better because after the Columbia University sit-ins I knew 'sitting in' was like sitting in on a bomb! A no-win tactic. In any case, I wasn't about to get into a situation like that for union organizing but insisted that if I were to come then there had to be a feminist issue. This issue was picked out as "pornography" because the publisher of Grove had a huge collection and published porn under another name.

And so, in April 1970, activists did a sit-in at the Grove Press offices. Ti-Grace continued, "There were maybe a dozen women involved. It turned out predictably badly. We sat in and were trapped. The publisher didn't hesitate to call the cops. The other protesters went limp and I resisted. So I was charged with a 'felony.'"[79] Nine women were arrested on charges of criminal trespass, destruction of property, and resisting arrest.[80]

Ti-Grace recounted the horrors of her time in jail:

It's a long story, but we ended up in a precinct in the middle of the night. When we got there, they confronted us with the "strip and squat." I had heard about this from Black Panther women over the past years, and also from some of the Columbia women. I realized this was a test case opportunity. I refused. As a result, I was spread-eagled on the front of a cell block and stripped and handcuffed. I would have been shackled also but the prostitutes nearby threatened the cops. Well, there's lots more. I was just there overnight but it was a memorable experience. Definitely shifted my brain and political attitude. What you'd call a "learning" experience.[81]

Ti-Grace described how she coped with that experience in jail: "I just thought, *Well, that's the way it was; step over it.* What else can you do? But you don't step over it. It changes a lot and it affects you, and now I go back to this archive of mine and I can really see it. I just really dealt with it recently—how important it was, how it radicalized me in certain kinds of ways."[82]

Ti-Grace's description of her arrests serves as a reminder that tactical approaches require commitment and dedication to the movement even when facing personal risks and the possibility of trauma. In an unusually quiet and reflective part of our 2008 conversation, Ti-Grace said, "I think people think sometimes that you should only do things if you're not afraid—or if you're afraid, then you should quit. You can be terrified, but if you made a commitment about something, you do it. Because it's the only way anything's gonna happen. Even if you're not successful, unless everybody does what they said they were going to do, it doesn't happen otherwise. It can be very tragic."[83]

(LEFT) Ti-Grace Atkinson gives a lecture at Arizona State University entitled "The Autonomous Woman: Sex, Love, and Feminism" in March 2013. Photo by Stephanie Robinson

(BELOW) Conservative Patricia Buckley Bozell slaps Ti-Grace Atkinson during Atkinson's speech at Catholic University, March 10, 1971.

(LEFT ABOVE) Ti-Grace Atkinson as photographed by her friend Diane Arbus in 1969. Photo courtesy of the estate of Diane Arbus

(LEFT BELOW) Radical feminist Ti-Grace Atkinson and famed civil rights feminist lawyer Florynce Kennedy sing together from one of Kennedy's humorous radical songsheets in 1977.

(ABOVE) Ti-Grace Atkinson gets arrested at the Kiss Off Nixon protest in front of the Richard Nixon campaign headquarters, New York City, 1972.

Ti-Grace Atkinson, September 1971

Ti-Grace Atkinson at her home in Cambridge, Massachusetts. Photo courtesy
of Janna Giacoppo

(LEFT ABOVE) Ti-Grace Atkinson at two years old, held by her father, Francis Decker Atkinson, and surrounded by her mother, Thelma Broadus Atkinson, and her four sisters, Robin Louise, Mary-Wynne, Frances Gay ("Frani-Gay"), and Thelma Byrd ("Temi-Be"). Baton Rouge, Louisiana, 1940. Photo courtesy of Schlesinger Library, Radcliffe Institute, Harvard University

(LEFT BELOW) Ti-Grace Atkinson at two years old with her parents and sisters, 1940, Baton Rouge, Louisiana. In the background are photos of her two brothers: John, who drowned in a swimming pool at age eight, and on the right, Richard (Dickie), who died of double spinal meningitis at one year of age. Photo courtesy of Schlesinger Library, Radcliffe Institute, Harvard University

(ABOVE) Radical feminist Kathie Sarachild at Arizona State University in March 2013, giving her lecture "Feminist Revolution: Toward a Science of Women's Freedom." Photo by Stephanie Robinson

(LEFT) Kathie Sarachild at age twenty-five in New York City, 1968. Photo by Bev Grant

(ABOVE) Kathie Sarachild at the 1968 Miss America pageant protest planning meeting, New York City. Photo by Bev Grant

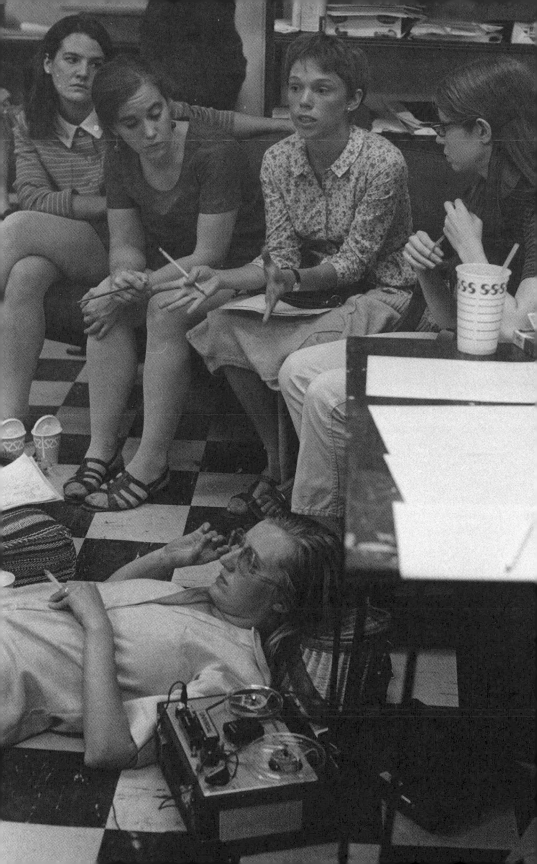

(LEFT) Kathie Sarachild (middle), Peggy Dobbins (floor), Marion Davidson (right), and Judith Duffett (left) plan the Miss America pageant protests, New York City. Photo by Bev Grant

(ABOVE) Kathie Sarachild travels to the Miss America pageant protest in Atlantic City, New Jersey, September 1968. Photo by Bev Grant

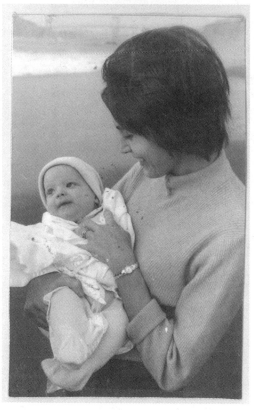

(TOP) Roxanne's first passport,
January 1967, Mexico City

(LEFT) Roxanne with her baby
girl Michelle at four months old,
February 1965

(RIGHT) Roxanne in Mexico City,
May 1968

Roxanne Dunbar at four years old in rural Oklahoma

Roxanne Dunbar-Ortiz in fall 2015 at the Yerba Buena Center for the Arts in San Francisco, at age seventy-nine

Roxanne Dunbar-Ortiz as photographed by Diane Arbus

(TOP) Dana Densmore practices martial arts.
(BOTTOM) Dana Densmore today

4 |

Sex, Love, and Bodies

> Women are no more subject to this system of corporeal production
> than men; they are no more cultural, no more natural, than men.
> Patriarchal power relations do not function to make women the
> objects of disciplinary control while men remain outside of disci-
> plinary surveillance. It is a question not of more or less but of dif-
> ferential production.
>
> —ELIZABETH GROSZ, *Volatile Bodies*

EARLY RADICAL FEMINISM TOOK AIM AT TOPICS TYPICALLY CON-
sidered, especially in the late 1960s, unworthy of or off limits for political
attack. The legacy of these feminists' critiques of familial institutions is
most keenly felt in the resonances of how they reimagined sex, love, and
ways of seeing women's bodies. Links between women and their bodies,
and men and their minds, have long informed the philosophical and theoretical roots of discussions about gender. What does it mean if women
get linked to their (irrational, leaky, troublesome) bodies and sexualities
while men, implicitly and by default, get linked to their (rational, sound,
nontroublesome) minds, thoughts, and spirits? Who determines the
meanings and merits of the body, and how does the body serve as a key
site for political struggle? How did early radical feminists unravel pre-
sumptions and ideas about the body and sexuality, and what implications
did those efforts have?

This chapter takes up the tension around sex, love, and the body—
sites imbued with cultural baggage around women's "proper" roles alongside clear notions of how power is (and should be) deployed to maintain

and manage those "proper" roles. I first trace the debates about the impact of linking women to their (sexualized/erotic) bodies, exploring particularly what it means that women get associated with their bodies while men seemingly do not. I then look closely at radical feminist debates about sex and sexuality, examining institutions that produce sex and sexuality. The chapter then moves into a highly controversial examination of love as a potentially troubling or regressive space, followed by a more lengthy description of how radical feminists have used celibacy, nonsexualities, and asexuality to fight back against patriarchal assumptions about women's sexual availability. Finally, I trace discussions around the phrase "The personal is political" and how sex, love, and bodies inform this core feminist philosophy.

LINKING WOMEN TO THEIR BODIES

The long history of connecting women to their bodies, while men get linked to their minds, has informed feminist politics for many decades. Inherited from the legacies of religious, philosophical, and medical texts—from nineteenth-century medical discourses of "hysteria" to Descartes's assertion that women had a fundamental link to their bodies— this belief in the dualism between male/female and mind/body has persisted. Elizabeth Grosz, in her critical reading of this mind/body split and the gendered qualities of such a dualism, wrote of these early assumptions, "Women are somehow *more* biological, *more* corporeal, and *more* natural than men."[1]

Roxanne Dunbar-Ortiz, discussing this association, criticized the automatic assumptions about the body that inform contemporary body politics: "When you say *body*, it's such a feminine noun. When you say *body*, you don't really immediately think of a male body. I think maybe a gay man would—but it's so *womanly*, as body, as flesh, as nurturance, as to be entered and opened and sucked on. It's the passive body." Roxanne likened this, at its root, to the patriarchal control over bodies both in terms of gender (e.g., women as wives, prostitutes, and caretakers) and race (e.g., Africans as slave labor): "The body in slavery is a commodity, too, bought and sold, and that's the similarity with the woman's body. It's fungible. It has value in itself before it even works, and with its labor, you can take it and sell it. That's so freakish that people don't even want to think about it, but when you think about it, that's really the position of women. It's like the enslaved Africans and the slave trade that developed under capitalism, or that created capitalism. It's the fungible body." Worried that radical feminists missed these connections between slavery and sexism at first, she added, "I think we tried to make those comparisons—between gender and race, sexism and racism—and now that the body is a subject of theory, it's important to see those linkages."[2]

Emphasizing the way that women's value is assigned to their physical bodies, Roxanne worried about the commodification of women's bodies: "We commodify ourselves now. In so many ways, that's still going on. In the 1960s, there were so many comparisons that were made. The idea of the sex caste and class system, the roles women played, these mattered—but also, the *actual body*. Only white men, propertied men, can really own their own bodies. That's another thread that links all women together, because even the very rich women, they're often just trophies, trophy wives, or much younger than the men. It's their body that's the value, the prize, the commodity."[3]

Ti-Grace Atkinson echoed these concerns, cautioning about the hazards of feminists reinforcing these historical links today: "It would be good to not have to be so concerned with our bodies, but I still think the distinction between being seductive versus being positive in your appearance is important. I look at you; you look at me. I don't look at myself, for the most part. So if somebody is really grungy and dirty, it makes a statement often about where their heads are. It can be kind of a hostile statement. You want something in between." She continued by saying that body acceptance can lead to less obsession with the body and better feminist politics: "So much emphasis on the body is not good. It's very tricky, because I think that women accepting their bodies as they really are—not as somebody has tried to say it *should* be—is also a way of getting rid of that focus, of making the body have less weight, less importance."[4]

Ti-Grace was a poster child of radical feminism—something the mainstream media often said during the late 1960s and early 1970s when covering the emerging feminist movement—and her body and appearance attracted much attention and publicity in media reports. For example, Marilyn Bender of the *New York Times* wrote of Atkinson, "Where Mrs.

Friedan is low-pitched and brusque, Ti-Grace Atkinson, president of NOW's New York Chapter, emotes in a dreamy, softly sexy style."[5] Known for wearing a white fur coat to many of the early radical feminist meetings, Ti-Grace saw her beauty (one newspaper article referred to her simply as a "tall blond") considered in the media as a contradiction to her politics. A *Life* magazine reporter, Sara Davidson, interviewed Ti-Grace and several other activists, lamenting in a 1969 piece on the women's liberation movement, "Some of them are quite beautiful, which creates political contradictions. Women's liberation rejects the glossy magazines' vision of the liberated girl, who wears see-through clothes, smokes Virginia Slims and gives free love. The feminists say this fake liberated girl is a sex object, a bigger and better prostitute, not a human being. Women's liberation members avoid makeup, fancy hair styles and seductive clothes."[6]

Looking back, Ti-Grace reflected on her own relationship with her body: "I've been part of the society, so I've had to think about it. I try to think about it just enough to pass, because when I went through periods where I was pure in that respect [rejecting the belief that appearance matters], it attracted too much attention, and that's not what I wanted. I wanted people to leave me alone in that way. If I put on lip gloss or if I broke too many norms of appearance, this attracted attention, and I wanted to get rid of that." Thinking about how her body image has changed with aging, Ti-Grace said, "I've always thought, unlike my friends, that aging got me out of certain situations. I remember a friend of mine, Ruby Rohrlich,[7] she said, 'Yes, but you're either a sex object or you're nothing.' And there is that. You're not seen. That, to me, is preferable."[8]

During our first interview in 2008, when I told Ti-Grace that as a researcher I studied women's sexuality, she objected to feminists devoting their scholarship to the study of women's sexuality in part because it implicitly linked together women, sexuality, and the body. She did not want sexuality (and sex itself) to have more emphasis than necessary: "It's tricky, because to give sex primacy of place is itself a whole problem. I certainly fell in that trap—but it is a good way to get people angry. When I wrote that piece on vaginal orgasm as a mass hysterical survival response, I had been asked to speak to this group of liberal doctors on sex and feminism. They wanted to be titillated, so I wrote a whole paper on it!" Ti-Grace cautioned that conservatives maintained a near-constant obsession with sex, which undermined feminist activism. She described her time picketing the *New York Times* for their sex-segregated want ads as an action reduced by conservatives to sex: "If you said anything about equal rights for women, people would say, 'Oh, you must be a lesbian.' I mean, you're thinking, *Where did that come from?* It made no sense at all. Is it a threat? Well, now, what I think it meant was that they were obsessed with sex! Either they look at you and see you with a man, or they look at you and see you with a woman. That's how they see you—as a disembodied cunt." Still, Ti-Grace felt conflict about avoiding discussions of sex altogether. In the late 1960s, she recalled, NOW desperately wanted to avoid discussing sex, but Ti-Grace had disagreed: "Even with abortion, they kept saying to stay away from sex issues—but you can't stay away from sex!"[9]

Issues of women's sexuality and the body also became less interesting to Kathie Sarachild over time. In a public forum where I conversed with Kathie and Ti-Grace about gender and power, Kathie expressed that she once saw issues of women's bodies as more relevant, but now saw them as trivial: "When I was a young feminist, I was really passionate about this stuff. I loved talking about it. I didn't think it was trivial at all. Now it's hard for me to talk about it, because I really don't care as much about these kinds of issues." Kathie emphasized that her interests had evolved even while she recognized the importance of continuing to analyze sexuality: "I'm much more interested in these economic chess games, and how are we going to have the power to decide about economic matters. I *do* think you have to talk about issues of sex and bodies, because they are a great source of worry for young women. It's really a very important part of life, and women suffer terribly because of it. It keeps them from being able to pay attention to other things." Thinking about the issues young women face today, Kathie said, "I've been very distressed about the stories I hear. Pressure on women to have to shave their pubic hair? That's outrageous! I can't believe that we are going back further than we had it before in certain areas. There are changes. The spread of porn worries me, too."[10]

Ti-Grace responded to Kathie's statements by expressing hesitation and caution about the true aims of the sexual revolution during the

1960s: "The problem is that the women's movement came up in a time when the so-called sexual liberation movement arrived. It was free love. I remember you proved that you were a liberated woman by sleeping with somebody you didn't even like! You don't have to think a long time before you figure out that that was bullshit. Free love? Free love for *whom*? What's going on here? There was exploitation going on here, and talking about it was important in terms of self-protection from being exploited." She continued by wondering whether it was better to be sexually exploited or not seen at all:

> My friend and I were eating in a restaurant, and this guy was referring to us as "honey," and she got quite riled at this and said something like "I didn't like it," and I said, "You know, it'd be really good to reach an age where no one is calling you 'honey' like that," and she said, "Well, the problem is that you will go from people not calling you 'honey' to not seeing you at all. You won't even exist." I thought that would be okay, because I could do my own thing. I would say that as I've gotten older, I'm not seen in the same way. It's nice to be rid of that, and it's something that affects most people in this room more than you are conscious of. We are constantly reminded that our values are based on our appearance, and that's not very humane.[11]

TAKING AIM AT SEX AND MARRIAGE

Ti-Grace argued that sex and love form the bases of women's oppression, and that many of the qualities of sex that seem physiological actually relate to women's oppression. In many ways, these claims foreshadowed what would eventually become an entire movement dedicated to the recognition of asexuality, nonsexualities, and celibacy as valid identities and forms of (non)sexual expression that would occur forty years later. In their 2010 essay on imagining asexuality, Karli June Cerankowski and Megan Milks ask, "How do we begin to analyze and contextualize a sexuality that by its very definition undermines perhaps the most fundamental assumption about human sexuality: that all people experience, or *should* experience, sexual desire?"[12] Second-wave theorizing about sex and love helped to provide a framework for thinking about asexuality as a form of *political* resistance.

Ti-Grace's famed 1968 speech (and later essay), "Vaginal Orgasm as a Mass Hysterical Survival Response,"[13] includes a statement where she recognized the irony of talking about sex while trying to dismantle assumptions about women's sexuality. In this speech she said, "What could be more amusing than a Feminist talking about sex? Obviously, if Feminism has any logic in it at all, it must be working for a sexless society. But sex you want? Sex you're going to get."[14] She went on to argue that women learn to orgasm vaginally not for themselves but as a means of pleasing men and of survival: "Why *should* she learn vaginal orgasm? Because that's what men want. How about a facial tic? What's the difference?" For Ti-Grace, sex had no place in a free society: "In a free society, you cannot have the family, marriage, sex, or love. You will have your Vietnams, and more, you will have your murdered Martin King's, and more, you will have your Revolution unless your wives and mothers free themselves, because that's where the foundations of oppression and exploitation are laid. You are going to have to have your power wrenched away from you right where you live, and you're not going to like it. And that's tough shit."[15]

Nearly fifty years later, Ti-Grace still argued that sex (and romance) *as an institution* must be challenged: "Sex and love is the dynamic that keeps women's oppression going, and the sex-class institutions will just keep recreating themselves unless you get at the deeper dynamics of this thing. But I don't think—until you challenge those institutions—that probably you can know much for sure. Women loving women has to be good, right? You can see it from that perspective. But when you see the role-playing, you realize, well, it doesn't seem to be the best choice for everybody."[16]

For decades, Ti-Grace has publicly called upon women to question the reasons that they want to have sex or fall in love, asking why friendship does not have more value to women: "I think sex and love often revolve around what is acceptable in appearance and in the body. We need social contact, so I'm not sure where that line is—what is sexual or not—and I think that will be transformed over time. I think ultimately friendship is more important."[17] Thinking back on the late 1960s, when sex seemed mandatory in an unchangeable way, Ti-Grace said, "Look at how our ideas about sexuality have changed since then—and that's something we did not think of as malleable. It was *not* malleable. It was like, 'Well, you gotta have sex.' I always thought, if your options for sex carry too much weight or are negative, you don't have to be negative. Better to pass on sex altogether. It was certainly an option I saw, but I got a lot of resistance to it, which surprised me. The other women in the movement felt that you have to have sex. I disagree."[18]

For Ti-Grace, sex and love took away from the communal aspects of political activism, while friendship allowed for coalition-building and expansion of the movement: "When people say that there's no movement, part of it is that there aren't bodies. We used to do this almost 24/7. We put everything into it, and that meant a physical commitment to it, and it also meant working with other people and not being individually driven. We didn't invest only in our personal relationships. That takes you away from community." She went on to say, "The idea about possession of people—other people—is built into these institutions. It's a value that we don't have with friendship. Friendships aren't exclusive. But when we talk about sex, it tends to get into possessiveness. *Mine. That's mine.* Now, what could that mean?"[19]

Sexual relationships and marriages, particularly traditional ones, often disempower women and lead to men treating women as property, something Ti-Grace objected strongly to:

It's delusion. It's a false belief that leads people to control other people, and it seems to be very capitalistic. It's treating people like property, and it's treating people like they don't change, that life doesn't change, and it does. I was married at seventeen and if I had stopped growing then, it might have worked out—but people grow and change, and their relationships to others change. But if you make a commitment for life, to do the best we can, is that permanent? I mean, I always thought that marriage would be a lifetime thing, and oh my God, was I wrong.[20]

Ti-Grace said that being pushed into her short-lived marriage by her mother was something she could never forgive: "That was my mother's doing, 'cause she thought I was wild. I was unhappy, sullen, and difficult, and she thought I was rebellious. And I was, I guess. I would get into trouble, and she was angry because I had embarrassed her. Years later she would say to me, 'Do you forgive me for that?' . . . I said, 'Mom, I will never forgive you for that. It was unforgivable!' She understood." Within her marriage, Ti-Grace realized she no longer had control over her own life: "It was not easy to get divorced. Back then, you had to have a reason. It's the only contract of its kind where the terms aren't listed in it. I knew I'd never get married again. Later, people would say, when you went for financial support in philosophy, 'We can't waste our money. We have to give it to the men, because you'll get married again.' 'I'm not going to do that again,' I'd tell them. But they don't want to give it to you." She went on, "I did realize, at seventeen, *Gee, I'm going downhill at seventeen . . . I'm married.* The wedding is the high point of your life, and from then on it's downhill. I thought, *Wow.* That seemed sort of depressing and odd."[21]

Her political resistance to sex and marriage sometimes contradicted her emotional impulses toward sex. Thinking back on her feelings about sexuality and desire, Ti-Grace said:

> There are times in your life when—if you look at it, say, before you're very conscious or whatever—that you're more sex-obsessed than at other times. It usually has something to do with, in my case, what else was going on in my life. I remember that when I was painting, when I was really *into* a painting, you had an experience that was almost like an orgasm for me. Things were really going well. I think any kind of creative work takes that kind of energy. With some people, it makes them more sexual. But I think the idea of libidinal energy has something to do with it, although I would rather it not be called that.

Ti-Grace argued that, while sexual impulses emerge, women should still work against the ways that sex oppresses women: "You're not going to live in the society where sex never comes up—that's not realistic—so in that way, you have to be able to accept that you have sexual feelings. Just because it's important to you doesn't mean that it's what you think it is—'natural.' Sexual feelings change. But I think ideally you have to be able to say, 'There are some things we just don't know, and we have to live with that. There are some things we know are bad, and we have to get rid of those things."[22]

When I asked Ti-Grace about what we need to get rid of as a society, she responded, "We have to get rid of marriage, poverty, different institutions that harm people. And I have a really hard time accepting that S&M [sadomasochism] and the rest of it can be a good thing. Insofar as I understand this issue about performance, I think that certain practices reify them or justify that structure. I think this idea of power, of competition, of these things as the meaning of life and your value as a person, how much money you have, or your value is based on fame, or your value is not internal but driven externally—that's a bad twist." She reiterated her claim that marriage is about survival: "Marriage leads people, whether subconsciously or not, to a permanent relationship where you have somebody to take care of you, even though in our economy most families need two incomes. In terms of the rewarding character of work, the guy's job is usually put first because he's making more money, and a woman rarely can really have a career because it often requires you move and there's no job for her. It starts to unravel."[23]

While the sexual revolution paved the way for women to have sexual pleasure, multiple sex partners, and more sexual freedom, Ti-Grace worried about the post-sexual-revolution impact on women's sexual lives. When discussing "hookup culture," or women having a lot of casual sex with multiple sex partners, Ti-Grace felt conflicted about the utility of this approach: "I guess my primary critique would be: It puts too much importance on sex. I like it in terms of 'People don't get entangled,' but the idea of casual and multiple, that's sort of not defined. That's what makes it interesting, too, because that entire word, *hookup*, is so undefined. It seems like a performance of 'not feeling,' the performance of 'it doesn't matter.'" Ti-Grace emphasized the importance of finding internal value, not defined by others (particularly men), as a key to fulfillment:

> I keep thinking: *Why would you do that [hookup] instead of masturbating?* To feel attractive? Desirable? That leaves your value as determined from the outside all of the time when you need more balance

and to get your value more internally. To get internal value, you're going to seek out relationships with people who think similarly, who also have thought about what's important to them, and I think that people who think independently are more reliable, actually! If you're in a conversation with a woman who gets her value from the outside rather than the inside, her thoughts are really going to be reflections of the values of that society. You're not going to get what she's worked out for herself, and if she's worked it out for herself, her commitment is much greater to those things so you can rely on that more. I think this has some importance. Of course, in a society that was more communistic, that would change everything, in terms of people not needing other people to materially survive.[24]

Ti-Grace adamantly emphasized that women should seek pleasure for themselves and not see casual sexual relationships as liberatory:

What passes for some kinds of third-wave feminism, really, is a kind of going back to the old sexual revolution where we sort of turned the tables—I did it briefly, too—where you think, *Well, I'll just sleep with somebody once*, and then you say goodbye and think, *I'll be liberated*. But then I asked myself, *Am I enjoying this?* and I thought, *No*. Then why are you doing it? Well, most women didn't go through that process of saying, "Is this something I want to do?" And if it isn't, I shouldn't do it, because certainly if sex is supposed to be anything, it should be about pleasure, and if I'm not getting pleasure from it, then I shouldn't do it.[25]

Imagining a vision for women's sexuality, Ti-Grace wanted women to think more carefully about their own interests, needs, and pleasures: "I think women need much more attention paid to what interests them and what they want to do and what they want to pursue, what they would like to do by themselves. What would they like to do if it were just up to them, if they were really free to choose? Part of that is feeling like you're important to yourself—putting yourself first and what interests you. It doesn't matter if anybody else is interested in it or not. I think we're pressured into defining things from that angle much more by conventions than we realize."[26]

Recounting a story of a woman she knew with an abusive boyfriend, Ti-Grace advised women to leave any bad relationship and instead become self-reliant:

> I said, "Leave him! You make the money. There's no way you're dependent on him. He's not behaving nicely. You've tried. Leave him! Get rid of him. Toss him out!" Well, this wasn't helpful. So the next time we hear the same story, I said, "What is going on here? I'm being demeaned by listening to this again. Why are you still here?" Well, everybody turned to me: "Well, you've got to have sex!" I said, "Have you ever heard of masturbation? Or if you have to have a partner, what about another woman? Sex is not like food or sleep!"[27]

PROBLEMATIZING LOVE

The question of how love might inform feminist politics has been taken up in vastly different ways by scholars in the last several decades. While scholars have largely ignored love as a target for feminist analysis, recent work that frames love as part of an ethic for women of color has reimagined the role of love and its political implications in forging solidarities and alliances. For example, feminist writer bell hooks, in *All About Love*, writes, "Indeed, all the great movements for social justice in our society have strongly emphasized a love ethic. Yet young listeners remain reluctant to embrace the idea of love as a transformative force. To them, love is for the naïve, the weak, the hopelessly romantic. Their attitude is mirrored in the grown-ups they turn to for explanations."[28] She goes on to write, "There can be no love without justice. Until we live in a culture that not only respects but also upholds basic civil rights for children, most children will not know love."[29] For hooks, love stands as the opposite of lying, selfishness, consumerism, and despair. Similarly, activist and scholar Ai-jen Poo, writing of organizing domestic workers, says of love and politics: "Like great love affairs, great campaigns provide us with an opportunity for transformation. They connect us to our deeper purpose and to the commonalities we share, even in the face of tremendous differences. They highlight our interdependence, and they help us to see the potential that our relationships have to create real change in our lives and in the world around us."[30] This framing of love moves away from romantic love as a target and instead frames love as a broader ethic that can unite women politically. This distinction maps onto Ti-Grace's conceptualization of the difference between romantic love, for which she has great suspicion and caution, and friendship/solidarity, which she more openly embraces.

In March 2013, Ti-Grace and Kathie both visited Arizona State University for a series of events that included two keynote lectures and a joint panel discussion about contemporary feminist issues. Ti-Grace chose to give her keynote about the problems of love, a talk she entitled "The Autonomous Woman: Sex, Love, and Feminism." She began the talk with a series of critiques about dependency, saying that autonomy allowed women to have freedoms otherwise denied to them through dependence: "An autonomous woman has choices. A dependent one does not. When a woman is dependent, her ability to get out of an abusive relationship, for example, is greatly compromised. Even worse, this dependency may prevent her from even *seeing* that she is being oppressed by institutions. Even the ability to see that she is being discriminated against is diminished, perhaps even obliterated; in other words, she is no longer able to objectively assess her situation. Why 'see' what she has no power to change?"[31]

Breaking with hooks and Poo, Ti-Grace saw love as a trap for women and assessed the problems of the women's movement as a problem of cultural identity too reliant on love at its core: "The women's movement quickly devolved into a women's culture, or our version of cultural nationalism. And women's culture is a culture of 'love.' The paradigm for this love quickly became the mother-child relation, an asymmetrical relationship by definition wherein the mother loves the child *unconditionally*. Basically, no matter what you do, it's fine! It's hard to imagine a more deadly principle to live by if your goal in life is to effect political change!"[32]

Tracing the history of love, Ti-Grace began in the eighth century BC in Greece, where Chaos and Eros were the ultimate powers: "'Love' (Eros) has as his task the appeasement of these overwhelming and terrifyingly destructive forces (Chaos). 'Love' is described as the fear response of mortals to Chaos; Eros expresses this love through sacrifice. And sacrifice of every kind is made. Love is an attitude of awe and then, in its more active forms, supplication and surrender. . . . Love is an emotion—an admission of helplessness. It is opposed to reason and understanding." She then cited the transition in the Middle Ages from love as a fear response to love as "the act of a credulous person who can be led by the nose by anyone's whim."

She added:

In the early Middle Ages, there is a crisis in religion about how men can *understand* God. By this time, reason has assumed a more prominent place in society, and there are questions: How does anyone know there *is* a God? Or at least that God is who and/or what you describe and worship? Of course, it follows that whomsoever has a grip on the definition of the *right* God wins, and that sect takes power in the temporal world. Saint Augustine (fourth century) was very vexed by these problems. How can we *know* God? How can you ask someone to *believe* in God if you can't *understand* Him? So Augustine is wrestling with how to resolve this problem. And he comes up with an amazingly clever sleight of hand by flipping the two sides of this conditional. It is no longer "I will believe in God *if* I can understand Him." Rather, it is "In order to *understand* God, you must first believe." And "belief" is achieved *not* through reason but through *faith* (another word here for "love"). And *faith* is a gift from God. You either have it or you don't. . . . Faith and love become synonymous with the *irrational*, and *this* is good! Faith and love become the *source* of understanding, no longer the *result* of understanding.[33]

Tracing her argument to religious mysticism, Ti-Grace emphasized the clear eroticism in mystical literature and art: "It is a very small step from here to religious mysticism, which is the practice of an ecstatic loss of self. Both mystical literature and art are heavily erotic, although the Church denies this. The idea that you can achieve an *immediate* (intuitive) knowledge of God through mysticism is evident here. And mysticism is the process of giving yourself up to the experience (mostly women engaged in this particular practice). The climax of the love of God was self-annihilation." Moving forward in history, Ti-Grace said:

> In the Renaissance, there are further developments, but really just a tweaking of the concept of love. Love became an end in itself and was not necessarily to be gratified by sexual experience. In "courtly" love, women are "elevated" to a position of unquestionable sovereignty over men—but of course women must be like the Virgin Mary, and strict obedience goes along with this "sovereignty." . . . Schopenhauer[34] says that sexual union is for the benefit of the species, not for the individuals involved in it: "Love drives men and women to suicide, madness, and extremes of sacrifice." Basically Schopenhauer is repeating here what has already been understood about love: It is about a loss of self.[35]

Shifting to an analysis of contemporary feminist perspectives on love, Ti-Grace provided a scathing critique of the loss of critical attention toward love:

> How is it that love has not enjoyed more of a critical analysis in feminism? Isn't love a secret goal—which everyone assumes anyway—of most women, in terms of fulfillment and finding happiness? It's the prize at the end of the rainbow. It is, for the most part, a chimera and a delusion. What I am proposing is that "love" is a major obstacle to women's liberation. Can we be agents of our own destinies, as long as we hang on to our part in the oppression between the sexes? No. Flat out! No. We *either* face up to our own collusion in this particular variation of the pathology of oppression *or* we should forget the whole enterprise of liberating women.[36]

Further nuancing her critiques of love, Ti-Grace advocated caution about emotions and the magical thinking behind them:

We tend to think of "love" as atomic or as a primitive impulse—something irreducible. No one believes you have to "define" love. You know it when you *feel* it. (Remember the theological tricks around this "argument.") However, philosophical psychology has tried to tackle this phenomenon. Emotions are based on feelings. Feelings don't come out of the blue: We are indoctrinated as to what the appropriate responses are in various contexts. In other words, our feelings—which are experienced only subjectively—are predetermined by our minds: what we have been taught or programmed about in terms of what we *should* desire, what we *should* avoid. Ultimately, the context of our minds, which contain impressions from all our previous education and experiences, determine our "magical" emotions. Women like to think of "love" as an escape from harsh reality—a kind of transcendence—whereas in actuality it makes us victims of this same reality. Is this trade worth the price? This is the question we must all answer for ourselves.[37]

Always self-critical and able to describe her own limitations, Ti-Grace assessed her own love experiences as problematic: "I've had my share of 'love' experiences. I have noticed that there felt like an element of surrender in these experiences; I became more passive, whereas my partner was energized by this experience. That was a clue for me. Not a complete shield against it, but a brake against such self-annihilation."[38] Ti-Grace emphatically critiqued romantic love and the implications of romantic love: "I get nervous with the love. I think it's delusional, just from my own experience, but I'm not saying that it isn't pleasurable! Maybe we can't get through life without some delusions or illusions—but, looking for love, as women are supposed to do, that's the big quest. *That* is bad. It justifies getting into bad situations—not taking responsibility for yourself, in terms of situations you put yourself in, and so on. Being self-reliant is key."[39]

When I asked about whether same-sex marriage might differ from the heterosexual contexts in which marriage has previously been seen or defined, Ti-Grace (responding prior to the 2015 Supreme Court passage of marriage equality legislation) still expressed reluctance about contexts where control and possession dominate the discourse: "When I taught political philosophy and feminism, I always bring up the idea of ownership. I have a number of friends—Mary [Eastwood], Shulie [Firestone], and Anne [Koedt]—and they're on this tier. For example, women often have many friends, but with romance we talk about '*my* boyfriend' or '*my* girlfriend' in a different way. They can't be lots of other people's boyfriend or girlfriend at the same time. There's possession here. How can that be good? I don't know. It's exhausting."[40]

CELIBACY AS POLITICAL RESISTANCE

As one possible solution to undermining the institutions of heterosexuality, sex, and love, political celibacy (or choosing to not have sex for political reasons) is integral to a radical feminist politics and has a long history in radical feminist visions of sexual possibilities. Nevertheless, little has been written about political celibacy as a tactic, in part because the refusal of sex often gets erased from complicated stories that attach women to their sexuality (even within resistance movements). As sexuality scholar Nicola Gavey argues, this may be in part due to the coital imperative so deeply embedded into thinking about women's sexuality, where penile-vaginal penetration is assumed, all other sexual acts are deemed "foreplay," and nonsexualities are largely forgotten or erased.[41] Asexuality scholar Ela Przybylo writes, "If the routine disbelief and disqualification of asexuality as a legitimate sexual identification spurs from the belief that sex and sexuality are central organizing forces for all modern subjects, then the concomitant absenting of political feminist celibacy as well as its framing as a threat to contemporary sex positive feminism stems from a feminist conviction or feeling that sex and sexuality are central to all feminist subjects."[42] In short, feminists need to be called out for their assumptions that the behavioral practices of sex are central to feminism.

Other recent work on asexuality and its links to feminism have noted that pro-sex feminism problematically frames anti-sex positions and asexuality as pathological or inferior. Asexuality scholars Karli June Cerankowski and Megan Milks write, "The crucial problem of the discourse surrounding the anti-porn/pro-sex debates is that it situates female sexuality as either empowered or repressed: the attendant assumption is that anti- or asexuality is inherently repressive or dysfunctional. The asexual movement challenges that assumption, working to distance asexuality from pathology and in doing so challenging many of the basic tenets of pro-sex feminism—most obviously its privileging of transgressive female sexualities that are always already defined against repressive or 'anti-sex' sexualities."[43] Further, asexuality as imagined today likely draws from second-wave radical feminism in its root structure, particularly in its claims that other kinds of connections, affections, and solidarities might have more value or salience than traditional notions of sex and sexuality. As Przybylo writes, "We thus see asexuals holding the tools for transfiguring sexuality, through emphasizing acts other than 'sex,' and transfiguring relational networks, through circumventing the importance of exclusive dyadic units."[44] Thus, messing with sex, and assumptions about women's sexual access, had paramount importance in early second-wave radical feminist thinking about political celibacy, influencing later generations' conceptualizations of sexual resistance and sexual refusal.

Radical feminist group Cell 16 prioritized sexual refusals and celibacy as necessary and important to moving feminist politics forward. Dana Densmore felt adamantly that celibacy represented a way for women to claim agency and that having sex was neither necessary or important for empowerment: "There were two other major areas in which we made assertions of our agency. One was in rejecting abusive relationships some women were entering into out of the ideology (promoted by psychologists) that we 'needed' sex." She continued: "Celibacy, we said, was preferable to unhealthy relationships, and was an honorable alternative until such time (should it come) as one found a love relationship that supported and celebrated one's human character and dignity. This came out in reaction to our dismay of seeing women sacrifice their feminist principles and their energies to struggle with a man who could not accept an equal. Willingness to honor celibacy allowed women to leave abusive men. Then men could choose to become decent or not, but if not, they would not have women's psychological and domestic support."[45]

One of the most controversial forms of rebellion that came out of Cell 16 was its position on celibacy as a political action or choice. Framed as a political identity and decision rather than a personal one, intentional pre-determined celibacy was put forth by the group as a valid form of resistance to sexual norms that mandated men's sexual access to women. When I asked Roxanne and Dana about their vision for the future of sexuality, they took stock of the relationship between Cell 16 and its unique ideas about sexuality and celibacy. Dana started by disavowing the relationship between Cell 16 and female separatism: "First of all, we were not separatists. The celibacy thing is about options. There's nothing wrong with it if the alternative is an oppressive relationship. Men cannot be permitted to have relationships with women—intimate relationships with women—if they can't behave themselves. If they're abusive, oppressive, or just disrespectful, we have to deny them our energies and our service."[46]

When I asked how the idea for politically motivated celibacy first came about, Dana answered:

The idea of celibacy came about because we saw at [the 1968] Sandy Springs [conference] that it was explicitly being cited that "We cannot leave abusive relationships!" *Abusive* relationships! Some women thought that leaving abusive relationships was a kind of separatism. We thought, *What are you staying here for? You have to leave!* This isn't slavery. *Leave.* They said, "Oh, we couldn't." We said, *"Leave them."* Some of the women believed that if they wanted to have sex, they had to be with them (and the idea of sex with women, of course, was not to be thought of at that time yet—not by them, and not by Redstockings even now). [The women at Sandy Springs] would say, "We need sex, so we're stuck in these abusive relationships."[47]

Dana situated the high stakes of sexual refusal at the time:

There was an ideology at the time that sex was necessary or you'd dry up. If you didn't have sex, you would not be a woman, you would be nothing. That's what we were opposing. First of all, it's not essential. You can have a perfectly good life without sex, but if you have a good situation and you want it whether with a man or a woman, great. But if it is not good, or it is break-ing you down and it is limiting you, preventing you from being who you are, then you don't want to do that. If it is siphoning off your energy, if you have to spend all your time struggling, you have an alternative.[48]

Dana added that the idea of refusing sex allowed women to question all sorts of other prescriptions about gender and what it meant to be women:

Women have been sat on by these categories—chained and bul-lied so much that we don't even know what a "woman" is or wants. We might personally have some suspicions that women are more nurturing or more oriented toward relationships or sexually accessible or peaceable—and there is some evidence for these things—but in fact how about if we just got rid of the prescriptions and just let women be human beings? Categories are very limiting for women. You get rid of those categories and there is going to be a whole human range, and perhaps much overlap between men and women. But it makes no sense to be prescriptive.[49]

Roxanne discussed the controversial decision to embrace celibacy as a feminist tactic and remembered Cell 16's early conversations about women's oppression as connected to sexuality:

We thought they were really important at the time. I think our whole group, it's a process we went through, where we were deal-ing at the same time with all the stereotypes of women, and here the countercultural movement has a new version of liberation—the "Big Tit," as Valerie [Solanas] might call it—of what women should be, but in a more attractive form, with lots of jewelry and long dresses and stuff that's attractive. But it's still the *woman* in the position of, as always, definitely being totally and always open to sex with anyone. Women are supposed to convince them-selves that they're empowered by this.[50]

Of Cell 16's decision to embrace celibacy, Roxanne said, "I think we were really the only group that felt that the 'sexual liberation' taking place was just an iteration of a new face of misogyny." When I asked her whether this meant women were expected to be always ready for sex, she replied:

Yeah—always available. Sexual liberation came in the form of a Virginia Slims ad: "Yeah, you can have your own cigarette," the whole consumer thing, the pleasure of it. Women could now express themselves sexually. The problem is that women's groups felt that they had to go along with that, even if they were women's liberationists, because they didn't want to appear as prudes, like the stereotyping associated with the suffragists— straight-laced, dour, boring people. They didn't want that. We were really thinking about *Is this what I want?* and we came up with the right to celibacy. It was just shocking to the women in the other groups. They were absolutely floored. If we had said, "Let's build some bombs and blow up the Playboy Club," they would have been less shocked![51]

Championing celibacy clearly hit a nerve as a kind of refusal that many women did not know how to respond to. What would it mean for women to refuse sex—to refuse something they had just earned the right to have openly and shamelessly in the "sexual revolution"? Roxanne remembered that, once Cell 16 argued for celibacy, they then had to reckon with all sorts of previously unseen injustices that women experienced in their sexual lives:

Our group was really the first that brought up that rape could happen to a prostitute, because we took that case to court. A member of our group who was a prostitute—an escort—she was raped and she had no sense she could get any justice. She was raped by this Harvard writer who had wooed her to be in his work- shop, saying, "Let's go talk about it," and he just forcibly raped her. It wasn't consensual. We won the case, but I don't think we

won the battle because there's still this point of view happening—
that women should be totally empowered sexually, but no one
should *ever, ever* refuse sex. They'll say it's like food—that we
need it. But it's not like food. Without food, you die. You don't
die if you don't have sex. It's different.[52]

Though not affiliated with Cell 16, Ti-Grace embraced sexual refusal
as a way for women to *see* their lives differently. She believed that refusing
sex could raise consciousness in important ways for feminists, even while
it presented emotional and logistical challenges to sustain celibacy:

Refusing to have sex or refusing to have one's body in certain
places, speaking from my own experience—they are steps on
the way to seeing. They're consciousness-raising. . . . The thing
about sex and love and the body and community—people are
social animals and we certainly need contact. It's difficult to see
how you're going to avoid all these pernicious things and have
connection with other people in your society. Oppression can't
work unless men and women have made a deal somehow. It's
a collusion, for survival. I mean, you don't want people to be
suicidal, so there is a point at which you do things to survive—
take jobs that are "selling out," work for an institution, agree
to sex or love or marriage, and so on.[53]

When I asked Ti-Grace how radical feminists can cope with the irony
of critiquing institutions at their core and then being a part of the system
they wanted to destroy (at least to a certain extent), she said:

Well, you're going to be a part of the society, and society in the
United States is horrendous. People say that we shouldn't have
anything to do with big business or this or that, but tell me
where it *isn't*. I mean, there's big money even at the university—
Wall Street money—so this is what we have. We live in a capitalistic society and that's what governs it, so I guess you could
say what you don't see makes it better, but that's really self-
deception. We are constantly opting out in every way we can,

and yet compromising ourselves nonetheless. Valerie [Solanas] tried to opt out constantly, but then, I would say, compromised herself with the prostitution. Everyone's in that situation. I like the fact that she never gave up critiquing it. That's what's important.[54]

In fact, tensions between Boston's Cell 16 and New York City's Redstockings came to the fore over this issue. As Roxanne remembered:

Kathie [Sarachild] and Redstockings went so far as to push marriage contracts.[55] They pushed marriage, saying that it was an obligation women could hold over men and make them behave better. It's interesting how it's gone totally in a different direction. There are more divorces than marriages. People get married to have the ceremony. Honestly! Gay marriage has changed everything. The right wing is right: It has destroyed the whole traditional concept of marriage by making it just a fun ceremony [where] you decide you're gonna be together and make this commitment. It just totally undermines the patriarchal power of it all in the best possible way.[56]

Roxanne recalled former San Francisco mayor Gavin Newsom's authorization of legal gay marriage and discussed how that act radically shifted cultural understanding and definitions: "My God, if you could have been there on Valentine's Day in 2004 in San Francisco when the mayor decided to allow gay marriage. I stood and watched—my daughter was getting a business license that day, so it just so happened that we were outside the courts, and they kept thinking we were waiting to get married! I said, 'No, we're waiting for a business license,' but we got to observe the whole thing. And I'll tell you, it was gay. This is the end of traditional marriage, sure enough, and like dominoes, it's gone!"[57] Dana laughed and said, "Good riddance. Good riddance!"[58]

Reflecting on her own marriage, Dana said, "I'm married, and I like being married, but marriage as an institution has so much bad, bad baggage. A bad history. It should be a nice history—it should be like that, about a nice thing between two people that are liking each other for as long as they like each other."[59] Roxanne said, "Yeah, like just a fun thing to do, like going to a resort or something. Just fun and not heavy."[60] Dana reiterated the problem of connecting marriage to so many tangible benefits and rights: "But here's the thing about marriage and why it's such a big thing. It *could be* a small thing, but it's a big, big, big thing because of all the laws—you know, your partner is in critical care, in the hospital, you can't get to see them. There's inheritance, stock options, retirement, Social Security, the tax code, and so on. If the right wing had jumped in twenty years ago and made those things universal, maybe there wouldn't have had to be gay marriage, but there wasn't, and so the right wing is now dealing with gay marriage."[61]

Roxanne expressed dismay that men cared more about their daughters than their wives in terms of supporting liberation movements:

> Everyone, even in the right wing, has someone close in their family who's gay. Even [former vice president of the United States] Dick Cheney, an all-time fascist! Even he, with his artificial heart, couldn't quite take renouncing his daughter [Mary Cheney], his gay daughter, his outwardly gay daughter. I think a lot of men did become pro-feminist with our movement because of their daughters. They had daughters—not so much wives—but their sisters and daughters. Maybe it's kind of a primal thing. You don't want bad things to happen to those you love, and you really revere your daughter. I think we also had that effect, but less so with marriage relationships. Marriage doesn't seem to radicalize men to care about their wives.[62]

A RETURN TO "THE PERSONAL IS POLITICAL"

Conversations about sex, love, and bodies—particularly surrounding their relationship to feminist politics and larger institutional frameworks that inform these aspects of women's lives—inevitably force a return to the feminist phrase "The personal is political." In a later conversation with Dana and Roxanne, I asked them about the origins of that phrase, particularly as related to the development of a feminist politics of the body and sexuality. Dana responded by emphasizing the diverse meanings of the so-called *personal* and her perceived (though quite controversial) sense of how third-wave and second-wave feminism might differ on this:

> I think that the third-wave people, they're going on the assumption that the personal is political, except that they wouldn't phrase it that way. I personally don't like the phrasing because it's too vague. What is *personal*? What does *personal* mean? *Personal* means a lot of different things to different people, but if what you're getting at is whether feminism (which can be quite radical) can coincide with fun and games—maybe be sexy, or dress sexy, or be interested in celebrity this and that; all the pop culture trappings— that's more of a third-wave understanding of "The personal is political."[63]

Dana added that radical feminists in the 1960s and 1970s thought of this quite differently, emphasizing a sense of shared suffering or shared oppression: "You thought it was just you. You thought it was *your* problem— you weren't satisfied, your husband did this or that oppressive thing, you didn't have an orgasm, and, you know, all these things you thought were personal but are, in fact, political."[64]

Roxanne emphasized that early radical feminism did not quite fit in with second-wave liberal feminist ideas about social change and mobilization:

> We're a little odd. We're not really 'second-wave' in the sense that Sara Evans describes in *Personal Politics*.[65] She says "The personal is political" came out of SNCC [and was adopted by] Redstockings, but I disagree with some of the claims about race. Redstockings often said that they were tired of working in SNCC for "other people's causes" and wanted to have their own thing. I mean, I hear this language that says, "Oh, I'm tired of it." Well, see, I wasn't tired of it, because I didn't feel like I was going out for other people when I was doing antiapartheid work. I never felt like I was carrying on someone else's struggle. I felt like it was *my* struggle for liberation in the world, so I have very different views.[66]

Radical feminists cared deeply about the minutiae of women's lives, seeing in the mundane and ordinary tasks women engaged in an immense amount of possibility for social change. On housework, for example, Roxanne added, "I *can* see how, abstractly, housework is political, because it's a social more that's imposed artificially on people—so it's in the political realm and has to be fought politically, and not personally. I just didn't think a good solution was Wages for Housework.[67] I'm for communal kitchens and men learning these tasks, which has mobilized a lot of young men to start cooking! Many of these men have feminist mothers."[68] Dana added, "They've just arrived by time capsule!"[69]

Roxanne recounted a disagreement in early radical feminism over what to do about men caring for children in day care centers or in the family: "I remember at Sandy Springs when we brought up that men have to work in these day care centers and learn to nurture children, and that we could not take the position that women were special because they nurture. Men have to learn it, too. They said, 'Well, we wouldn't trust men with children.' I said, 'God, you really hate men more than I do! You call me a 'man-hater,' but I trust all the men I know in my family and extended family to be with children. What kind of men do you know?'"[70] Dana said, "Why would you have children with somebody you wouldn't trust to take care of them?"[71]

Dana insisted that women should separate from oppressive relationships of any kind:

> Women do put up with more than they would under ideal conditions, but it's so much better now, at least. What's ideal is that women would get to be authentic. We'd get to have an orgasm or not. No more protecting the male ego and puffing him up so he feels like he did the thing for us. That hasn't completely disappeared everywhere, but it's actually much more possible for somebody that wants to be straight and clear and honest in communication and ask for what she wants and needs and to say what seems loving to her. There's much more room for that now.

Thinking about the bridge between the past and future of women's sexuality, Dana said wistfully, "The thing that turned out to be revolutionary was the refusal of women to be in bad relationships, *not* the sex part of the sexual revolution. That's what made the difference. That's what made the shift. We have to *not* agree to anything that feels wrong. And when that spreads enough, men's consciousness had to change. First of all, their behavior had to change because they were losing the domestic service, the sex, the caretaking. Then, slowly, they started to see it a little differently." As a final thought on the overlap between sex, love, and justice, Dana said, "We learned what liberation was, what justice was, what it was to respect the rights of the downtrodden. Celibacy was the proper and self-respecting stance if the only alternative was oppressive, demeaning, unsatisfying relationships."[72]

| 5

Women as a Social and Political Class

> The freedom we want, for ourselves and for others, is not an absolute
> metaphysical, abstract freedom which in practice is inevitably trans-
> lated into the oppression of the weak; but it is real freedom, possible
> freedom, which is the conscious community of interests, voluntary
> solidarity.
>
> —ERRICO MALATESTA, *Anarchy*

AS A SIGN OF THE CHANGING TIMES, TRANS RIGHTS[1] HAVE COME
to the fore in recent years, showcasing the intensity of the social justice
struggle of those disadvantaged by transphobia and oppression based on
gender identity. Along with this, radical feminism has been aggressively
dismissed by some people as "trans-exclusionary" or "transphobic," pre-
cluding spaces where radical feminism and trans rights coexist, overlap,
and work together. Since its inception, radical feminism has worked to
reject gender essentialism (the notion that women have a fixed essence)
and ideas about women's and men's "natures"; as Ellen Willis[2] wrote,
radical feminism "began as a political movement to end male supremacy
in all areas of social and economic life."[3] These contradictions—on the
one hand, a commitment to reject oppressive constraints placed upon
women through gender dichotomies, and, on the other, an interest in
imagining women as a social class (and thus constructing some version
of a gender binary)—form the crux of this chapter on the controversies,
benefits, and problems of conceptualizing women as a social and political class.

This chapter takes up the difficult question of whether feminists should conceptualize women as a distinct social and/or political class—that is, a group of people that should lobby for rights as a collective body. On the one hand, such a framework allows for women to lobby as a group for reproductive rights, just as it allows for class action lawsuits and a clear sense that women and their bodies (particularly uteruses and vaginas) meet with systematic, misogynistic discrimination. On the other hand, the large amount of diversity of experiences and social locations within the category of "women" might prevent a unified vision for women as a cohesive social and political class, particularly in its more liberal ("within-system") iterations.

I first take up the questions of how to define women and how that definition has changed since the beginning of radical feminism, followed by a discussion of "female liberation" becoming "women's liberation." I consider sex and gender differences, radical feminist conversations around such distinctions, and the utility of these conversations for political activism. Next, I question the claim of "trans exclusivity" by looking at radical feminist attitudes toward trans men and trans women, along with the role of trans rights within (radical) feminism. I then converse with these activists about the value and pitfalls of imagining women as a social and political class (or "caste," as Ti-Grace says), and examine "women-only spaces" and their value in the late 1960s and early 1970s. I specifically take up the question of the stakes of the Michigan Womyn's Music Festival (recently ended in August 2015) and the future of women-only spaces in light of controversies about radical feminism and "trans exclusion."

EXPANDING DEFINITIONS OF "WOMAN"

While third-wave feminists mostly imagine the category of "woman" as a flexible, multiply configured, shifting, and expansive category, second-wave feminists did not yet have as much flexibility when defining "woman" (in part because a person's sex led to flagrant privileges and disadvantages that are, in part, more hidden and subtextual now). Third-wave feminists championed intersectionality and notions of interlocking systems of oppression, while second-wave feminists were starting to plant the seeds of this thinking.[4] As a scientist and scholar, Dana wondered about the changing role of women once feminism undermined the caricatured and stereotyped ways of thinking about women and gender. She disallowed the possibility of any inherent differences between men and women: "Was there an innate difference between male humans and female humans? The prescriptive demands and the incessant training from birth and even before was so heavy that there seems to be no way to know. We proposed that after our whole moratorium on the whole concept of male and female, a prolonged allowing of everyone to just be who they were—perhaps extending over several generations—might be enough to do it. Maybe some tendencies would emerge."[5]

Recognizing that too much diversity exists within the category "woman" to allow for a consistent definition or characterization, Dana acknowledged the difficulty in forming a political movement based on a category of people too diverse to properly define: "Even under the present heavy conditioning, some women are more of a given masculine quality than most men, and some men showed more of any given feminine quality than most women. Surely under free expression, we wouldn't expect to form any consistent pattern—but some tendencies might emerge statistically, or not. That was the important thing." For Dana, freedom of gender expression felt like the most urgent goal: "The important thing was that patriarchy takes its foot off our necks and let us be whatever range of human qualities felt right to us. Instead of dividing all human qualities into male and female, which for some bizarre reason documented society seemed to have done, why not let the human range play itself out? Human diversity is enormous. We see it not just among ourselves, despite social pressure to conform to gender stereotypes, but among different cultures around the globe." She added that women must demand their freedom because men will not give it to women: "We must insist on the terms of our own liberation. Women are not responsible for saving men. Just as men can't *give* women liberation, we can't give it to men. Unless it is taken, seized, it isn't real. As long as men hold on to their privileges, they can't be truly liberated or be truly human themselves. They must lie to themselves about the nature of reality."[6]

Both Dana and Roxanne recalled that conversations about the connectedness between women informed the inception of the journal *No*

More Fun and Games. Dana said that their debates about the journal's name and whether to use "women," "female," or "feminist" closely revealed the problem of situating radical feminist politics within existing structures of language:

> First, we might note that it was a journal. It was intended
> to be serious, to work out theory. Second, it was a journal
> of *female* liberation, not women's liberation. If we could have
> brought it even more to the bare bones of who we were, we
> would have, but at least we could chuck off the phony label
> *women.* Why not *feminist*? We respected the history of the word,
> but it was too close to the undignified *feminine* to sit well with
> us. Practically every word associated with women had baggage
> in the language made by patriarchy for its purposes. It was hard
> to find something neutral, let alone dignified. And finally, there
> was the main title: *No More Fun and Games.* A refusal to be trivial-
> ized, to be played with, and to not function as entertainment and
> sport to men.[7]

Histories of the late 1960s and early 1970s have widely documented patterns of trivializing women and not taking them seriously. Women faced a staggering number of barriers and sites of discrimination: pregnancy could be a fireable offense, many jobs specified body weight requirements, women could not open lines of credit unless their husbands cosigned with them, and women were routinely excluded from top universities (Harvard, for example, did not even admit women until 1977, when it merged with Radcliffe College). Women could not serve on juries in all fifty states until 1973; unmarried women could not get birth control pills until several years after the FDA approved the pill for married women; and job ads were segregated by gender (with the worst jobs assigned to women). Flight attendants had a mandatory retirement age of thirty-two, pay equity of fifty-nine cents to the dollar was standard, and women lacked access to abortion and domestic violence shelters. Marital rape laws were not put in place in all fifty states until 1993.[8]

Thinking about the differences between third-wave and second-wave ways of approaching women's liberation, Dana framed the struggle of second-wave feminism as a struggle to be taken seriously, noting that activism needed a serious, earnest tone: "The third-wavers are often confident enough to take a humorous tone. They can make fun of the ridiculous attempts to suppress women, despite the real damage often being done. For us in the late '60s, humor was, while not entirely absent, in shorter supply in our writings. We didn't know how it would turn out. What would men be willing to do? Would it be fighting to the death over the barricades, as men's violent reactions and rhetoric seemed to threaten? As it turned out, it didn't come to that." Dana worried immensely about the outcomes of calling for women's separatism or celibacy:

> Our call for women to refuse to stay with men who were abusive or disrespectful turned out to be powerful incentive for reevaluation of behavior, if not a full turning-over of consciousness. Today there are many more male allies, and many more female allies as well. Some of us can even arrange to move in circles where the worst outrages of misogyny don't have a large impact on us in day-to-day ways. This frees us to fight the remaining challenges with a bit of detachment, and throw our efforts in support of those whose situation in life does not allow them that same protection.[9]

Dana and her Cell 16 colleagues wanted to tap into women's oppression by reaching out to women themselves, rather than to men:

> We were trying to sort out and hone and clarify what the tapestry of problems were by which the oppression of women reached into every aspect of life. We wanted to get it so searingly transparent that even women with the most to lose (the privileges of playing the role, the threats that had to be risked to refuse or resist)—that even those women would recognize their lives and the power relations that held sway and the price they were paying in human dignity. That was what we could do to cause the movement to spread widely enough that men would be forced to reevaluate—or if not that, to accept that they could not control women's human drive to life.

She went on, "We weren't speaking to men; we were speaking to women. We trusted, and were proved right in this, that when enough women said 'No' they could not be forced to carry on. It was only when we ourselves took the deal—accepted the ideology, each one of us isolated—that such gross injustice could prevail."[10]

Early radical feminists in the late 1960s also did not have the luxury of drawing upon an archive of academic theorizing about sex and gender. Judith Butler's *Gender Trouble*,[11] Judith Lorber's *Paradoxes of Gender*,[12] and much of queer and trans theory (especially within academia) did not yet exist. The early days of imagining sex as not always aligned with gender were quite radical. Simone de Beauvoir's famous claim in *The Second Sex* that "One is not born, but rather becomes, a woman"[13] inspired second-wave thinking about the distinctions between sex and gender, and created momentum for later works that further shattered and complicated the relationship between sex and gender (particularly Butler's *Gender Trouble*). Kathie Sarachild argued that sex and gender were useful distinctions that helped to lay the groundwork of early radical feminist thought: "There was a big case using *gender* to mean the 'cultural superstructure' or material oppression or the things that were not truly biological differences. *Gender* was the socially constructed, politically constructed differences between men and women, as opposed to just plain real biological differences. That seemed useful as a sort of framework."[14]

The early versions of recognizing and valuing a divide between sex and gender emerged when radical feminists wanted to bring in differences between men and women as one of the bases of women's oppression. Kathie situated this as a discussion around reproductive rights: "Radical feminists were criticized by socialist feminists for acknowledging that there was some biological basis for the rise of male supremacy and it had to do not with strength differences but with the reproductive role of women. I remember I always loved this question that Ti-Grace raised in one of her writings: 'Do all women have the right *not* to bear children?' In order to live and survive, there has to be a workforce, and the workforce has to be replenished."[15]

Kathie then explained that this basis for reproduction leading to the oppression of women has been diluted by thinking more about gender and less about sex: "Once gender came in and gender identity came in, it was as if it eliminated the fact that there was an oppression of women, or the goal of trying to get to the bottom of what it was really based on. Since I was in the camp that felt that biology actually *did* have something to do with it—in this area of reproduction and the idea that there *is* the human female regardless of what you think you are—I also think that we are basically the blue-collar workers of reproduction." Kathie went on to argue that, if radical feminists want to organize women based on their reproductive lack of freedom, trans rights issues may divert from this goal: "There are so many aspects of this. Not every woman has children, but we are kind of the labor pool of reproduction: menstruation, eggs are for sale—it's harder to get an egg out of a human female than sperm out of a male. Our whole social economic system is built around the fact that females are needed for this and we want to work this system out in a just way, so I see that transgender issues are sometimes diverting from that goal, not helping it."[16]

In response to Kathie's statement, Ti-Grace expressed caution about many aspects of cultural feminism (celebration of women's differences from men). While cultural feminism had many overlaps with radical feminism—for example, refusing mainstream culture and establishing feminist cultural places like bookstores, restaurants, and record labels—it also often veered into a politics that valued women's "innate" differences from men as something deserving of celebration.[17] Ti-Grace considered this latter version to be especially dangerous: "There was a move in the women's movement which was really what I would call 'female nationalism' where differences between men and women were valorized and exaggerated. That is part of what led into female cultural nationalism—that we are sitting in all of this shit but it is actually good, right? That was the revolution. Instead of just moaning and saying, 'Oh, we're so special. We can do this and nobody else can do this because the differences make us superior rather than inferior,' there were a lot of tricky things happening around difference."[18]

Reiterating Kathie's point about women producing laborers for a capitalist system—and thus, their reproductive bodies being needed to support the dominance and power of the elite and wealthy classes—Ti-Grace reiterated the political significance of looking closely at reproductive politics. Drawing heavily from Shulamith Firestone's early claims that women should stop reproducing children entirely,[19] Ti-Grace described the links between not having children and feminist politics:

> The differences between men and women have greater sig-
> nificance because they provide workers to capitalism. I've been
> saving clippings on test-tube babies since 1963 in part because
> I knew I didn't really want to have children. It's hard on the
> body, having children. And this has happened in some European
> countries, where they can't bribe women to have children. Some
> women say they love having children and love the experience of
> pregnancy and motherhood. While I find that foreign, I have to
> accept their testimony just as I have asked them to accept mine.
> But, as women come into their own more and more, fewer and
> fewer would want to interrupt their lives in this way. What then?

When imagining what would improve women's lives, Ti-Grace, like Shu-lamith Firestone, believed that anything that *reduced* gender differences or freed women up to function as equals to men would improve their lives greatly: "If you have some alternative means of reproducing, differ-encc is reduced. I find a lot of women are threatened by this idea of this difference being reduced. What if there were an alternative? How would we see sex roles and sex itself differently?"[20]

TRANS EXCLUSION?

To understand the shift from early radical feminist goals of thinking meaningfully about sex and gender, seeking to reduce gender differences, and working against gender essentialism to the more recent accusations of radical feminism as "trans-exclusionary" (sometimes expressed via the acronym TERF, or "trans-exclusionary radical feminist"[21]), we must first understand the ideological challenges of the second wave. In the late 1960s and early 1970s, radical feminism emerged as a way to push liberal feminism into considering a more expansive and rebellious set of goals and priorities. Looking at the private sphere became paramount to under-standing women's oppression, particularly around things like marital rape, abortion, day care, the media's objectification of women, and domestic unhappiness.[22] Radical feminists critiqued liberal feminists for working to achieve equality for women while ignoring racial and class stratification and women's subordination in the family (again, with an emphasis on the private sphere).[23]

By the mid-1970s, however, when the women's movement no longer drew heavily on its radical edges (for example, women's liberation had by now successfully lobbied for the creation of women's studies programs *within* academia, giving the movement institutional support but losing some of its activist roots), radical feminism had shifted toward cultural feminism. This move toward cultural feminist values of celebrating essential femaleness (e.g., celebrating women as nurturing mothers) contrasted starkly with early radical feminist goals of deconstructing gender and gender relations and undoing the sex-class system.[24] More importantly, cultural feminism ushered in more liberal (instead of radical) ideas of individual empowerment instead of thinking about women's oppression on a structural level.[25]

As conservative ideologies grew in the late 1970s and early 1980s, political radicalism across social movements was dealt a serious blow, in part because groups feared retaliation of state violence. As scholar/activist Rose Coursey argues, "This further marginalized far left socialist (Marxist, Leninist, Maoist) factions within the feminist movement along with radical feminists who had created their own breed of feminist politics, disassociated from the male-dominated far left."[26] Further, radical feminists split into two camps, a divide cited by radical feminist Ellen Willis as the "politico-feminist split."[27] While the politicos argued that capitalism led to women's oppression, the (radical) feminists believed that male supremacy constituted a "systemic form of domination."[28] In short, radical feminists believed that they had to showcase the role of power imbalances between men and women in order to truly embody an antiracist, anticapitalist, anti-imperialist radical politics.[29]

Within this political framework, then, early radical feminists argued for the value of seeing women as a coherent social and political class, just as they also advocated political lesbianism and lesbian separatism. These two early frameworks of radical feminism led, however unwittingly, to modern interpretations of *all* radical feminism as trans-exclusionary, even though these early frameworks existed in a much different time and place than contemporary understandings of gender and the gender continuum.[30] (Remember, this was *before* sex and gender were widely theorized as distinct entities; Simone de Beauvoir had only recently introduced the idea of women *becoming* women rather than womanhood being innate.)

Recent scholarship from Cristan Williams has actually argued that radical feminism has a long history of trans *inclusivity* and advocacy for gender variation.[31] Further, rapid change has occurred in approaches, conversations, and lexicons surrounding trans identities and gender fluidity, with (for example) sharp increases in people identifying as nonbinary, pushbacks against gender as itself problematic to maintain as a stable construct, more political lobbying for trans visibility and recognition, and changes to academic curricula within women's studies to include more trans-affirmative critical writings and scholarship.

Reflecting back on changes in thinking about trans identity, Ti-Grace described what she saw as the gendered continuum and how trans people fit into it without necessarily changing the fundamental premises of gender inequality:

> There is a continuum in terms of male and female, and some people are much more just physically feminine, and some are more masculine-looking. It's not just two sexes, in that sense— but in a way, gender is an artificial construct, much like black and white. Knowing this doesn't change the fact that for a millennium women have been the pivot of the family and that responsibility, and their oppression comes from that role, and it's not going to be changed easily or that quickly. Generally, transgender people and transvestites choose a role—choose one or the other roles to identify with—but it doesn't fundamentally alter the sex role system. It's just part of it.[32]

Kathie said that she feared that transgender identities may actually reinforce rather than undermine gender differences: "It celebrates it. To see [trans women] dressing in women's stereotyped clothing—what we call the 'instruments of female torture'—is difficult. I mean, when we had the Miss America protest we were throwing high heels and all the false ways we had to dress into the freedom trash can! Now you have these [trans women] celebrating these 'slave' characteristics!"[33]

When asked about whether trans rights are a civil rights issue, Ti-Grace responded tepidly: "I don't think it's a civil rights issue, but I do think that if that's what people want to do, that's their right. They have a right to jobs. They have a right to not be discriminated against."[34]

For Ti-Grace, many trans women (people transitioning from male to female) did not, particularly for those not feminist-identified, have enough critical analysis about what "being a woman" meant, particularly in the sense that being a woman is often a difficult, painful, and oppressed status: "I also think that, on the whole, they really don't see being a woman as a *problem*, which is pretty offensive. They wouldn't say women are oppressed. They might say there's some discrimination but they don't see any downside. That's where our interests diverge. They need to recognize women's oppression and fight against it."[35]

When thinking about trans women who do *not* identify as feminist, Ti-Grace emphasized that feminist identity and social identities often do not overlap: "That doesn't seem a contradiction to me. Feminism is a critique of masculinity. [Trans women] don't always want to critique masculinity. Although their identities are implicitly a critique, they don't want to directly attack masculinity, but it *is* a rejection of masculinity to be trans. When my friend said, 'It's about women as love, they are soft,' and so on, this is implicitly a critique of the stereotype of masculinity, but they don't want to see it this way. Feminists are, rightly, complainers."[36]

When I asked Ti-Grace about her response to trans women who adopt a firmly feminist political stance and construct their identities as an overt rejection of masculinity, she said that such a framing would more closely align with radical feminist goals: "Yes, because one of the complaints was that we [as early radical feminists] were critiquing sex roles."[37] Ti-Grace added that the cultural backlash about feminism often connects to problems of critiquing masculinity: "That's why [men in the late 1960s and early 1970s] got so upset—the critique of masculinity. Feminism is a critique of masculinity. And masculinity is directly connected to capitalism and power politics. It's essential to it. Power, dominance, hierarchy—these all go together. Our whole class system is based on sex roles. It's *all* about power."[38]

When discussing why it seems that trans rights struggles have come to define radical feminism, Ti-Grace responded that an emphasis on trans identities, while themselves important, can sometimes obscure the totality of discrimination against women: "I think it's interesting how popular the trans issue has become. I think it's a way of escaping from anything feminist. If these borders are so malleable, then it really isn't sex discrimination (or it really undermines it). If men can be women, it takes away the whole *analysis* of the process of becoming a woman in this society and being trained." And, indeed, some trans people do argue that their experiences of being recognized as a man or woman did change their experiences of discrimination. Ti-Grace also felt that trans women's claims of discrimination actually highlighted the (less glamorous) experiences of cisgender women: "I mean, we could say to trans [women], when they complain about being discriminated against as trans, we can say, 'No, you're being treated just like a woman.' It's true! Welcome! Join the club! Being excluded, undermined, not hired."[39]

When I asked Ti-Grace about her sense of whether trans men (people who transition from female to male) offered a different framework for thinking about trans identities, she said that she could relate to the impulse of not wanting to be limited as women: "Well, that's a much smaller number, and I think that's more an attempt to escape being a woman, which is understandable. You could say a lot of feminists who were accused of wearing pants and all that were 'wanting to be men.' No. We just wanted to not be *limited* by being a woman." Analyzing the gender dichotomy, Ti-Grace said, "I also don't like the idea that there are only two genders. Some people would like to think that trans is an attack on the dichotomy, but I don't think so. It reinforces that dichotomy. With trans, we also move away from 51 percent of the population to focus on a tiny percent of the population, which obscures the critique." When reflecting on violence against trans women, Ti-Grace expressed sympathy and solidarity: "Violence against trans women in sex work is enormous; that's the kind of work where there's also a lot of violence against women. We also need unisex bathrooms."[40]

Roxanne had a more nuanced view of how trans identities fit within radical feminism and early radical feminist goals: "I think it's really complicated. I've been on a learning curve for a couple of years now, really trying to reconstruct our early goals. One of them was to destroy anything socially based on sexual differences. I don't think we imagined the variety of gender identifications that already existed, or that people were so excluded (like trans women), or that you didn't even need to formally exclude them because they weren't noticed or even mentioned!" Feeling solidarity with the struggle of trans people, Roxanne likened their erasure to the erasures of Native Americans:

> So now trans women have brought attention to themselves: "We're here! We may not be many, but we exist!" So when you say this, it feels familiar from the point of view of a Native American. It's instilled in me to listen to this rhetoric. I can understand how a transgender person or a gender-neutral person—the identity they've taken—gets erased. In the past they would be forced to think, 'There's something wrong with you,' and be treated with therapy or drugs or something. I've been trying to apply my Native perception to what I'm hearing from these trans women (and it's trans women more than trans men).[41]

In this sense, Roxanne could vividly tie her experiences of being erased or made invisible as a woman of color to the experiences of trans peoples' struggle for social justice. Although trans identities complicate the framework of gender, they also align with radical feminist goals of forging alliances with like-minded feminists and pushing for collective action.

WOMEN AS A SOCIAL AND POLITICAL CLASS

The notion that women have shared political power, shared interests, and shared oppressions seems, on the surface, an easy and logical claim. Still, the idea that women can (or could) fight together as a political bloc is fraught with assumptions about women's similar experiences. Can women recognize their shared experiences and band together for a unified feminist attack on sexism? Can a group who has been socialized toward deference, politeness, and the prioritization of others' (particularly men's) needs instead focus their energies on confrontation and impolite political interventions that value women's experiences as a collective? In the 2016 US presidential election, when Donald Trump said on tape that he felt entitled to "grab [women] by the pussy"[42] and kiss women without their permission, many news commentators argued that such an outrageous statement would solidify women in opposition to Trump. While this happened in some instances (including the Female Collective creation of a "Pussy Grabs Back" shirt[43] and the grassroots Women's March, which was the largest-ever feminist protest in the United States), women largely continued to vote along party lines; Republican women, particularly white women without college educations, overwhelmingly supported Trump despite Trump's frankly misogynistic comments.[44]

The academic question of how to take seriously, and understand, women's differences from each other while still recognizing the overlaps between them began in earnest during the early 1980s. At that time, black feminists started to craft what would eventually become one of the most prominent and important theories of feminism: intersectionality theory. Audre Lorde wrote in her now-famous 1980 essay "Age, Race, Class, and Sex: Women Redefining Difference": "[W]e have all been programmed to respond to the human differences between us with fear and loathing and to handle that difference in one of three ways: ignore it, and if that is not possible, copy it if we think it is dominant, or destroy it if we think it is subordinate. But we have no patterns for relating across our human differences as equals. As a result, those differences have been misnamed and misused in the service of separation and confusion."[45] In subsequent years, legal scholar Kimberlé Crenshaw developed intersectionality theory as a useful framework for understanding how women of color, in particular, were disadvantaged by the lack of legal recognition for their intersecting identities (for example, legal rulings often found that there was no sex discrimination if white women alone were promoted, and they found that there was no racial discrimination if black men alone were promoted, largely ignoring black women).[46] These frameworks continue to inform discussions of how scholars and activists understand women's differences.

Ti-Grace Atkinson argued that women constitute a social and political class based on many interlocking identities: "Women are a social class, or, more importantly, a *political* class. We have never worked out that problem of 'Every woman is a mix of different class identifications'—not just race and sex, but maybe fifteen categories that we identify with. We are an amalgamation of these; each of us is an amalgam of our different class identifications, and this accounts for many of the differences we have. If we don't understand that, we can't organize effectively." Thinking about her time organizing with other women, Ti-Grace said that they recognized their differences while also looking for areas of overlap: "The degree to which you feel oppressed is based on a multitude of things. Because there were these differences, people looked for things that we could agree on—so rape, domestic violence, whatever, there wouldn't be an argument about." When I asked her how we could both recognize women as a social class *and* recognize differences between women, she said, "[Early second-wave feminists] wanted differences *not* to emerge, but the differences are nonetheless there. We have to find ways other than denial to get at these—to acknowledge them and to figure out strategies based on them."[47]

The importance of recognizing women's many multiple and interlocking statuses emerged in Ti-Grace's description of women as a political class: "Women are a political class. But they're not the only one. And women belong to many different classes—not just economic, not just racial, but religious or other external factors affect how they are valued or devalued. Certainly body image comes into that, marriage, all of these things." When I asked her about the value of identifying women as a political class, Ti-Grace talked about shared experiences: "We have unity around certain things. But we have to recognize that there is disunity based on other class identifications, which are obvious, but we never want to talk about it."[48]

Roxanne Dunbar-Ortiz thought the concept of women as a social class had value but also produced a strange side effect of minimizing or glossing over class differences among women: "Back at the time when we were developing theoretical approaches, I didn't like using *class* for anything except socioeconomic class. If you're talking about all women as a class, I don't think I have anything in common with really ruling-class women. There may be a few freaks among them, but they're so few you can almost name them all. It's kind of a dangerous proposition." In agreement with Ti-Grace, Roxanne framed the word *caste* as more appropriate for thinking about women as a collective: "I think the term *caste*, borrowed from places like India (where it means a specific thing) is better.

It *does* have the meaning of certain occupations being assigned by caste—men are mechanics, women are telephone operators—and it dictates what you do in your life. Women are mothers; men are hunters. To me, *caste* is a better word, so we always used 'sex caste' in our journal to mean what people were saying when they used *class*."[49]

Roxanne went on to explain what a "sex caste" would look like: "It's a common thread for all women; there are typecast roles. It still exists, but it has changed, too. About 40 percent of nurses are now men. It's well-paid and it takes a lot of training. It used to be something women could depend on, but now they have to compete with a whole other group. Schoolteachers, too—women were always a huge majority, and now it's about half and half. With doctors and lawyers and law school, there are more and more women doctors and lawyers. Housework is changing, too. The 'sex caste' is shifting and evolving."[50]

When I asked Roxanne if it would make sense for women to lobby as a caste, she said that it would absolutely be appropriate for reproductive rights issues: "Within the reproductive rights part of it, yes. Whether they like it or not, women have to menstruate. Women get denied reproductive medical care. They need the right to abortion. In that sense, they are definitely lobbying as a caste. I think it's complicated by gender now, too. When you get outside of the purely biological and reproductive rights issues and into the gender spectrum, it's different. Caste would probably be too flattening to deal with the multiple gender oppressions. But for reproductive rights, yes."[51] Kathie also adamantly supported the notion that women band together to solve the problems of their oppression:

> We have a problem as women all right, a problem which renders
> us powerless and ineffective over the issues of war and peace,
> as well as over our own lives. . . . We must see that we can only
> solve our problem together, that we cannot solve it individually
> as earlier feminist generations attempted to do. We women must
> organize so that for man there can be no "other woman" when
> we begin expressing ourselves and acting politically, when we
> insist to men that they share the housework and child care, fully
> and equally, so that we can have independent lives as well. . . .
> We want our freedom as full human beings.[52]

WOMEN-ONLY SPACES

> Women generally are not the people who do the defining, and
> we cannot from our isolation and powerlessness simply commence
> saying different things than others say and make it stick. There is a
> humpty-dumpty problem in that. But we are able to arrogate definition
> to ourselves when we repattern access. Assuming control of access,
> we draw new boundaries and create new roles and relationships.
> This, though it causes some strain, puzzlement, and hostility, is to
> a fair extent within the scope of individuals and small gangs, as out-
> right verbal redefinition is not, at least in the first instance.
>
> —MARILYN FRYE, "SOME REFLECTIONS
> ON SEPARATISM AND POWER"

Controversies about women's separatism or "women-only spaces" have pervaded disagreements about trans exclusion and women's shared collective organizing experiences. Those advocating women's separatism— the possibility of living without, or excluding, men (or living without conditions in which men assume access to women)—have argued that such spaces allow women to have freedom and autonomy from traditionally oppressive modes of relating. They say that women-only spaces free up women's time for women's own pursuits and allow a more full and rich exploration of gender roles and women's oppression than do spaces that require women to provide emotional, physical, psychological, and sexual labor to men.

Marilyn Frye, in her work on separatism and power, argued that separation fundamentally underlies the broad character of feminism:

Feminism seems to me to be kaleidoscopic—something whose shapes, structures, and patterns alter with every turn of feminist creativity; and one element which is present through all the changes is an element of separation. . . . The theme of separation, in its multitude variations, is there in everything from divorce to exclusive lesbian separatist communities, from shelters for battered women to witch covens, from women's studies programs to women's bars, from expansion of daycare to abortion on demand. The presence of this theme is vigorously obscured, trivialized, mystified, and outright denied by many feminist apologists, who seem to find it embarrassing, while it is embraced, explored, expanded, and ramified by most of the more-inspiring theorists and activists.[53]

The topic of women's separation from men, or the creation of women-only spaces, is fraught not only with emotional disagreements about the meaning of such separations, but with ideological disputes about the value of separation itself.

Ti-Grace described immense ambivalence about women-only spaces, citing some clear benefits while also recognizing the downsides: "The benefits of women-only shared spaces are that you can sort of share your experiences, your life experiences, with other women. If men are present, that's really tamped down. A disadvantage is that fighting through these differences, confronting these things, is also important. It's sort of like women's educational institutions. Women thrive within them, but when they go out into the world, they're less equipped because they haven't been honing these skills. But I still think women-only spaces promote people being, or feeling, like they can say more things. But it's complicated!"[54]

The attacks on women-only spaces have come from a plethora of places: institutions that claim these spaces discriminate against men; cisgender men who argue against exclusion; and, recently, trans women who claim that these spaces are trans-exclusionary. This collectively raises the question of who has the *right* to be included in women-only spaces and what such spaces signify. Ti-Grace expressed particular pain about any attacks directed at women-only spaces, particularly given how uncommon they are in the first place. She cited, in part, largely unrecognized male privilege as one culprit for trans women's critiques of these spaces: "The whole thing of trying to break down or attack these spaces is very hostile. They're so rare to begin with! I resent it in terms of trans groups, particularly trans women. Look at how some of the trans activists behave! They are like a personification of the *worst* attributes of men: privileged, violent, disruptive. It would be funny if it weren't so offensive and sometimes scary, you know? The worst part of it is that they're effective because that sort of behavior is *always* effective with women."[55]

When I asked Roxanne why she thought that trans women were more vocally critical of "women-only" spaces than trans men, she explained that women carry immense trauma around sexual violence and specifically the penis:

> Already we have the figure of the butch and the femme in lesbianism—so becoming a man is just, you know, a little bit more than that. It's almost like it's in our built-in thinking that men are superior—that's it's okay to go up, but not down. I think trans women don't realize that the presence of the penis is really terrifying to some women. There's a lot of trauma, and I think it's very hard for trans women to know their trauma, and it's hard for them to know some of the specific traumas of women (like those expressed by Andrea Dworkin). I found it even hard to fathom how she could have been abused and raped so many times and still be a brilliant woman and a brilliant writer and theorist.[56]

Citing the symbolic meaning of the penis, Roxanne went on: "In a misogynistic society, the penis is that symbol, so someone who is trans who comes into a women's-designated bathroom will inspire some women to freak out. It happens all the time in San Francisco, and it doesn't bother me at all. A lot of bathrooms are for both genders, or just unigender, and no one seems to mind." Noticing a perception gap between herself and her feminist friends, Roxanne lamented, "My own friends— long-term friends—it's almost like we can't talk about it because they feel that this is just men trying to undermine feminism and the oppression of women." For Roxanne, recognizing privilege based on being cisgender and having a vulva felt incredibly foreign to her: "I felt that way myself, being called *cisgender*. It doesn't matter if you're a lesbian or heterosexual or abstentious—if you have a vulva, you're cisgender. That is a privilege? It's very hard to get my head around that—having a vulva being a privilege—but I'm working on it."[57]

As one key example of tensions around women's separation from men and how that factors in trans identity, the Michigan Womyn's Music Festival—an annual festival known as the "the Original Womyn's

Woodstock" that ran from 1976 to 2015 in Oceana County, Michigan—recently ended after controversies about its trans-exclusionary politics created such strife and tension that organizers decided to stop it altogether. The festival had been, for four decades, a haven for embracing and creating space for the vast diversity of women's experiences, particularly as it wholly embraced lesbian feminism. Women organized, planned, set up, and worked at the festival, and all attendees were "women-born women," with the intention of creating safety for all women at the festival. Playwright Carolyn Gage wrote of the festival: "At Michfest, she can experience a degree of safety that is not available to any woman any time anywhere except at the festival. And what does that mean? It means she achieves a level of relaxation, physical, psychic, cellular, that she had never experienced before. She is free, sisters. She is free. Often for the first time in her life."[58]

In the 1990s, the issue of whether trans women could attend the festival began to appear more visibly, particularly as trans women protesters set up Camp Trans in the national forest across from the festival. In response to accusations that the festival excluded trans women, founder Lisa Vogel wrote in 2014, "As the 39th Festival closes and we turn our hearts and minds to our landmark 40th anniversary, we reiterate that Michfest recognizes trans women as women—and they are our sisters. We do not fear their presence among us, a false claim repeatedly made. What we resist—and what we will never stop fighting—is the continued erasure and disrespect for the specific experience of being born and living as female in a patriarchal, misogynist world." Vogel continued, "Again, it is not the inclusion of trans women at Festival that we resist; it is the erasure of the specificity of female experience in the discussion of the space itself that stifles progress in this conversation. As long as those who boycott and threaten Michfest do not acknowledge the reasons why the space was created in the first place, and has remained vital for four decades, the conversation remains deadlocked."[59]

Scholar Kath Brown, in her interviews with 238 attendees of the festival, highlighted what she saw as the *productive* paradoxes and contradictions of women-only spaces and trans protest of those spaces. She wrote, "Such oppositions may reproduce particular relations, which demand the separation of the dominant from the marginalized, and omit positive tensions and pleasures of marginal spaces. Yet marginal social spaces created by those rendered 'out of place' can cultivate alternative ways of living which not only reproduce forms of power, but also redress societal hierarchies."[60]

When speaking about the Michigan Womyn's Music Festival, Roxanne said, "I think [leaving out trans women is] kind of extreme. It happened with one of the lesbian communes in Washington, DC, in the sixties. Some of them were getting pretty essentialist." Roxanne remembered that opening up space for other gender expressions was productive, even if confusing: "Sarah Lawrence was one of the early places that accepted transgender people—trans men, trans women, and gender-neutral. They do not inquire about gender at all. They leave a space and say, 'If you wish, identify your gender.' It's a bit confusing for gender-neutral . . . It's sort of like being an atheist—it's an absence of gender."[61]

Thinking broadly about the goals of radical feminism, Roxanne remembered a desire for a world where gender no longer dictated rights and privileges: "I do think that that's where we wanted people to get to—where gender just didn't really matter anymore—but I *don't* think that ever meant that attention wouldn't be paid to the needs of lactating women, pregnant women, raped women, and the possibility of impregnation with rape and so on." In the late 1960s, radical feminists like Shulamith Firestone argued that women should abandon reproduction altogether in order to free themselves from gender differences (and disadvantages). Roxanne said, of Firestone's claims:

> Shulamith took it all the way to saying that childbearing was barbaric and should be phased out completely! Maybe that will be the only way to really bring about gender neutrality—but it's so class-based that it's hard for me to accept it, at least in a capitalist society, that gender neutrality should be implemented or that we should support implanting and cloning and so forth. You can't really trust the motives there. A society where you have no say over those things could be dangerous. But I do think that the philosophical idea of gender neutrality or choosing your gender is interesting.[62]

On August 12, 2013, Carol Hanisch, Kathy Scarbrough, Ti-Grace Atkinson, and Kathie Sarachild wrote a sharply worded open letter entitled "Forbidden Discourse: The Silencing of Feminist Criticism of 'Gender.'"[63] They emphasized the problems of ignoring the real, material consequences of oppression for women, saying, "Radical feminist analysis and activism focus on unequal power relations between men and women under male supremacy, with real, material benefits going to the oppressor group (men) at the expense of the oppressed group (women)." Calling for the right to organize and maintain spaces that exclude men (and trans women) based on seeing women as a social and political class whose bodies are used for reproduction in sex-based discrimination, they wrote: "There will have to be many advances in science and technology before the bodies of female humans will no longer be needed for the complicated and dangerous jobs of supplying eggs and gestating and bearing ongoing generations to carry on the work of the world. There will also, no doubt, be struggles to ensure that women are not oppressed in new ways under these new circumstances." The letter also catalogued recent episodes related to Deep Green Resistance (a radical feminist environmental and social justice group that has openly embraced political viewpoints opposing trans inclusion) and RadFem (a UK-based group of radical feminist activists), particularly conferences in which radical feminists who wanted to organize women-only events and spaces were threatened with attacks, assaults, and slurs.[64]

Arguing that women's liberation requires both freedom from gender but also a recognition of the material bases for women's oppression, the letter concluded: "We look forward to freedom from gender. The 'freedom for gender' movement, whatever the intentions of its supporters, is reinforcing the culture and institutions of gender that are oppressing women. We reject the notion that this analysis is transphobic. We uphold the radical feminist principle that women are oppressed by male supremacy in both its individual and institutional forms. We continue to support the radical feminist strategy of organizing an independent power base and speaking the basic truths of our experience out of earshot of the oppressor. We hold these principles and strategies essential for advancing toward women's liberation."

While Ti-Grace and Kathie signed the letter, Roxanne and Dana chose not to sign. When thinking about her response to the letter, later signed by thirty-seven feminists around the world, Roxanne said that she had become far more interested and sympathetic with trans rights struggles over the past several decades: "[The authors of the open letter] think it's the most absurd thing in the world to think that there could be in the mind a sense of oneself that's different from your biology—that you could just wish it away with surgery or hormones. As I've thought about it and read about it, I don't see it as absurd."[65]

Ultimately, the struggle to make a coherent statement about the connection between radical feminism and trans communities—particularly given that being trans does not necessarily mean that one has a feminist identity (and being feminist does not necessarily mean that one is trans-friendly or trans-affirmative)—has been a daunting one. And yet, the push toward evolving into an understanding where trans rights can coexist with radical feminism seems ever more possible. Recounting a recent experience with a family friend, Roxanne expressed how views about trans struggles continue to evolve:

My daughter's friend came out as trans. I think when you have that personal experience of something—and her transmitting that to me—I've seen her really change, and I've become more defensive of trans people and gender neutrality. You don't pay attention to this kind of phobia until you're tuned in, so I think that kind of fierceness in the [trans rights] movement is sort of like what we were in the '60s. You make so much noise that people eventually have to listen—the gay movement for gay marriage, the prisoner rights movement in the prison industrial complex. There's a different kind of spirit—a "take no prisoners" kind of calling out of stuff—and I've come to see that radical feminists can't just rest on their laurels. They have to evolve with the times and understand that that wasn't the end of everything back then.[66]

6 |

Intergenerational Dialogues and the Future of Radical Feminism

> I know that suffering does not ennoble. It destroys. To resist destruction, self-hatred, or lifelong hopelessness, we have to throw off the conditioning of being despised, the fear of becoming the *they* that is talked about so dismissively, to refuse lying myths and easy moralities, to see ourselves as human, flawed, and extraordinary. All of us—extraordinary.
>
> —DOROTHY ALLISON, *Skin*

IN MANY WAYS, EARLY RADICAL FEMINISTS LIKE TI-GRACE Atkinson, Roxanne Dunbar-Ortiz, Kathie Sarachild, and Dana Densmore served as historians of a feminist future. They sought to see outside of themselves and their own time and instead looked toward something in the far distant future, vaguely visible, only beginning to take form. Radically reimagining gender—the conditions of women's lives, the power imbalances that imbued gendered relationships, the unspoken and unexamined beliefs about women's roles and social statuses—required an almost uncanny ability to adequately assess the problems of their time and then push toward something new. As such, this chapter examines the connective tissue between second- and third-wave feminisms and imagines this connection as a productive site for knowledge-making. In short, I take up in this chapter the question of what has been done and, more importantly, *what is to be done* (as the recent radical feminist conference in honor of Shulamith Firestone postulated back in 2013).[1]

The chapter begins by critically examining the institutionalization of feminism via the development of women's studies programs within universities. Conflicts about the problems and potentials of women's studies as a field of inquiry begin this chapter. Next, I examine conversations about the meaning and processes of building a radical feminist archive as a tool of memory and generativity. I then consider the process of *looking back* as these women reflect on the successes and failures of early second-wave radical feminist activism, including an examination of what younger radical feminists should learn from early radical feminist organizing. The chapter concludes by looking forward into the future of radical feminism in order to imagine the new edges and contours of a radical feminism yet to come. Ultimately, by exploring the politics, regrets, mistakes, successes, joys, and continued struggles of radical feminism, this chapter offers a broad conversation about how to preserve the work and lessons of early radical feminism. We imagine together generative feminist futures for our own willful daughters and for all people invested in the politics of social justice.

INSTITUTIONALIZING WOMEN'S STUDIES

At the start of the second wave (late 1960s), women were grossly underrepresented at major universities as undergraduates, with the percentages of women dropping significantly further at the graduate student and faculty levels.[2] In 1975, for example, even after benefiting from the gains made through feminist activism, only 22.5 percent of professors were women.[3] The essential texts in any given field overwhelmingly emphasized men's contributions and men's works, often neglecting women's histories, literary contributions, philosophies, and writings. This meant that women had to fight for entrance into graduate programs and assignment to professorships (with their numbers dwindling even further at the level of *tenured* professorships). One of the dreams of the feminist movement—liberal and radical—was to have women's experiences at the center rather than the margins of educational attainment.

Shortly after the start of the women's liberation movement, feminists fought hard to develop the first women's studies curricula and create a formal space within the institution for students to directly engage with women's issues and women's lives.[4] The first women's studies course was held at Cornell University in 1969 and, after a year of rallies, petition-circulating, intense organizing of women's consciousness-raising groups, and operating unofficial classes and presentations, the first women's studies program was established in 1970 at San Diego State College (now University).[5] This sparked a host of other new programs in women's studies around the country: Cornell University (1970), Humboldt State University (1972), Sonoma State University (1973), and San Francisco State University (1976).[6] The first journal in women's studies, *Feminist Studies*, began in 1972, and the National Women's Studies Association, the first professional academic organization dedicated to this emerging field, started in 1977. The first PhD program in women's studies earned approval at Emory University in 1990. These programs, publications, and organizations offered a diverse set of courses and goals with the primary aim of moving the activist spirit of the feminist movement into the classroom.

Women's studies programs did not arise from administrative or faculty efforts; instead, student demand propelled them along, with forces like the civil rights, free speech, antiwar, New Left, and student activist movements all contributing to the early formation of women's studies. Early women's studies programs wanted to help women examine their history and understand overlaps between feminism and other social movements and modes of resistance; as such, students were heavily involved in the making of the curricula (and ensuring the success of the programs), and the programs had a strong grassroots feel to them.[7]

For women involved in radical feminist activism, the successful establishment of women's studies as a formally recognized academic field—complete with programs, faculty, curricula, and an emerging canon—was seen as a double-edged sword. While formal recognition in this manner allowed feminism to reach new audiences, and validated many of the experiences women had by encouraging new narratives about the role of women in a variety of disciplines, it also opened up new possibilities for feminism to be appropriated, distorted, or exploited. What would it mean for women's studies to move from outsider to insider status in this way? How could feminists ensure that they retained control over the curriculum? Given that institutions are inherently conservative, how could radicals maintain influence over them? What would happen to the activist and grassroots origins of the feminist movement when it became institutionalized in these ways?

Echoes of this discomfort and wariness continue today in assessments of the role and impact of the women's movement on women's studies (and vice versa). Kathie Sarachild, speaking at Arizona State University, described the uneasy process of feminist activism becoming feminist scholarship:

> Our being here today is really a cross between a political action
> and a scholarly inquiry—but that's the core of women's studies,
> actually. Women's studies is not just a cross between the two,
> but a crossover. Activism to academia. Women's liberation activism was at the birth of, the root of, women's studies. Can a plant
> continue to grow when it's cut off at its roots? There are many
> ways a plant could get cut from its roots. It can be uprooted, of
> course. It can be co-opted—the pretty flowers—and part of the
> plant put into a fancy jar. Even with plenty of water, the flowers
> will eventually die without the roots.[8]

Kathie continued by emphasizing the potential pitfalls of this crossover from activism to academia:

> Women's studies has long had this problem of being a hybrid. It
> was born out of the women's liberation uprising. It was started
> as a struggle to restore truth. "Write women back into history"
> was the cry of women's history. "Find names for the anonymous.
> Make visible the women in history rendered invisible, erased."
> *Women's studies*, as a name, was a little less clear to me, a little
> prone to be hijacked into objectifying women, peering at women,
> a little static—for what is the purpose of studying where we are
> unless it's to move us to where we should be?

Kathie wanted these programs to instead bear a name reflecting the field's liberatory roots: "Women's studies should really be seen as and called 'women's liberation studies.' It should embrace in its name what its roots are, and its purpose should be the pursuit and improvement in theory and practice needed to make feminist revolution. That's what the science of women's liberation is about—the theory and practice and the pursuit of it that we will learn and try again and again in how we can succeed at being free."[9]

Seeing a loss of coherence in the movement as a whole, Kathie said of the institutionalization of feminist activism: "I think the main problem with women's studies is that the movement as a whole weakened and had kind of a crisis of success. If the radical feminist movement had managed to stay together, there would have been a constant force keeping women's studies serving the movement more." Noting that the women's liberation movement lasted only for a few years and that radical feminism failed to consider how its work would be appropriated, Kathie described blind spots: "It wasn't until women's liberation started doing its innovative actions and launching these slogans and everything—which became household words for a while—that we were recognized. We have quotes from President Ford saying, 'We are against male chauvinism'! He would use terms that we women's liberationists and radical feminists had introduced. That was when women's liberation groups were all over the country; lots of small cities all over the country were producing tabloid-sized underground women's liberation newspapers. We had journals everywhere."[10]

For Kathie, women's liberation had a crisis of success that imperiled its future: "I think one of the big problems was that we missed the boat on organization of the radical wing. Now we have anti-structured, anti-leader groups, and I think that's one reason we fell apart. We had a crisis of success. Who would have guessed that the contents of these mimeographed publications were going to go on to commercial anthologies when things began to sell?" Thinking about the hazards of institutionalizing something with activist roots, Kathie continued, "In a sense, women's studies was part of this 'crisis of success.' Suddenly in the academy you could make a living doing this work. We wanted to increase women's ability to make a living. That was part of the purpose of the movement—to have equal pay and access to jobs—but there was a tricky area when it came to making a living based on the movement that introduced a conflict of interest almost."[11]

The pressure to speak in more scholarly ways also lessened the potential radical impact of women's studies. Kathie bridled at the idea of obscure theoretical language being used within women's studies: "But the other problem is that there was not a strong outside pressure where you really told truthful things in a kind of clear way, the way you do when you are not worried about keeping your job. We need a force out there, opening up space inside the establishment, but we also need to have created more space in those institutions for stronger, truer positions on things. That's the problem." She added that pressure to publish in many ways created serious hazards for the quality of feminist scholarship within academia: "I do think women's studies has in some ways maintained feminism after these radical groups fell apart. It was more liberal, and that is the problem— the 'publish or perish' of academia does lead to irrelevant writings or 'acababble.' You've got to publish just to publish something, and there is this pressure. You lose concern for real quality because you need it for your PhD or to stay in academia or whatever. I think the main problem is that we don't have a strong enough radical feminist movement on the outside which would impact the inside."[12]

Dana, too, described an intensely conflicted relationship with academia, saying that she had originally hoped that academic journals would nurture women's diverse ideas about women's liberation:

> Then the first academic journals started coming out of women's studies departments and I thought, *This is just a bunch of jargon!* At the end, what do you have? Nothing real—or there is something, but after all this talk and conversation and a million citations and footnotes of what somebody else said, it's the most primitive thing. It is just like a germ of an insight into an idea that the actual female liberation activists had [taken] way, way, way further. They think the whole field of feminism is just their conversation in the department! Haven't they read any of this other stuff from the activists?[13]

Dana admitted that she stopped reading the journals because she found them disappointing, abstract, distant, boring, not grounded in the real world of political struggles, and filled with assumptions she did not find compelling: "In academia, people don't talk to people outside their group very much. Many of the history books that come out may mention

Cell 16, but they never talked to me, or any of us, really. I thought, *Wait a minute. I'm in the phone book. I'm all over the Internet. It's the easiest thing in the world to find me.* But it's sort of a journalist's mentality: 'I'll just write what I have or what I think.'" Dana went on, "It's very hard to explain what it was like to be on the barricades to young people. They cannot see that they, too, have social pressures that they buckle under, and they don't want to think about who did the work before them. Many women in history didn't get very far by speaking up, but then sometimes they did and wrote interesting stuff. Sometimes they were very influential, but we don't hear about them."[14]

Ti-Grace also felt that mixing radicalism with academia was a dangerous combination: "Radicals mostly avoided formal organizations because we didn't want to lock things in. That made it difficult. If you have a formal organization, you incorporated all the rest of it, like NOW did. This is something that seemed a contradiction to us at the time, and also there was so much energy you couldn't imagine that at some point things would disintegrate to the degree that they did." Speaking of the problem of working formally within women's studies, Ti-Grace questioned the motives of those working within the field: "I think there's a real problem with opportunism. There is a danger of people self-censoring, seeing it as a 'career move.' If you're going to be in a liberation movement and you think it's consistent with upward mobility and career, you've got problems. You could always be blackmailed in some way. In academia, you're always receiving hints that you should self-censor or 'better not go there.'"[15]

As someone who has had a foot both in and out of academia, Ti-Grace recalled a personal experience of trying to receive a grant to study discrimination against women:

> In the late '60s and early '70s, they were pretty overt about discrimination in academia. I got called in by the dean at Columbia [University] and he said, "You know, we want to give you this money, but what is this crazy idea you have that women are discriminated against? People think you're not balanced, and we can't give financial support to somebody who's unstable." He said, "I only tell you this because I'm so fond of you." I don't know what you call that kind of mechanism, and somebody who

was more intelligent might have shut her mouth, but it just made me really angry. Certainly other people had to see the example. If you want to get ahead in certain ways, you better not say something that is not going to be popular.[16]

(And, of course, Ti-Grace found herself at the center of many controversies—both within and outside of the movement—for speaking up about what she saw as unjust. She fiercely resisted anything that lessened the impact of her ideas and cared little for notions of "respectability" at the expense of truth.)

Ti-Grace also strongly believed that academia and activism teach people different, sometimes incompatible, lessons: "If you haven't been in the street and you have not tried, hands-on, to change something, that is an educational experience no book can give you. You have to try to think about how to change something. Try it—see what response you get, how you feel when that happens, what you're going to do next—and it just gives you a different sensibility and acuteness and smartness that is lacking from most women's studies people now, although navigating academia is an art form in itself."[17]

Speaking from her experiences within academia, Ti-Grace described the ways in which feminist academics are sometimes out of touch with real-life activist struggles. She described as a key example the Sears, Roebuck and Company class action lawsuit where the Equal Employment Opportunity Commission (EEOC) represented thousands of women who accused Sears of sex discrimination for channeling female workers into lower-paid salaried jobs instead of the higher-paying (and higher-prestige) commission jobs.[18] Sears did not dispute the lack of women in commission sales jobs, but said that those jobs were justifiably more suited for men because the work involved selling "traditionally male" products like plumbing, automotive supplies, and furnaces, and because they required evening and weekend hours. Sears relied upon the expert witness testimony of women's historian Rosalind Rosenberg, who argued that women's commitment to home and family and their internalization of relationship-centered values undermined their work commitments and specifically their ability to work in commission-based positions. To counter this, the EEOC brought historian Alice Kessler-Harris to testify that women's work opportunities have been blocked and that working women typically choose higher-paying jobs when those jobs are available. Further, Kessler-Harris argued that not all women have the luxury of having "feminine" values of home and domesticity—especially single mothers and women in couples where both people must work.[19]

Speaking of the Sears case, Ti-Grace expressed disdain for women in academia who are individualistic, competitive, and antagonistic toward other women: "Academia is awfully small, and it can get really petty. Women in academia do not represent women as a class. They are not representing those in the Sears case who brought about a class action suit against Sears because they had been restricted to jobs where they couldn't sell big-ticket items and therefore couldn't get big commissions. That was a working-class issue, and most women had families they were supporting. Sears wanted to fight back against these women, so they went to women's studies departments to get someone to testify about why this would not be sex discrimination." Not able to find a women's studies professor, Sears did find Rosenberg, a women's historian based at Barnard College, who, according to Ti-Grace, "argued that women have higher values than men and don't value money in the way men do, so it's plausible that women don't really want those higher paying jobs. Now, this is what I mean when I say that people in women's studies sometimes lack a certain political acuteness. . . . Now as it happened, Sears won the case and it did a lot of damage. This was a good example of what my reservations are and why there's impatience from feminist activists toward women's studies. This example is not isolated."[20] (Notably, Rosenberg was a historian, not a women's studies professor, though Atkinson's point about the lack of political acuteness is well taken.)

Since the start of women's studies, radical feminists had expressed doubts about the field's merits, as Ti-Grace recalled: "In 1973, some radical women were attacking women's studies and warning the women's movement, 'You know, these are parasites and they are conservative and they are bad news,' and my view was, 'Well, you know, they are kind of conservative—but they're ambitious, and they're academic, and give them a break. We don't have to go after them.' That was a mistake. We should have kept them honest. They would gut the important things and their politics were basically antithetical to the sorts of politics you have to have if you're going to make change for women." For Ti-Grace, early radical feminist activism, on the other hand, emphasized the synergistic relationship between activism and theory: "We were building theory at the same time we were acting. Women's studies people were very conservative and couldn't be trusted with the history of feminism. They wanted to get ahead within the academy and they would sell out feminism in a heartbeat, if they grasped it at all (and almost none of them had ever been involved). Except for Catharine Stimpson,[21] who's a woman I respect. She has lots of character."[22]

Ti-Grace admired Stimpson's honesty and forthrightness:

This respect was not generated by Catharine's women's studies work (that occurred later) but rather by our shared activism in early NOW (1967–1968). My impression is/was that Catharine's original conception of women's studies, while academic, was more political and feminist than was later reflected in many later programs. Catharine was always honest about where she stood on issues. . . . We all make choices at certain points in our lives—quite understandable ones. All women, especially, reach various forks in the road where they have to make choices. These choices are determined by our ultimate goals and what we believe we need to do to achieve these. Sometimes, our choices do not confirm with our stated aims, which are often merged with a certain image we want to project, both to ourselves and to the world. I respect those who have the courage to say where they are at honestly, especially when this impacts other people's lives. There are many factors involved in such situations, such as idealism versus pragmatism. Sometimes it's hard to say which is the *right* choice. This depends ultimately on the individual. But the tension between idealism and pragmatism can be particularly stark in an historical period such as the late 1960s.[23]

Imagining how to improve women's studies or return it more to its activist roots, Kathie advocated for a vision for women's studies that would include more political praxis along with direct ties to outside organizations:

Women and women's studies should help these outside forces, and hopefully the outside force would open political space in the department for women's studies people themselves to be able to write more freely. A lot of interesting work has been done in women's studies and women's history. The problem is that there's little activism. The link between activism and women's studies should be stronger, where outside groups could present or could work with people inside, saying, "We need research on this. Can someone write a paper on this?" or that some of the guidance for research and study could be coming from the outside groups that were involved in activism. If we could get organized at that level, it could happen.[24]

BUILDING AN ARCHIVE

Questions of how to preserve radical feminist history—particularly given that no existing center or library is exclusively dedicated to that history's preservation—has also posed new challenges to early radical feminists. The process of building an archive—far from boring or apolitical—has long troubled feminist and queer scholars.[25] Some of the issues at stake include who can and should access an archive; how to have global reach when building archives; whether papers should be purchased by university libraries or public libraries; who defines or gives narrative to archives; how to archive invisible or marginalized voices and lives; and what it means to create institutional memory.[26] Additionally, building an archive from something that existed largely outside of institutional frameworks (or which has been silenced, ignored, mischaracterized, or forgotten) presents a series of problems and challenges for those interested in accessing documents from early radical feminism.[27]

Kathie Sarachild has spent a great deal of time and energy supporting Redstockings' independently run, non-university-affiliated Archives for Action project, which argues that women's liberation studies must make "history for activist use," employing the slogan "Building on What's Been Won by Knowing What's Been Done!"[28] These archives operate from a mostly volunteer grassroots effort and include a variety of materials related to the early women's liberation movement, Redstockings, and freedom organizing from the 1960s. In short, "The Archives for Action emphasizes the distinct power of engaging with primary sources to learn from, analyze, and advance the gains won from past freedom struggles."[29]

Kathie's interest in preserving the history of radical feminism—and Redstockings in particular—began early. She published, with Carol Hanisch, Faye Levine, Barbara Leon, and Colette Price, an edited collection called *Feminist Revolution* in 1978[30] that included a variety of documents from early radical feminism and sought to create an early sense of memory for the work of Redstockings. In her essay "The Power of History," Kathie wrote:

> How can women's history ever get written if women system-
> atically "forget" or obliterate the origin of the conceptions that
> change their lives—whether out of fear of remembering and
> thus taking a real political stand for the movement or in order
> to appropriate them as their own for career purposes. The origins
> of the most influential ideas are blurred and suppressed the fast-
> est by those who see them as a competitive threat. These are not
> the kinds of careers feminism is trying to win for women, and, in
> any case, they will be exceedingly short-lived and will die as soon
> as they kill the movement off first.[31]

She went on to argue for the importance of studying radical feminism: "The loss of the movement's history, both recent and past, is now a key problem which is stopping its momentum and the revision of its original ideas is one of the prime reasons for its dilution and weakness. Therefore raising the political issue of revisionism is necessary for the agenda of action. What this essentially means is raising the issue and defining it—defining what it is, when it occurs and alerting people to the toll it takes on women's history and the movement—and then defeating it."[32]

Fighting against the forgetting and erasure of grassroots organizing and action, Kathie said:

> In terms of legacy, and how do we preserve the facts that have
> been erased from history (that really 'radical women' were the

popular ones!), people don't know about these details. We've started this 'Archives for Action' concept. Some of it is just promoting the idea and the materials. We've combined [the feminist organization] National Women's Liberation and Redstockings, where Redstockings is the kind of think-tank wing and National Women's Liberation is the activist group. We combined them. We are holding classes now. We're trying to apply another lesson, that this time we are not going to just let everything out in an unorganized way. We want to build the organization at the same time we get the material out, so that slows the process down a little bit.[33]

Redstockings has indeed had a resurgence in recent years, particularly following the election of Donald Trump. Redstockings worked with National Women's Liberation to organize the January 20–21 Women's Strike.[34] Over seven thousand women and their allies pledged to strike in order to protest Trump, Pence, and the Republican Congress's antiwoman agenda.[35] Further, Redstockings has actively generated the Archives for Action project, started in 1989, "to make the formative and radical 1960s experience of the movement more widely available for the taking stock needed for new understandings and improved strategies."[36] Of all of the radical feminist groups active in the second wave, Redstockings has taken most seriously the task of making, forming, and sustaining an archive alongside continuing activist work that speaks to the challenges of the times. For example, in addition to their anti-Trump activism, they have designed a consciousness-raising organizing packet, organized a rally at the United Nations on International Women's Day in 2007 to demand rights for women, and have worked toward single-payer healthcare as a feminist issue. (Notably, they have also documented these efforts as part of their online archive.)

Looking back on the history of Cell 16, Roxanne Dunbar-Ortiz also emphasized the importance of archival forms of memory: "I think one thing that Cell 16 and other groups did was to emphasize the importance of documentation, the importance of developing an archive. The archive is not just paper and words but something that will sustain itself. There's that urge to not be forgotten. I think that's how Native Americans have survived and resistance has occurred, because they create that memory that continues." Thinking about the aspects of the archive she felt most proud of, Roxanne said, "The things I liked best were how we worked on the journal—how we worked together to make this artifact which we could give to people. It was like a little bomb inside that would blow their minds. I mean, that was a part of the '60s culture that was really good! All of these underground papers were being created. There were so many deficiencies on the left—the sex ads, the misogyny, the male dominance— so what women produced in this way was really truly *radical*."[37]

Lamenting the loss of radical documents, zines, and self-published journals, Roxanne framed today's feminism as less interested in archival works of radical thought: "That's not being done so much now. There are all these women's studies journals and all, but they're all very academic. We don't have this kind of populist literature. It all seems very slick now. I get all of these Planned Parenthood materials and I think, 'Who would get *excited* about this?' It's just so boring to me, and I'm someone who's already interested in it!"[38]

Roxanne went on to think about the role of language in radical feminism, particularly as feminists recast their history in the archive:

> I think we need to rethink language. We need to insist upon appropriate language to describe things and to castigate that which is demeaning. Whether you think it is or not, if someone says, "That demeans me," okay, you stop doing that. Sorry, you don't get a choice of whether to call Cassius Clay Muhammad Ali. That's his name. Call him that. There's still pushback from the right wing and others, saying, "This is being so picky and irrelevant," but it's not. Language matters. There's always this attempt in imperialism, colonialism. Language is everything. I think that the women's liberation movement really had a lot of women who were writers. It was no accident that radical feminists had a deep respect for language. That was really a hallmark of the movement. If you look at other movements, it was "Fuck this" and "Fuck that"—a really small vocabulary. We had quite an intricate rhetoric, and this was an important tactic for us.[39]

Assessing the historical impact, successes, struggles, and failures of early radical feminism has been an ongoing project as women active in the early second wave now age into their seventies, eighties, and nineties. Roxanne reflected on the distance traveled between then and now and emphasized the important links between different generations of feminists: "I guess we're even more a fourth wave now—the millennials. I see differences in what these millennials feel in comparison to third-wave feminists. They're really returning to the movement and changing it. Many of them have feminist mothers. They are pretty solid. Others have not been introduced to feminism yet." She went on, "I've seen that with teaching. Some of my students really wanted mentorship from me. They just wanted everything they could suck out of me—to understand how to think like we did at that time and read everything. . . . Because when we were creating it, that was very exciting. But to hand it over to someone else in practice when we didn't really practice it—we just created it, the ideas—and they're expected to practice what we preached . . . I think it is very complicated passing down knowledge, teaching about radical feminism."[40]

She recalled with fondness the early days of Cell 16 and its inspirational impact on her: "Those first few months were exciting—starting the journal, starting the organization, the tae kwon do, hitting the streets. We also did a protest at the Playboy Club on opening night and kind of rained on their party. We didn't even think of it as publicity. I just really wanted to make a statement about what we thought about women being objectified. Hugh Hefner was our number one target. It was a lot of fun. And every time there would be any kind of public thing, it would attract a lot of new women."[41]

Contemplating the successes and failures of second-wave radical feminism, Ti-Grace lamented the many setbacks that feminists have faced when trying to push forward their agenda. She revisited the question of why the radical feminist movement stalled: "So I have been troubled by the following question: Given such promising beginnings, why did the movement suffer this failure of nerve in the mid-1970s and decline thereafter both in terms of goals and activities? Of course, there were some external causes for this: for example, male supremacy, a decline in other progressive movements as contextual supports, periodic fluctuations in the economy. But these obstacles were there from the beginning." Returning to her original claim that women represent the *majority* in the world, Ti-Grace said:

> But there is one overriding fact that most feminists seem to want to avoid. Women are half the population. We are smart. We are nearly as physically strong as men—so nearly as to make little difference. So what happened? What did we fail to come to grips with? What did we miss? Why have we failed, as a movement, to achieve our goals or even to maintain those achievements we *did* gain? . . . Women are a colonized people. A caste. A class. So why haven't women physically revolted over so many millennia? Why are only 6.5 percent of the prison population women?[42]

Thinking about why women have largely internalized their own oppression rather than fighting back, Ti-Grace framed women's oppression using the postcolonial literature of Frantz Fanon and Albert Memmi[43]: "The themes of both these writers—and Fanon was active in the Algerian Revolution itself—are colonialism, decolonialism (the process of the colonized freeing themselves from colonialism); and finally *neo*-colonialism. All three topics turn on the interdependency between the oppressor and the oppressed. Colonialism depends upon both the colonizer and the colonized playing their assigned roles to the fullest; otherwise, colonialism cannot survive." After explaining the various stages of colonization, Ti-Grace said, "How do the colonized accept and/or bear their condition? Obviously, no human being can tolerate living with constant and systematic abuse. Doesn't it make sense that the systematically discriminated against or oppressed *has* to transform her life experience into something else?"[44]

She went on to frame women's oppression as a parallel to slavery by referencing the master-slave dialectic in Hegel's *Phenomenology of Mind*.[45] Ti-Grace said, "If you are a religious believer, on its face, this looks like a good trade: a miserable moment, on the one hand, contrasted with an eternity on the other. By the time the slave discovers the trick, it's too late. On the other hand, this 'miserable moment' will be over anyway. . . .

The slave may be 'contented.' But does he have a 'life'? So is contentment *or* life satisfaction more important? Doesn't this depend on the ego-strength, sensitivity, and awareness of the slave?"[46] Ti-Grace believed that women's internal colonization mimicked some of the processes of colonization more broadly, particularly as women were pushed to accept their oppression and not to challenge it.

Shifting the conversation into the realm of regret and what she wished had gone differently in early radical feminism, Ti-Grace explained how her perspectives have changed as she has grown older: "Not regret, exactly. There are very few things I could say I feel regret about. But, for example, I was very impatient with these women who were older and who were very upset about feminism touching anything that had to do with sex. I thought, 'Well, that's just silly!' I had no empathy for where they were coming from at all. I just brushed it off like it was crazy." Ti-Grace added, "They wanted to restrict feminism to things like taxes, education, and employment. Nothing else. Now I have a little more understanding of why they were upset or what they were fearful about in reducing feminism to the sexual. This was certainly not my intention. But they had lived most of their adult lives with people trying to negate women's situation by simply saying, 'You're all cunts,' and that's it. I have more understanding of them, more empathy."[47] She later admitted sadness about losing touch with some of her early fellow activists: "I regret certain personal connections I didn't keep up, but a lot of that had to do with time. I wish I had maintained more of those old connections—that I had written back more to people who wrote me. But otherwise, I think I went pretty much to the edge on things. I don't have that regret."[48]

Of the shifts that happened in radical feminism, Ti-Grace said that appropriation and distortion of the tactics and rhetoric caused her the most pain: "There were women who later became attracted to the movement more because it was something chic and because it was so-called 'radical.' It became more co-opted. By the mid-1970s, we were having a lot of intramovement fighting. It was a constant struggle. Probably what was called 'radical feminism' by the mid-1970s really did not even resemble its origins."[49] Thinking about her mistakes with the changing radical movement, Ti-Grace said, "As far as mistakes, I think at some point I was too optimistic. At first I think I had my feet on the ground and I knew it was going to take forever, but then when all of these women joined, it just seemed like mobs of people came to the movement. I thought, 'Oh, I've underestimated.' But I think I had looked at what was happening with other movements, and that they were starting to dissolve, and so we were getting people who were more 'lifestyle' rather than committed feminists." Ti-Grace added: "You have to have an analysis before you know what needs to be done, and you have to agree on that analysis."[50]

As the years went by, early radical feminism got more distorted. For example, Ti-Grace recalled the shift toward maternal thinking and motherhood within radical feminism: "In most ways, later incarnations were the opposite of earlier radical feminism. For example, if matriarchy becomes radical feminism, you find that power dynamic again. It wasn't a challenge. It certainly wasn't a challenge to sex roles, because it was sex roles with a vengeance. Motherhood is a heavily permeated sex role. God help you if you refused the tit; they'd really kill you. It seemed benevolent only if you went along; it's a real heavy power trip."[51]

When I asked if she thought there were relationships that don't involve power or have lessened power, she responded:

> I think people can get closer to that if they're very conscious
> of it and if they're working at it. I do think that relationships
> are uneven. I used to be obsessed with my relationship with Flo
> [Kennedy].[52] I'd make a list of all I got from her and then what
> I gave to her, and it always seemed to be very lopsided. It seemed
> like she gave everything to me, and I didn't give to her. She prob-
> ably thought that I was very silly. In friendships that go on, I
> think it goes back and forth. In other words, I think that one per-
> son can be more needy at one time than the other and the other's
> more supportive, but it should even out over a period of time.
> I think there are times when it is uneven, but if people are con-
> scious of it, if they have some idea about in what ways it's evened
> out, it's better.[53]

Ti-Grace emphasized reciprocity and friendship as crucial outgrowths of radical feminist politics—ones that sustain individuals and the struggle more broadly. She summed this up by saying:

I think that reciprocity is important. I think we need each other. I think life's hard. Especially in this country. I think it's hard. I find it very hard to live with Iraq, knowing what we're doing there. Some Weatherpeople [radical militant activists known as the Weather Underground][54] have been saying, "Oh, we went too far." But was it really too far or wasn't it? What is adequate? We talk about "good Germans,"[55] right? They didn't do enough. Why didn't they stop things? Why aren't *we* stopping things? Just because we're aware this is terrible, is this enough? I feel like we're all "good Germans" here, and the atrocities are mind-boggling.[56]

Ti-Grace discussed what she wished the early radical feminists had learned from earlier movements: "From studying the last women's movement, I realized that women have gotten together to make change when everything else is on top of them, like a war or other class systems. When everything is moving and shaking, this gives us a space where we can start to see, 'Oh, yeah, things aren't really good with us.' When those problems—slavery or whatever—seemed to reach a sort of impasse (or, I wouldn't say, 'resolution,' but something similar), that space closes over. Then the whole weight of it seems to come down again on women."[57]

Ti-Grace emphatically argued that women must take advantage of those small periods of turbulent social change and recognize windows of opportunity when they happen: "I felt strongly that we have a smallish window of time to make change in; we've got to make our most important gains fast. We have to really seize this time. I felt compelled by this, so there was no time for any socializing or fun and games—none of that. We had to keep digging and figure out what we want to do, do it, push, keep digging, and so on, because we don't have forever here. It's not the worst premise."[58]

Speaking more broadly about social change and the role of radical feminists in making social change, Ti-Grace said:

What we're trying to do is really change the whole world, and it's not going to be in any one generation. Yet, you have to push hard and constantly as if you're going to see it in your lifetime. That's the big order. It would be really important if we could stand on the shoulders of people who have gone before us and not make some of the same mistakes. You can't reinvent the wheel every time. Until you clear away some of the debris of any kind—the material aspects of oppression—it's very difficult to see internalized oppression because there's so much other shit on top of it. There might be yet another layer, but there may be all sorts of other things also.[59]

Ti-Grace also reiterated the need for fun, praise, rewards, friendships, and celebration, things she initially struggled to value:

I learned a lot from Flo, a lot in retrospect. Flo always mixed the social in with the political. For example, she always had a pot of chili on the stove. She always had some sort of cake that she cut into a hundred pieces so that everybody got just a teeny bit, but there was something for everyone. There was a little reward. And she would always say, "Well, the best revenge is if we have fun. We also have to have fun. You have to fight, but you have to have a good time while you're doing it." She was very serious, but she had a lot of wit, and she always understood you can burn out. I felt so much pressure that I thought, "We don't have time for that." But I see this differently now. I see now how much has to be done, that you can't finish no matter how hard you push, no matter if you never sleep. There's too much we don't even know yet about what has to be undone, so you've got to play it so that you can last.[60]

LOOKING FORWARD TO RADICAL FEMINIST FUTURES

As second- and third-wave feminists look to the next generations of feminists and the lessons they must learn, bridge-building continues to pose challenges. Discussing her concerns about contemporary social arrangements, Dana Densmore said:

Some of the same things are still happening. The "I'm not a feminist, but . . ." or various kinds of double standards. Men are so frequently murdering their children, but one woman kills her children and it is all over the media. We see the same patterns at work, though back then every man you respected had these attitudes—dismissive, contemptuous attitudes toward women. Now, it's different. You can practically arrange your life to only be around men that will not have any egregious behaviors, and will give lip service to a woman's right to be human. When it's not everybody, you are free to say, "That guy is a jerk."[61]

When thinking about her hopes for future generations of radical feminists, Ti-Grace again emphasized attentiveness to broader social upheaval as an ideal window for enacting social change. She said, "Women's best shot is when the whole society is changing—when you have a revolution. That's when we really have to get our demands in there. The women's movement had a lot to do with the degree of unrest in society as a whole. It really made spaces for women's ideas. It's probably not going to shift substantially until there's more of that again."[62] At the same time, Ti-Grace argued that feminist activism has persisted beyond the "wave" model of three different periods of social change. Directing suspicion toward that characterization of feminist history, Ti-Grace said:

There aren't really "waves" of feminism, either. People raised a lot of issues in the so-called first wave beyond the vote. There was a lot more to it. Some of the questioning these women were doing can be illuminating. They were critiquing a lot more, but what can you get a lot of people organized around? That ended up being the vote—people not thinking as deeply. I always thought *The Woman's Bible*[63] was a wild, wild enterprise. I also found it an odd pair—Elizabeth Cady Stanton and her partner, Susan B. Anthony.[64] It was an interesting pair. They had so many differences. I don't know how they worked those out.[65]

Looking ahead to future generations of radical feminists and the life choices they must make, Ti-Grace said:

When women are about to graduate from college, that's a really critical point, because they're going to make some choices about where they're going to put their energies. Are they going to put it into finding a mate or finding themselves? Do those conflict? You can't go back. I think there's this whole self-deception about 'Well, I can have a career and I can be married and have kids. I can do it all.' You're not going to do it all. There is no Wonder Woman. You can't. And you can't take ten years out of your life and then pick up and be at the same place. It's partly about coming to terms with that and thinking in a different way. That's the sort of thing I think was so important about Flo. She really understood building pleasure and rewards into the movements.[66]

When speaking about the difficulty of making life choices within a framework of radical feminism, Ti-Grace said:

I think it makes it easier to live with the consequences of your choices if you're conscious of making them and if you've weighed the options and have done the best thing for you, even though it might not be the choice somebody else makes. The most painful thing is to do things that somebody else wants you to do. If bad things happen but *you* made the choice, it's a lot easier because you can see what you'll change. I mean, you live in a society where you're victimized by all sorts of things, but it's important to try to avoid making choices to please others. I worry, for example, about violence against women. The best way to avoid it is to not be dependent.[67]

Assessing why radical feminism as imagined in the 1960s and early 1970s died down, Ti-Grace said, "A lot of it was that there were too few people carrying it. We've got to talk about it all, try to explore it. There are so many questions. I start seeing people start to get so-called 'radical' again, and they're picking up exactly where we left off, making the same mistakes again and again. That's no good. There was a lot that we started with that was right." She added that coalitions, alliances, and evolving perspectives on the movement keep it alive:

You're going to have to cut across other movements. Your alliances are going to be with other people who understand that *they* need profound change. If women aren't fighting for their own freedom, they're the most conservative, backward force in society. Everybody wants to have a decent life, and to tell people, "You're going to have to face that everything that has been planned for you is terrible, and you have to envision what change would be without being able to see it"—that's a problem that we must cope with. It's a big one. You've got to have something to keep going.[68]

To sustain the movement, then, women need to sustain each other, as Ti-Grace said: "That's why I keep thinking about Flo's ideas about community and about rebuilding each other and about supporting each other in that psychological, sociological sense. We've got to do it, got to figure out how that's going to work, because otherwise you self-destruct. We're also ahistorical and we don't learn. I think it's part of being very reactionary, being ahistorical, because nobody wants you to learn."[69]

The process of generativity and creating different feminist futures also depends on learning from the vast archive of women who have come before.[70] When thinking about the qualities of feminists she most admired, Ti-Grace said, "Very, very independent women. Even though they might appear sort of shy or this or that, they had strength. They knew what they thought, and they were stubborn about it. It was a strength I really liked. They had weathered things. They would stand up. They had courage, conviction—strong conviction. They knew there wasn't any other option. I find that people like that are more tolerant, oddly enough." Seeing some of these qualities in herself, Ti-Grace said, "One thing I know about myself is that if I'm interested in something, I dig and dig and dig and dig; I need a great deal of information. And then when I get it, I know what I have to do. And if I'm in a frightening situation, I'm the same way. First I ask, 'What is the problem?' and then I ask, 'What do I need to know to resolve it?' There's usually a lot of research and work involved."[71]

Roxanne, too, felt simultaneously encouraged by the progress women have made and still quite concerned about rampant misogyny in this culture: "Things are so much better now than they were before. There are so many more opportunities for women to be able to be self-determined, but the violence against women is really unabated—what I call 'woman-hating'—and I think we have to talk about that more. I really do think men on the whole hate women, and even the ones who profess to love women often don't. It's time for a men's movement of solidarity." She paused and then continued, "I think we have gone as far as we can as women—structurally, anyway—but at a certain point, like with race, the oppressor has to get involved. It's not by sympathy. There needs to be another strong women's movement that just demands support. We have the unique position of being individualized in men's lives, and unless we opt out of that and get into a separatist community, men will have to get involved."[72]

Cautious and worried about the infectious qualities of "beauty culture" and the use of medical procedures to change female appearances, Roxanne said, "The beauty culture that has entered even the working-class minority communities—you know, the plastic surgery, the nips and tucks—that worries me. There's something about having your feet operated on so you can have your feet fit a certain size that worries me. Or vaginal surgeries, bulimia, anorexia. It's a new narcissism of women and the subtle, antifeminist qualities of those things that worries me."[73]

Thinking of the body as a social text, Roxanne admired the bravery of women and felt optimistic about young women: "When I think of young women today, some say that they're regressing, but I think they're doing feminism in a different way. I think they're pretty self-confident in their bodies—and they're all shapes and sizes and colors—so it's just different. I see young women who are so confident that in the past would have been shrinking from being seen. I think they're on good grounding." When imagining the priorities for future generations of feminists, Roxanne said that antiwar activism is an essential part of our future: "What's really important is to reinvestigate and reimagine the importance of women in relation to the militarism in war, because the first instinct of women—it goes back to the suffragist movement—is that they were pacifists during World War I. They started Women Strike for Peace. It was all the antinuclear movements, because they were all led by women."[74]

Donna Allen, Dana Densmore's mother, founded Women Strike for Peace and later became Roxanne's friend and mentor. Allen was a prominent activist with the American Federation of Labor, the League of Women Voters, and anti-Vietnam protests.[75] Roxanne described the work of Women Strike for Peace as crucial for radical feminism: "They were brazen individual women, powerhouses, because they didn't have a collective but they saw the need for it. They were very lonely sometimes, because it's hard to keep a man around when you're out there organizing all the time. They often became single moms."[76]

Speaking of today's young activists fighting against militarization and the prison-industrial complex, Roxanne said:

> For women to engage—in prison rights, for example—is exciting. Angela Davis[77] had a lot to do with it over the years from her own incarcerations. She is inspiring, especially to young black women—to be in the leadership of that. It came from a lot of different directions. One day I saw it and said, "Wow, this is amazing!" I know I had nothing to do with it—maybe a few seeds, back then—but it does make me think that we need that same kind of connection. Really looking at how we can stop the United States from destroying others and that we have a responsibility to the world—these are priorities that the next generation of feminists are taking on.[78]

Roxanne framed the sabotage and undermining of US imperialism as one of the key priorities for new generations of feminists.[79] Describing the United States and its political problems, Roxanne said, "The United States is a predator, preying on the weak people all over the world. It's got to stop. I think that consciousness-raising can go far, and I think women will be the leadership. They have been in the past, and we discredit their roles in that. It's disappointing to think that we imagine the advances of feminism as being women in combat and women in the military rather than women being in the leadership of *antiwar* movements." Of antiwar activism, Roxanne said:

> I think we have to go in that direction, in part because of climate change. It can't really be separated—the struggle for reversing climate change and to completely remake what the military is

for. [The military] should be an institution working for restoring the planet. We saw that during the tsunami—the terrible Indonesian tsunami—that really only the US had the equipment to go and really rescue people, and that's not what they're usually doing with that equipment. Those who have the desire to help others are brainwashed to use that equipment for war instead of really helping the planet. I think they'd be happier soldiers otherwise. I'd start thinking that way. Rather than just demilitarization, it's a complete reformation of the role of the military in the world. If the militaries of the world used their equipment to assist with climate change rather than to fight each other, if it could be redirected, with women at the helm, we'd be saving people.[80]

Ti-Grace also adamantly insisted that the United States embrace and nurture a legitimate third party to undermine the power of the two-party system we currently operate within. She said, "I think that both parties are corrupt so I sort of hold my nose and vote for the least bad, and I'm not happy about it. I would like to see a third party. I can't help but want to get rid of the Electoral College. I would like for us to have preferential voting, where you could give your priorities so you could vote for a minor party and not feel like you were electing George W. Bush or feeling like you were committing a crime for voting for a third party." Taking on the Republican Party, Ti-Grace said, will also serve as an important future step for young radical feminists: "The Republicans were so astronomically stupid about rape and the tax law, Planned Parenthood, and ACORN.[81] Their obsession with sex is so sick. It's disturbed. I don't want to be in a small room with them because it's so bizarre."[82]

When considering the whole of what has happened and what is to be done—in short, what we *must* learn from early radical feminism— Ti-Grace mused, "Sometimes you ask yourself, 'Well, just how far out can I get from the time and context in which I live?' When do you just get tired and say, 'I'm not living up to the standard I set. I'm tired and I know that'? I liked what I liked. I like who I liked, who was interesting. I don't know how to explain it—except if you live long enough maybe that's how it sorts out, if you are independent in your tastes and such. I liked [photographer] Diane Arbus." Reflecting on losing touch with people but also wanting closeness, Ti-Grace said:

I think I often regret that I didn't spend more time on different relationships. We have this standard, especially for women, where we expect them to water and nurture relationships more, and I don't know if I did that as much as I should have. I was interested in something somebody was doing at a given time, and then years and years later it turns out, "Wow." Then later I think, *Well, why didn't people say "Wow" when they were alive?* Why does life have to be so hard for people who are different, like Valerie [Solanas]? Sometimes I think that it's like being an artist. The artist dies, and then the work is complete, and that is when the value shoots up. Diane [Arbus] didn't have enough money to buy photographic paper. Almost no one would buy her work. She said that people thought her photos were of freaks, but she thought they were beautiful. She said, "If I'm dead, you watch—the prices will go sky high." It's true. This is a pattern with artists, again and again and again. With radical feminism, I feel that people are afraid of it in terms of their getting too close to the living thing in terms of its contemporary relevance.[83]

When considering the biggest lessons of her life's work, Ti-Grace said:

I think that if you have anything really corrupt—like sexism, like the way women are treated—and it's accepted, you have a poison. You have something at the core. It's going to infect everyone, and it's the foundation. You have to get all the way back into it, and you start to understand things. I understood other oppressions when I understood the oppression of women. I think that the most horrifying part is that we are at least half of the problem, because if we only say "no" and just refuse, it's over! It's over! Just a few people speaking up—the whole world practically came to an end. It's amazing! It can't be all that secure.[84]

Speaking of the work left to be done and the long and winding road toward women's liberation, Ti-Grace insisted:

Women's oppression has been going on so long, and it's had so many twists and turns. There are so many layers to it that there's a huge amount of work to be done. All the layers, all of the other institutions in society that we've seen that have obscured for us what's going on with women—no matter how deep we dig, we're going to have another perception, another insight, and we have to accept that we do our very best and get it as right as we can. Maybe in another ten years, if we all press on and never let up, we may see it differently. We may see that we didn't see deeply enough then. We've got to dig deeper, and you have to understand what you're dealing with.[85]

As a final thought—one that epitomizes the necessity of radical feminism and the insights embedded in the oral histories of radical feminist politics—Ti-Grace returned to the lessons of Flo Kennedy to lay a foundation for the work that is yet to come:

Now, how do you keep going? That's when I turn to Flo. You've got to build in a way to keep going, and not knowing that was my mistake. I thought you just work, work, work, work, work, like we're doing now. Are we just going to fall over, exhausted? We have to figure out how we're going to fulfill each other, and hopefully nurture each other. Nobody is going to be interested in what it takes out of us except us. We have to figure how we can make up for it somehow, so that we can build in rewards. That's what Flo did. Flo would make plaques, and it was sort of silly, but I was really pleased when I got a plaque. Once, she said, "Who else is going to appreciate us except us?" and she was very wise—very, very wise. I didn't get it at the time. It's like you need a different tempo or something. We can't just beat ourselves. There's just something almost battering about the ripping and ripping and ripping like we have to do. But there's also some way of restoring. We've got to be aware that this is very damaging. It's exciting, but we're ripping everything that we have known that keeps you secure. I don't believe anyone's going to find the truth, but I believe that there are things closer to the truth and things further away. We need to strive to get it right. We have to figure out some way to keep going.[86]

Epilogue

ON JANUARY 21, 2017, FUELED BY A COLLECTIVE RAGE ABOUT the inauguration of President Donald Trump, over five million women marched in cities and towns all over the world to protest the politics and policies that Trump and his presidency stood for. Reporters estimated that rallies in Los Angeles and Washington, DC, reached over three hundred thousand protesters each; marches in over 650 towns and cities in the United States, and many more throughout the world, signaled a newfound commitment to refusal, resistance, and defiance in the face of the Trump presidency.[1] Though the press coverage of these marches largely edited out the more edgy or "obscene" posters and signs (for example, "Karma Has a Pussy"), thus obscuring some of the more provocative components of the march, the experience of being physically present at the march showed a far different perspective: The Women's March embodied many facets of unabashedly radical feminism.

These marches were fanatically intersectional, highlighting feminist causes that ranged from climate change and reproductive justice to queer rights and prison reform. Protest signs talked openly and honestly about the body, and used "the pussy" as a weapon of resistance ("This Pussy Has Teeth") and accusations of "nastiness" as a means to fight back ("Nasty as We Wanna Be" and "You Haven't Seen Nasty Yet"). It also brought together an astonishing array of protesters: women, men, trans people, teenagers, college students, professionals, blue-collar workers, mothers, aunts, grandmothers, husbands, young boys, little girls, those in wheelchairs, seasoned protesters and those brand-new to activism (and everything in between). The march featured rhetorical tactics ("A

Woman's Place Is in the Revolution"), frank depictions of the body as resistance ("The Red Vadge of Courage"), careful wordplay ("Girls Just Wanna Have Fundamental Human Rights"; "Super Callous Fascist Racist Extra Bragga Docious"), overt rejections of Trump and his connections to Putin ("Make America Think Again" and "Stop Putin Your Hands Where They Don't Belong"), and a huge range of emotions and expressions (from "Grab Patriarchy by the Balls" to "Now You've Pissed Off Grandma"). The sheer size of the march was an overwhelming testament to something new emerging in the "post-Trump" period: a more confrontational feminism not as afraid of its anger and its edges, its intersections and its divergences, its complaining and its outrage.

The question of what we will do with this edgier, angrier, more collective feminism, and how it might transform the core of the (profoundly liberal) feminist movement thus far, remains to be seen. Suddenly, the stories of feminist rage outlined in this book seem uniquely timely, and tactics of an enduring radical movement seem especially relevant. Conversations about sustaining ourselves and each other, forging new alliances and solidarities, digging as deep as we can into the root structures of intersecting oppressions, and insisting on using the right tactics to resist all resonate more clearly. The prescient warnings that Ti-Grace, Roxanne, Kathie, and Dana have outlined in this book take on new significance in an era when pussy-grabbing, the elimination of the EPA, lethal attacks on abortion, appallingly homophobic vice presidents and cabinet members, attacks on old people's health care, overtly racist wall-building, and anti-intellectualism have ripped through the core of our political character.

The enduring spirit of radical feminism—its insistence on refusal; its belief that a firm *no* is often far more impactful than a postmodern argument that facts and truth and decisions can be always in motion or wishy-washy in nature—has arrived again in full force. Feminists (young and old) once again embrace the scariness of radicalism, its potential as a threatening force, now that we stare down the weighty, mighty threats made to us by the Trump-defined right wing. We once again look to the streets and the megaphone and the protest poster for solace and renewal, remembering that *impact* and *change* in our political world takes a twisting path paved with the blood and tears of radicals and their allies.

If radical feminist organizing persists today, it does so not only in the words and actions of the outraged masses but also in the spirited and defiant politics of several emerging (or strengthening) movements: Black Lives Matter, with its insistence on fighting police brutality and racial profiling, its links to the Panthers, and its tactics of avoiding surveillance;[2] Feminists Against Trump, which takes as its starting point the premise that "pussy grabs back" (following the October 2016 disclosure that Donald Trump bragged on a hot mic in 2005 about how he would "grab [women] by the pussy"); the anti-incarceration movement, which takes on the corporate and political investment in maintaining and extending a racist criminal justice system;[3] the overtly antiwar, pro-peace politics of women-run Code Pink;[4] the avidly anticapitalist politics of the Occupy movement;[5] the antifa ("antifascist") resistance movement; and the long-established but recently reinvigorated National Women's Liberation movement, which has thrown its weight behind the labor movement, organized women's strikes, single-payer healthcare, and radical new visions for fighting male supremacy and misogyny. Radical feminism also persists in the reinvigorated politics around fighting border politics and policies, the intensifying defiance of "bathroom laws" and lack of federal protection for trans people, the pushback against laws that slowly chip away at abortion rights, and the forging of new alliances between movements and causes (men fighting for feminist causes, heterosexuals fighting for queer rights, whites fighting alongside people of color at the border, etc.).[6] In each of these, the bubbling up of anger and the refusal to accept slow and incremental change lies at the core. As daughters of the first, second, and third waves, we understand now, I think, that there is urgency in these struggles, that "wait and see" or "just be patient" approaches to social change mean death, and that at the root of all forms of oppression is a politics of domination and destruction. We have, in part, early radical feminists to thank for trying to teach this to us.

In this most recent period—when misogyny and patriarchy have emerged as explicit values of Trump's presidency (and his personal behavior); where the president more closely resembles an internet troll or a radio shock jock than a dignified leader; where women who resist are explicitly targeted and denounced (e.g., Gamergate provocateur Anita Sarkeesian, or even conservative news anchor Megyn Kelly)—radical feminism has new salience. It offers a critique of the structure itself—of the very essence of what drives rape culture and trivialization of women's lives—rather than simply critiquing these politics at the surface. Radical feminists understand that misogyny stems from a deep investment in power imbalances, hierarchy, and inequality, that racism has its root structure in the belief that certain people are disposable, and that dominance and colonization are acceptable modes of human exchange. Radical feminists help us to understand not only *why* these things are happening but also what to do in response; a radical flank is necessary for real social change.[7]

There is no rational, reasonable, agreeable negotiating with the forces of white supremacy, sexism, capitalism, and racism, just as we cannot play nice with the phobias and insults and threats and violences that these things produce. We do not take on the powerful through skittish, "respectable" behavior. Rather, the fight must be taken up in intense and sustained ways, requiring the willpower to remain in a permanent state of defiance. We look to grassroots organizing in order to show collective strength, muscle, and guts. Radical movements require multiple tactical interventions in language, politics, theory, family and kinship structures, institutional practices, education, healthcare, violence, and the body, and we know that each of these interventions matter. New solidarities and alliances are crucial; working through differences, or valuing the tension of those differences, matters. Creating space for vigorous disagreement that disallows outright dismissal of unpopular radical ideas also matters. Making an archive of the work that is being done, and the people doing that work, matters. Defining and redefining the lines in the sand definitely matters. This is no time for polite, respectable, inclusive, emotionless, milquetoast "feminism is for everybody"; we need impolite, feral, emotional, risk-taking firebrand feminism.

We are, in a sense, living through history, burdened with the perpetual sensation that these are dangerous times, filled with the potential to crush or draw inward those who may have otherwise resisted in spirited and defiant ways. I am reminded of James Baldwin's claims about the *aliveness* of history, the necessity that we understand that all history—including radical feminist histories—is made and remade within us. Baldwin wrote, in "Unnamable Objects, Unspeakable Crimes," "History, as nearly no one seems to know, is not merely something to be read. And it does not refer merely, or even principally, to the past. On the contrary, the great force of history comes from the fact that we carry it within us, are unconsciously controlled by it in many ways, and history is literally present in all that we do. It could scarcely be otherwise, since it is to history that we owe our frames of reference, our identities, our aspirations. And it is with great pain and terror that one begins to realize this."[8] This is why, for me, the stories in this collection are not merely *history*, as in the telling of stories about the past, but instead serve as lessons for the present, stories for the future, tales made for understanding, surviving, and perhaps partially averting the disaster we are now living through.

The histories of women—stories buried in the silt and ashes of lives burned down, ignored, forgotten, or discarded—are, as Baldwin says, alive in all we do. The teachers, activists, scholars, and thinkers, brave and ahead of their time, form a crucial part of our identity as feminists. And while key tensions may still exist—between second- and third-wave feminism, for example—these differences betray the broader problem that second-wave feminism can only be understood, in this time and place, through the lens of this current third-wave movement. *History is alive within us.* In short, second-wave radical feminist histories only make sense when imagined through the present, when interrogated and examined in light of the politics of today. Their rage is our rage. Their struggles are, in many ways, our struggles.

And so, I invite you to carry these stories around with you, rummage through them, add texture to the characters and places and ideas featured here. We are charged with continuing the story further, trying to see as far ahead of our time as possible, mapping and outlining the urgent necessity of a radical feminist future. Such a future will likely include conflict and contradiction, rage and friendship, solidarities and painful divergences; it will be messy, exciting, and difficult. In the meantime, these firebrand feminists will carry us along, teach us a few tricks, and send us with full bellies on the long journey forward.

ACKNOWLEDGMENTS |

First and foremost, I thank Ti-Grace Atkinson, Roxanne Dunbar-Ortiz, Kathie Sarachild, and Dana Densmore for not only all they gave to this book but for our friendship and solidarity over these many years. I am, now and always, forever in their debt and filled with fondness and affection for each of them. I have deep gratitude for other radical feminist scholars and activists as well, particularly those whose work has inspired and shaped my own thinking about the necessity of radical feminism. Jane Caputi, equal part radical feminist and earth mother, thank you for your wisdom. Certainly the work of Flo Kennedy, Shulamith Firestone, Kate Millett, Anne Koedt, Carol Giardina, Ellen Willis, Carol Hanisch, Nancy Naples, Barbara Crow, Jo Freeman, Susan Brownmiller, Nancy Whittier, Loretta Ross, Mary Daly, Sara Evans, Linda Gordon, Amy Scholder, Andrea Dworkin, and Jacqueline Rhodes has infused the way I think and write about radical feminism. Alice Echols has shown particular generosity to me throughout this project, as have Eileen Boris, Estelle Freedman, Carol Srole, Mary Felstiner, Valerie Matsumoto, and the entire UCLA Teaching Workshop on Women's History group.

The wonderfully complex lives and works of other scholar-activists also support, directly and indirectly, the work I do on radical feminism. Leonore Tiefer, who brought the New View group into my life, thank you for embodying generosity, bravery, and humor in equal measure and for always validating this work. Chris Bobel, at the helm of the Society for Menstrual Cycle Research, you epitomize why sisterhood matters and why artists, activists, and scholars all need a place at the table. Virginia Braun, I am forever inspired by the many intersections of your truly radical work, not to mention your warm and generous mentorship and support. Thank you again and again to the menstrual mafia: Chris Bobel, Joan Chrisler, Ingrid Johnston, Elizabeth Kissling, Maureen McHugh, David Linton, Mindy Erchull, Heather Dillaway, Jerilynn Prior, Tomi-Ann Roberts, Peggy Stubbs, Jax Gonzalez, and Jane Ussher.

I had the tremendous fortune to receive institutional support through the Provost's Humanities Fellow Academy in 2015, where I met weekly with Elizabeth Brake, Jacqueline Martinez, and Kevin Sandler to discuss each of our books and to keep on writing, thinking, redrafting, imagining, and laughing. I owe each of you a great debt for this time together, particularly the extraordinarily gracious and generous Elizabeth. I cannot summon enough words to thank Marlene Tromp, who helped me secure this fellowship and who has had my back for many years. Thanks also to Duane Roen and George Justice for supporting this book formally and personally. I also thank Rebecca Plante and Andrew Smiler, my writing group friends, who helped me to imagine the book in the first place. Thanks to the Redstockings Women's Liberation Archives for Action (PO Box 744, Stuyvesant Station, New York, NY 10009; www.redstockings .org) for the important archival work they do about radical feminism. Thank you to Felicity Plester and Beth Bouloukos, and to Amy Scholder, radical feminist publisher extraordinaire, who prodded me to think about the bridge between these radical feminist women's lives and contemporary feminist issues—this project wouldn't exist without you. To my editor, Larin McLaughlin, who threw her weight behind me since the beginning (and who has a hand in so many wonderful book projects from coast to coast), you are simply the best of the best. Thank you also to the University of Washington Press gang—especially my thoughtful copyeditor Anne Mathews—for seeing this book through to the finish line.

To the Feminist Research on Gender and Sexuality Group ("the FROGS"): For your boundless energy, your true kindness, your generous sense of intellectual community with me and each other, and your commitment to nurturing radical feminist impulses in yourselves and the world, thank you a million times over. I have loved watching all of you dive headlong into difficult work while embodying the true spirit of feminist community. I just cannot ever explain how lovely and wonderful you all are. Thank you in the most heartfelt way to all of the FROGS: Madison Carlyle, Kimberly Koerth, Ayanna Shambe, Emma DiFrancesco, Crystal Zaragoza, Laura Martinez, Natali Blazevic, Michael Karger, Adrielle Munger, Jax Gonzalez, Stephanie Robinson, Rose Coursey, Chelsea Pixler Charbonneau, Corie Cisco, Elizabeth Wallace, Marisa Loiacono, Eva Sisko, Carissa Cunningham, Jennifer Bertagni, Alexis Starks, Tatiana Crespo, Laisa Schweigert, Sheldon Banks, and Decker Dunlop. Many of you—especially Madison, Kimberly, Alexis, and Ayanna—invested considerable time in fact-checking, editing, and compiling references for this book. Thank you! I owe an immense debt to Kimberly Koerth for indexing the book with such care.

Among my colleagues—near and far—of many years and many (weary) miles, I thank Louis Mendoza, Todd Sandrin, Sian Mooney, Sharon Kirsch, Michael Stancliff, Arthur Sabatini, Barry Moon, Ashley Gohr, Monica Casper, Gloria Cuadraz, Thea Cacchioni, Rose Carlson, Valerie Kemper, Deborah Tolman, Bernadette Barton, Carla Golden, Sandy Caron, Jennifer Baumgardner, Diana Álvarez, and Patrick Grzanka. Ela Przybylo, I am so grateful for your intelligence and kindness, your seriousness, and your affection. Thank you also to the many (here unnamed) clinical patients with whom I have shared numerous hours of deep and intense work and reflection. You will never know what you mean to me and to my work, and how much your imprint, your stories, and your struggles have influenced this book and everything I write.

There is perhaps nothing that makes the world feel more tolerable and full of hope than having mentors and friends who also understand the value and necessity of struggling together on the frontlines of feminism. To my mentors—Deb Martinson, Abby Stewart, Sarah Stage, and Elmer Griffin—thank you for believing in what I do and insisting on the value of my radical feminist spirit. Thank you to my friends, a feisty bunch of troublemakers who embody kindness, generosity, love, and goodness: Lori Errico-Seaman, Sean Seaman, Sara McClelland, Mary Dudy, Jennifer Tamir, Annika Mann, Denise Delgado, Garyn Tsuru, Jan Habarth, Marcy Winokur, Steve DuBois, Sadie Mohler, Connie Hardesty, Katie Goldey, Pat Hart, Karen Swank-Fitch, and David Frost. To my sister, Kristen, who works too hard for her own good, and to her radiant children, Simon and Ryan, I love you. To my aunts—Marilee, Michelle, Linda, and Julie—thank you for the deep roots that connect our tree. To Eric Swank, for the thousand ways you have supported this book—editing, nurturing, giggling, growling, overlooking, approving, forgiving, holding, pondering, talking, bonding—and for carrying each project through with your own beautifully radical spirit, you are too wonderful for words. I love you. Finally, I dedicate this book to my mother, who has always valued my willfulness and who taught me from a young age to listen carefully to the stories of old women.

NOTES |

PREFACE

1   See also Sherna Berger Gluck, "Has Feminist Oral History Lost Its Radical/
     Subversive Edge?" *Oral History* 39, no. 2 (2011): 63–72.

2   Susan Geiger, "What's So Feminist about Women's Oral History?" *Journal of
     Women's History* 2, no. 1 (1990): 180. See also Alessandro Portelli, "What Makes
     Oral History Different," in *Oral History, Oral Culture, and Italian Americans*, ed.
     Luisa Del Giudice (London: Palgrave, 2009), 21–30; Sherna Berger Gluck and
     Daphne Patai, *Women's Words: The Feminist Practice of Oral History* (New York:
     Routledge, 2013); Jeska Rees, "'Are You a Lesbian?': Challenges in Recording
     and Analysing the Women's Liberation Movement in England," *History Work-
     shop Journal* 69, no. 1 (2007): 177–87; and Joanna Bornat and Hanna Diamond,
     "Women's History and Oral History: Developments and Debates," *Women's
     History Review* 16, no. 1 (2007): 19–39.

3   Rachel F. Moran, "How Second-Wave Feminism Forgot the Single Woman,"
     Hofstra Law Review 33 (2004): 223–34; Rosalyn Baxandall and Linda Gordon,
     "Second-Wave Feminism," in *A Companion to American Women's History*, ed.
     Nancy A. Hewitt (New York: John Wiley and Sons, 2008): 414–32; Barbara A.
     Crow, *Radical Feminism: A Documentary Reader* (New York: New York University
     Press, 2000); Alice Echols, *Daring to be Bad: Radical Feminism in America, 1967–
     1975* (New York: Vintage Books, 1979); Jo Freeman and Victoria Johnson, *Waves
     of Protest: Social Movements since the Sixties* (New York: Rowman & Littlefield,
     1999); Estelle Freedman, *No Turning Back: The History of Feminism and the Future of
     Women* (New York: Random House, 2007); and Denise Thompson, *Radical Femi-
     nism Today* (London: Sage, 2001).

4   Lauren E. Duncan and Abigail J. Stewart, "A Generational Analysis of Women's
     Rights Activists," *Psychology of Women Quarterly* 24, no. 4 (2000): 297–308; Finn
     Mackay, *Radical Feminism: Feminist Activism in Movement* (London: Palgrave, 2015);
     Kate Eichorn, *The Archival Turn in Feminism: Outrage in Order* (Philadelphia: Temple

University Press, 2013); Nancy M. Henley, Karen Meng, Delores O'Brien, William J. McCarthy, and Robert J. Sockloskie, "Developing a Scale to Measure the Diversity of Feminist Attitudes," *Psychology of Women Quarterly* 22, no. 3 (1998): 317–48; Nancy Whittier, *Feminist Generations: The Persistence of the Radical Women's Movement* (Philadelphia: Temple University Press, 2010); and Stephanie Gilmore, "The Dynamics of Second-Wave Feminist Activism in Memphis, 1971–1982: Rethinking the Liberal/Radical Divide," *NWSA Journal* 15, no. 1 (2003): 94–117.

INTRODUCTION

1   Ti-Grace had a cat named Ruthless. See *Florence Morning News*, "Feminist Consulted Columbo," August 22, 1974, www.newspapers.com/newspage/68522437. In numerous encounters with these women, I witnessed their status as old women and their radical political politics converging in humorous ways. Roxanne, for example, asked me to return in a few hours when we had scheduled an in-person interview because she needed to take a nap. Another time, when I emailed Ti-Grace to ask if she needed anything while recovering from a hip surgery, she wrote, dryly, "A different body." (Atkinson, email to Breanne Fahs, October 6, 2016.)

2   Many retrospective accounts of feminism—particularly radical feminism—emphasize conflicts between women as a centerpiece of the movement. Carol Hanisch, for example, writes, "As its popularity grew, the feminist bandwagon became overcrowded with a myriad of offshoots: cultural feminists, lesbian feminists, lesbian separatist feminists, matriarchal feminists, eco-feminists, anti-nuke feminists, peace feminists, anarcho-feminists, animal rights feminists, third-wave feminists, Jewish feminists, and the list goes on—even the anti-abortion Feminists for Life. Some, in our view, bore little relationship to the real struggle for feminist or women's liberation demands, but were women self-segregating themselves to fight for other goals." ("Women's Liberation: Looking Back, Looking Forward," *On the Issues*, Winter 2011, http://ontheissues magazine.com/2011winter/2011_winter_Hanisch.php.) For other examples, see Jo Freeman, "The Tyranny of Structurelessness," *Women's Studies Quarterly* 41, no. 3–4 (2013): 231–46; Sara M. Evans, "Women's Liberation: Seeing the Revolution Clearly," *Feminist Studies* 41, no. 1 (2015): 138–59; and Victoria Hesford, *Feeling Women's Liberation* (Durham, NC: Duke University Press, 2013).

3   Interestingly, some scholarship argues that diversity and infighting within the feminist movement led to attacking sexism on multiple fronts—along with more creative, inclusive, and radical frameworks for thinking about social justice. See Suzanne Staggenborg and Verta Taylor, "Whatever Happened to the Women's Movement?" *Mobilization* 10, no. 1 (2005): 37–52; and Holly J. McCammon, Erin M. Bergner, and Sandra C. Arch, "'Are You One of Those Women?':

Within-Movement Conflict, Radical Flank Effects, and Social Movement Political Outcomes," *Mobilization* 20, no. 2 (2015): 157–78.

4   The obituary for Patricia Buckley Bozell captures some of these details. (See Adam Bernstein, "Patricia Buckley Bozell, 81; Activist Founded a Catholic Opinion Journal," *Washington Post*, July 14, 2008.) Further, in a March 10, 1971, speech in DC entitled "Catholic University," Ti-Grace said, "It was in this context that the issue of the Virgin Mary was raised. She was impregnated supernaturally, and was, therefore, forced to bear the responsibility and sorrow of her supernatural child more than if he had been conceived naturally. 'Knocked up' . . . She was impregnated; 'knocked down'—this son was a great source of grief to her; 'with no clues'—without sexual intercourse, my remarks depended on the virginity of the Blessed Mother. I was attacking the cruelty of her having to bear this sorrow alone. So much for what I said at Notre Dame."

5   Radical feminism, however, has significant variation in political priorities, tactical interventions, and specific goals—though radical feminism as a whole does share some common grounding assumptions about *not* prioritizing within-system change.

6   *Kathleen G. Donohue, Freedom from Want: American Liberalism and the Idea of the Consumer (Baltimore: Johns Hopkins University Press, 2003).*

7   Eric Alterman, *Why We're Liberals* (New York: Viking, 2008).

8   Michael Walzer, "The Communitarian Critique of Liberalism," *Political Theory* 18, no. 1 (1990): 6–23.

9   Mary Becker, "Patriarchy and Inequality: Towards a Substantive Feminism," *University of Chicago Legal Forum* 1 (1999): 21–22.

10 bell hooks, *Feminist Theory: From Margin to Center* (New York: Routledge, 2015), 19.

11 National Organization for Women, "About the NOW Foundation," http://now .org/now-foundation/about-now-foundation.

12 Amy Sherman, "Hillary Clinton's Changing Position on Same-Sex Marriage," PolitiFact, June 17, 2015, www.politifact.com/truth-o-meter/statements/2015 /jun/17/hillary-clinton/hillary-clinton-change-position-same-sex-marriage.

13 Ellen Willis, "Radical Feminism and Feminist Radicalism," *Social Text* 3, no. 3 (1984): 93.

14 Willis, "Women and the Left," *Notes from the Second Year: Women's Liberation*, 1970, 56, http://library.duke.edu/digitalcollections/wlmpc_wlmms01039.

15 Ruth Brine, "The New Feminists: Revolt Against 'Sexism,'" *Time*, November 21, 1969, 53. For a full analysis of this media coverage, see Patricia Bradley, *Mass Media and the Shaping of American Feminism, 1963–1975* (Jackson: University Press of Mississippi, 2004), 99.

16 Martha Weinman Lear, "The Second Feminist Wave," *New York Times*, March 10, 1968.

17 Sheryl Sandberg, *Lean In: Women, Work, and the Will to Lead* (New York: Knopf, 2013). Sandberg's book argues that women should be more assertive in business

and should "speak their truth," seek mentorship, accept compliments, and "fake it 'til you make it." The book (and the movement around the book) has been critiqued by prominent feminists like bell hooks and Susan Faludi, who argue that it produces "faux feminism" by framing women as marketable consumer objects and playing down systematic gender biases. See Susan Faludi, "Facebook Feminism, Like It or Not," *Baffler* 23 (2013), http://thebaffler.com/articles/facebook-feminism-like-it-or-not#; and bell hooks, "Dig Deep: Beyond 'Lean In,'" *Feminist Wire*, October 23, 2013, http://thefeministwire.com/2013/10/17973.

18   See Catherine Rottenberg, "The Rise of Neoliberal Feminism," *Cultural Studies* 28, no. 3 (2014): 418–37; Caroline C. Fitz, Alyssa N. Zucker, and Laina Bay-Cheng, "Not All Nonlabelers Are Created Equal: Distinguishing Between Quasi-Feminists and Neoliberals," *Psychology of Women Quarterly* 36, no. 3 (2012): 274–85.

19   See Fahs, "Dreaded 'Otherness': Heteronormative Patrolling in Women's Body Hair Rebellions," *Gender and Society* 24, no. 4 (2011): 451–72; Fahs, "Breaking Body Hair Boundaries: Classroom Exercises for Challenging Social Constructions of the Body and Sexuality," *Feminism and Psychology* 22, no. 4 (2012): 482–506; and Fahs, "Perilous Patches and Pitstaches: Imagined Versus Lived Experiences of Women's Body Hair Growth," *Psychology of Women Quarterly* 38, no. 2 (2014): 167–80.

20   Roxanne Dunbar-Ortiz, in "Outcasts and Outlaws: Cell 16, Valerie Solanas, and the History of Radical Feminism," panel presented with Dana Densmore and Breanne Fahs at A Revolutionary Moment: Women's Liberation in the Late 1960s and Early 1970s Conference, Boston, MA, March 29, 2014.

21   Maria Akchurin and Lee Cheol-Sung, "Pathways to Empowerment: Repertoires of Women's Activism and Gender Earnings Equality," *American Sociological Review* 78, no. 4 (2013): 679–701; Anne N. Costain and Steven Majstorovic, "Congress, Social Movements, and Public Opinion: Multiple Origins of Women's Rights Legislation," *Political Research Quarterly* 47, no. 1 (1994): 111–35; Lee Ann Banaszak and Heather L. Ondercin, "Public Opinion as a Movement Outcome: The Case of the US Women's Movement," *Mobilization* 21, no. 3 (2016): 361–78.

22   Steinem's new book, *My Life on the Road* (New York: Penguin Random House, 2016), continues to be a bestseller with a well-publicized national tour.

23   Ti-Grace Atkinson, "How to Defang a Movement: Replacing the Political with the Personal," paper presented at A Revolutionary Moment: Women's Liberation in the Late 1960s and Early 1970s Conference, March 29, 2014.

24   Ti-Grace Atkinson, interview by Breanne Fahs, Cambridge, MA, February 1, 2008.

25   Ibid.

26   Ibid.

27   Ibid.

28   Ibid.

29   Simone de Beauvoir (1908–1986) was a feminist writer and French intellectual from Paris. She was the youngest person at the time to have passed a highly

competitive postgraduate exam in philosophy at the University of Paris at the age of twenty-one. She spent the rest of her life writing, traveling, and engaging in political activism, publishing over twenty-five books. She was notorious for her long-term open romantic partnership with Jean-Paul Sartre (1905–1980), also a French philosopher, and for her unusual sexual liaisons with many of her female students. See Lawrence D. Krizman, ed., *Politics, Philosophy, Culture: Interviews and Other Writings, 1977–1984* (New York: Routledge, 1990); and Deirdre Bair, *Simone de Beauvoir: A Biography* (New York: Summit Books, 1990).

30 Atkinson, interview by Fahs, February 1, 2008.

31 Betty Friedan (1921–2006) wrote six books, including *The Feminine Mystique* (1963), and is credited with starting the second wave of American feminism. The book sold millions of copies following its release. She cofounded the National Organization for Women in 1966 and was elected its first president. Friedan also organized the Women's Strike for Equality in 1970 and helped to found the National Women's Political Caucus the following year. She supported the Equal Rights Amendment and founded the National Association for Repeal of Abortion Laws (now known as NARAL Pro-Choice America). See Margalit Fox, "Betty Friedan, Who Ignited Cause in *Feminine Mystique*, Dies at 85," *New York Times*, February 5, 2006.

32 "Red-diaper babies," a term coined by Judy Kaplan and Linn Shapiro, are children of parents who were members of the US Communist party. See Judy Kaplan and Linn Shapiro, *Red Diapers: Growing Up in the Communist Left* (Urbana: University of Illinois Press, 1998).

33 Atkinson, interview by Fahs, February 1, 2008.

34 Ti-Grace Atkinson, *Amazon Odyssey: The First Collection of Writings by the Political Pioneer of the Women's Movement* (New York: Links Books, 1974), 13.

35 The October 17th Movement took up the name The Feminists shortly after its creation on October 17, 1968. It was founded as a split from the New York City chapter of NOW by Ti-Grace Atkinson and included prominent members like Anne Koedt, Sheila Michaels, Barbara Mehrhof, Pamela Kearon, and Sheila Cronan. The Feminists later picketed the New York City marriage license bureau and worked on radical feminist social change. See Atkinson, interview by Fahs, February 1, 2008.

36 Atkinson, interview by Fahs, February 1, 2008.

37 Ti-Grace Atkinson, "Vaginal Orgasm as a Mass Hysterical Survival Response," public speech, Philadelphia, PA, April 6, 1968. The piece was later published in Atkinson, *Amazon Odyssey*, 5–7.

38 Ti-Grace was called feminism's "haute thinker" in Martha Weinman Lear, "The Second Feminist Wave," *New York Times Magazine*, March 10, 1968.

39 See the Schlesinger Library, www.radcliffe.harvard.edu/schlesinger-library; and the Dobkin Family Collection of Feminism, www.glennhorowitz.com/dobkin.

40 In June 2015, real estate development firm Boston Investments bought Ti-Grace's small apartment building on Harding Street in Cambridge, Massachusetts, and

raised rents to levels many tenants could not afford. Ti-Grace took action, engaging city council members and nonprofit legal organizations for guidance, distributing leaflets to call together tenants, and arranging meetings in her home so they could coordinate a response. This resulted in an eviction notice, which then inspired Ti-Grace to start the Harding Street Neighbors, who successfully lobbied the city's housing authority to create an emergency category of Section 8 housing vouchers for people facing immediate displacement by unaffordable rent increases. Ti-Grace told reporters, "My neighbors learned the hard way that being a nice tenant won't get the job done. They haven't been through the fire of the feminist movement that I have. . . . They messed with the wrong bitch." See Sarah Kwon, "Ti-Grace Atkinson, at Home in Cambridge, Adds Cause to Radical Feminism: Housing," *Cambridge Day*, January 6, 2016, www.cambridgeday.com/2016/01/06/ti-grace-atkinson-at-home-in-cambridge-adds-cause-to-radical-feminism-housing.

41 The Student Nonviolent Coordinating Committee (SNCC) was a youth organization inspired by the Woolworth's lunch counter sit-in; it was founded by Ella Baker in April 1960, at Shaw University, in order to fight for civil rights. As one the more radical wings of the civil rights movement, the group was instrumental in planning and facilitating freedom rides and sit-ins, registering black voters in Southern states, and integrating public facilities. An offshoot of the Southern Christian Leadership Conference (SCLC), SNCC disagreed with the SCLC's ideology of pacifism and eventually split off from it. During Freedom Summer, the 1964 Mississippi voter-registration project, three civil rights workers were murdered by the Ku Klux Klan. In 1966, Stokely Carmichael became the elected leader of SNCC and advocated for black power, self-reliance, and the use of violence as self-defense (a direct split from Martin Luther King Jr.'s tactics of nonviolence). In 1967, it was disbanded. See "SNCC," History.com, www.history.com/topics/black-history/sncc; and Emily Stoper, "The Student Nonviolent Coordinating Committee: Rise and Fall of a Redemptive Organization," *Journal of Black Studies* 8, no.1 (1977): 13–34.

42 The information on Kathie Sarachild in this book comes from her written speeches, public forums, published works, email correspondences, and website information; she did not allow a one-on-one interview, which limits throughout this book the depth and scope of her contributions.

43 Kathie Sarachild, email to Breanne Fahs, March 24, 2013.

44 Civil Rights Digital Library, "Kathie Sarachild," October 23, 2016, http://crdl .usg.edu/people/s/sarachild_kathie/?Welcome.

45 Barbara Love, *Feminists Who Changed America, 1963–1975* (Chicago: University of Illinois Press, 2006), 405; see also Redstockings, *Redstockings Women's Liberation Archive for Action Packet: Some Documents from and Media Responses to Redstockings Abortion Speakouts, 1969 and 1989* (New York: Archives Distribution Project); see also the cover from *Notes from the First Year*, Duke University Libraries Digital Collections, http://library.duke.edu/digitalcollections/wlmpc_wlmms01037.

46 Kathie Sarachild, "A Program for Feminist 'Consciousness-Raising,'" *Notes from the Second Year*, 78–80; see also Kathie Sarachild, "Consciousness-Raising: A Radical Weapon," in *Feminist Revolution*, ed. Redstockings (New York: Random House, 1978): 144–50.

47 Love, *Feminists Who Changed America*, 405; and Redstockings, "June 1969: A Blast of Redstockings Feminism," www.redstockings.org/index.php/june-1969-a-blast -of-redstockings-feminism.

48 Sarachild, email to Fahs, March 24, 2013.

49 Sarachild, "A Program for Feminist 'Consciousness-Raising,'" 78–80.

50 Sarachild, email to Fahs, April 13, 2017. The Miss America pageant protest occurred on September 7, 1968, and included many prominent feminists including Kathie Sarachild, Flo Kennedy, Alix Shulman, Carol Hanisch, Robin Morgan, Carol Giardina, Helen Kritzler, Bev Grant, Peggy Dobbins, and Florika Remetier.

51 For full details about the Miss America pageant and more, see Redstockings, *Feminist Revolution*, 209. (Also note that a complete PDF version of *Feminist Revolution* can be accessed on the Redstockings website at www.redstockings.org /index.php/main/feminist-revolution.)

52 Love, *Feminists Who Changed America*, 405.

53 Redstockings, "June 1969."

54 Love, *Feminists Who Changed America*, 405.

55 Love, *Feminists Who Changed America*, 12; and Redstockings, "About Redstockings of the Women's Liberation Movement," accessed October 22, 2016, www .redstockings.org/index.php/about-redstockings.

56 Love, *Feminists Who Changed America*, 405.

57 Aida Mallard, "Fame Recipient Fought for Equal Rights," *Gainesville Sun*, January 7, 2010.

58 Redstockings, "About Redstockings."

59 Roxanne Dunbar-Ortiz, *Red Dirt: Growing Up Okie* (Norman: University of Oklahoma Press, 2006), 12.

60 Red Dirt Site, "About Roxanne Dunbar-Ortiz," accessed November 2, 2016, www.reddirtsite.com/about.htm.

61 Dunbar-Ortiz, *Red Dirt*, 12.

62 Ibid.

63 Dunbar-Ortiz, interview by Fahs, San Francisco, CA, December 11, 2008.

64 Ibid.

65 Dunbar-Ortiz, *Red Dirt*, 130.

66 Ibid., 149.

67 Ibid., 152–58.

68 Ibid., 197.

69 Ibid., 159–224.

70 Ibid., 217.

71 Dunbar-Ortiz, *Outlaw Woman: A Memoir of the War Years, 1960–1975* (San Francisco: City Lights, 2001), 9.

72 Dunbar-Ortiz, interview by Fahs, December 11, 2008.

73 Howard Smith, "The Shot That Shattered the Velvet Underground," *Village Voice*, June 6, 1968.

74 Dunbar-Ortiz, *Outlaw Woman*, 119.

75 Dunbar-Ortiz, interview by Fahs, December 11, 2008.

76 Ibid.

77 For a fuller history of Cell 16, see Dunbar-Ortiz, *Outlaw Woman*.

78 Dunbar-Ortiz also remembers sending long letters to her then-husband, Jean-Louis, trying to transform him into the leader of a male feminist movement. "I did not succeed," she writes. One such letter included the following: "I haven't rejected Che [Guevara] in admiring Valerie Solanas. For me, Che will always be a saint, and I learn from him, try to be like him. Yet I know he did not mean what I have made of his message. He was dedicated to patria o muerte, and for me it's humanidad o muerte. Che, in using an old symbol and an inherently oppressive fixture, the nation-state, did not deal with patriarchy and how the state reproduces it and requires it. . . .Women are not taken seriously even when they die bravely for a cause. It is the same with Valerie. She is viewed as a psychopath even by radicals, the same ones who call Che a great revolutionary and Billy the Kid a social bandit, but a female rebel is neither—she is surely either a spy or a seductress, or at best a helpmate." Dunbar-Ortiz, letter to Jean-Louis, July 5, 1968, as cited in Dunbar-Ortiz, "From the Cradle to the Boat: A Feminist Historian Remembers Valerie Solanas," *San Francisco Bay Guardian*, January 5, 2000.

79 Dunbar-Ortiz, "From the Cradle to the Boat."

80 Sara Evans, as quoted in Echols, *Daring to be Bad*, 209.

81 Ti-Grace Atkinson, as quoted in Echols, *Daring to be Bad*, 107.

82 Dunbar-Ortiz, interview by Fahs, December 11, 2008.

83 Ibid.

84 Ibid.

85 *Native Times*, "Activist, Author Roxanne Dunbar-Ortiz Addresses Standing Room Only Crowd at University of Tulsa," May 5, 2013, www.nativetimes.com /life/people/8695-activist-author-roxanne-dunbar-ortiz-addresses-standing -room-only-crowd-at-university-of-tulsa.

86 Dunbar-Ortiz, *The Great Sioux Nation: An Oral History of the Sioux Nation and Its Struggle for Sovereignty* (New York: Random House, 1977), reprinted as *The Great Sioux Nation: Sitting in Judgment on America* (Lincoln: University of Nebraska Press, 2013).

87 Dunbar-Ortiz, interview by Fahs, December 11, 2008.

88 Ibid.

89 Red Dirt Site, "About Roxanne Dunbar-Ortiz."

90 Dunbar-Ortiz, interview by Fahs, December 11, 2008.

91 Michelle Callarman, "A Daughter's Story," in *The Conversation Begins*, ed.

Christina Looper Baker and Christina Baker Kline (New York: Bantam Books, 1996), 166–67.

92 Red Dirt Site, "About Roxanne Dunbar-Ortiz."

93 Women Strike For Peace (WSP) was inaugurated with a daylong strike by an estimated fifty thousand women in sixty cities, all pressing for nuclear disarmament. The group included many mothers, including Allen, who feared the effects of nuclear proliferation on the short and long-term health of their children. Their slogans, "End the Arms Race—Not the Human Race" and "Pure Milk, Not Poison," were prominently displayed at their rallies. They later worked against the Vietnam War, protested the draft, and worked to expose the war's effects on Vietnamese children. They also picketed the White House, the United Nations headquarters in New York City, and the Pentagon to demonstrate their opposition to nuclear weapons and war.

94 Densmore, interview by Fahs, Santa Fe, NM, October 24, 2009.

95 Ibid.

96 Ibid.

97 The Association of Western Pulp and Paper Workers (AWPPW) was created to help form a democratic labor union, get higher income, obtain safer working conditions and general worker's rights, and keep up with labor laws and environmental laws. It was created in 1964 to join together the International Brotherhood of Pulp, Sulphite, and Paper Mill Workers and the United Papermakers and Paperworkers unions. See Association of Western Pulp and Paper Workers, www.awppw.org/index.cfm.

98 The American Federation of Labor and Congress of Industrial Organizations (AFL-CIO) is a national trade union center and the largest federation of unions in the United States. Made up of fifty international unions and representing more than twelve million active and retired workers, the AFL-CIO has been a major influence on policy, activism, and political spending. See American Federation of Labor and Congress of Industrial Organizations, "About the AFL-CIO," www.aflcio.org/About.

99 Densmore, interview by Fahs, October 24, 2009.

100 The National Committee for a Sane Nuclear Policy (SANE) emerged as a reaction to the Eisenhower administration's heavy reliance on nuclear weapons development and procurement, combined with significant anxiety about the arms race. Founded in 1957 by Lenore Marshall, this grassroots movement formed student chapters and recruited celebrities to target mass audiences. SANE worked with the Kennedy and Johnson administrations and then merged with a fellow antinuclear group, the Nuclear Weapons Freeze Campaign, to become SANE/FREEZE, later renamed Peace Action. See George Washington University, "National Committee for a SANE Nuclear Policy," www2.gwu.edu /~erpapers/teachinger/glossary/nat-com-sane-nuc-pol.cfm.

101 In the 1960s, universities and cities set up draft counseling centers that offered

help and advice to those who refused to serve in the military. See Slayton Robert, "Don't Mourn, Organize!" *Huffington Post*, November 9, 2016, www .huffingtonpost.com/robert-slayton/dont-mourn-organize_b_12876600.html.

102 Betty Friedan, *The Feminine Mystique* (New York: W.W. Norton, 1963); Simone de Beauvoir, *The Second Sex*, trans. Constance Borde and Sheila Malovany-Chevallier (New York: Random House/Alfred A. Knopf, 1949).

103 The New Left, which drew heavily from the Students for a Democratic Society, was a movement of mostly college students who were inspired by the activism of the civil rights movement and the growing counterculture of the 1960s. Though there were many subgroups within the New Left, the movement was most well-known for protesting the Vietnam War, burning draft cards, and participating in activism on college campuses.

104 Densmore, interview by Fahs, October 24, 2009.

105 Ibid.

106 Ibid.

107 Bernardine Dohrn (1942–) was a radical political activist and a leader of the violent Weather Underground from 1970 to 1977. Active in Students for a Democratic Society (SDS) and Jobs or Income Now (JOIN), she went into hiding after three members of the Weather Underground blew themselves up with bombs that were supposed to be used on Fort Dix servicemen. She was placed on the FBI's Most Wanted list and later spent seven months in prison for refusing to cooperate with a grand jury when she resurfaced in 1980. She currently works as a lawyer. See Bill Ayers, Bernardine Dohrn, and Jeff Jones, eds., *Sing a Battle Song: The Revolutionary Poetry, Statements, and Communiqués of the Weather Underground, 1970–1974* (New York: Seven Stories Press, 2011).

108 Stokely Carmichael allegedly said, "The only position for women in SNCC is prone," at the organization's Waveland Conference in 1964. See Sara M. Evans, *Personal Politics: The Roots of Women's Liberation in the Civil Rights Movement and the New Left* (New York: Vintage Books, 1976).

109 Densmore, interview by Fahs, October 24, 2009.

110 Ruth Rosen, *The World Split Open: How the Modern Women's Movement Changed America* (New York: Penguin Books, 2006), 108–9.

111 Densmore, interview by Fahs, October 24, 2009.

112 Ibid.

113 Ibid.

114 Historians have convincingly shown that social movements are not distinct entities; as one example, many key organizers of the radical wing of second-wave feminism had connections to labor rights struggles. See Dorothy Sue Cobble, Linda Gordon, and Astrid Henry, *Feminism Unfinished: A Short, Surprising History of American Women's Movements* (New York: W.W. Norton, 2014); and Nella Van Dyke, "Crossing Movement Boundaries: Factors That Facilitate Coalition Protest by American College Students, 1930–1990," *Social Problems* 50, no. 2 (2003): 226–50.

1. FEMINIST RAGE

1   Dunbar-Ortiz, *Outlaw Woman*, 124.

2   Ibid., 124–25. Note that Roxanne left off last names on purpose.

3   Ibid., 127.

4   Ibid., 129.

5   Ibid., 123–45.

6   Densmore, in Dunbar-Ortiz and Densmore, interview by Fahs, Boston, MA, March 29, 2014.

7   Ibid.

8   Dunbar-Ortiz, in Dunbar-Ortiz and Densmore, interview by Fahs, March 29, 2014.

9   Dunbar-Ortiz, *Outlaw Woman*, 148–49.

10 Ibid.

11 Dunbar-Ortiz, in Dunbar-Ortiz and Densmore, interview by Fahs, March 29, 2014.

12 Ibid.

13 Ibid.

14 Atkinson, interview by Fahs, Boston, MA, March 29, 2014.

15 Frances Fox Piven and Richard A. Cloward, *Poor People's Movements: Why They Succeed, and How They Fail* (New York: Vintage, 1979); Mala Htun and S. Laurel Weldon, "The Civic Origins of Progressive Policy Change: Combatting Violence against Women in Global Perspective, 1975–2005," *American Political Science Review* 106, no. 3 (2012): 548–69.

16 Atkinson, "The Autonomous Woman: Sex, Love, and Feminism," lecture, Arizona State University, Phoenix, March 27, 2013.

17 Atkinson, with Fahs and Sarachild, "Feminist Provocations," public forum, Arizona State University, Phoenix, March 27, 2013.

18 Atkinson, "The Autonomous Woman."

19 Sarachild, "Feminist Revolution: Toward a Science of Women's Freedom," lecture, Arizona State University, Phoenix, March 26, 2013.

20 Ibid.

21 Atkinson, interview by Fahs, February 1, 2008.

22 Sarachild, "Feminist Revolution."

23 Fahs, *Valerie Solanas*, 44–155.

24 Ibid., 146.

25 Ibid., 156–95.

26 Ibid.

27 The feminist groups included the following prominent leaders: New York Radical Women (New York City)—Robin Morgan, Carol Hanisch, Shulamith Firestone, Chude Pam Allen, and Kathie Sarachild. The Feminists (New York City)—Ti-Grace Atkinson, Anne Koedt, Sheila Michaels, Barbara Mehrhof, Pamela Kearon, Sheila Cronan. New York Radical Feminists (New York

City)—Shulamith Firestone and Anne Koedt. Cell 16 (Boston)—Roxanne Dunbar-Ortiz and Dana Densmore. Redstockings (New York City)—Ellen Willis, Shulamith Firestone, and Kathie Sarachild. Chicago Women's Liberation Union (Chicago)—Naomi Weisstein, Vivian Rothstein, Heather Booth, and Ruth Surgal. National Black Feminist Organization (New York City)—Michelle Wallace, Faith Ringgold, Doris Wright, and Margaret Sloan-Hunter. Combahee River Collective (Boston)—Barbara Smith. See Echols, *Daring to Be Bad*; Bettye Collier-Thomas and V.P. Franklin, eds., *Sisters in the Struggle; African American Women in the Civil Rights–Black Power Movement* (New York: New York University Press, 2001); and Kayomi Wada, "National Black Feminist Organization (1973–1976)," *Black Past*, www.blackpast.org/aah/national-black-feminist-organization -1973-1976#sthash.T9Lj8kTA.dpuf.

28 Atkinson, interview by Fahs, February 1, 2008.

29 Ibid.

30 Sherie M. Randolph, *Florynce "Flo" Kennedy: The Life of a Black Feminist Radical* (Chapel Hill: University of North Carolina Press, 2015). See also Florynce Kennedy Papers, 1915–2004, Schlesinger Library, Radcliffe Institute, Harvard University, http://oasis.lib.harvard.edu/oasis/deliver/~sch01221.

31 Atkinson, interview by Fahs, February 1, 2008.

32 Ibid.

33 Ibid.

34 Densmore, in conversation with Dunbar-Ortiz and Fahs, "Oral History of Cell 16, Female Liberation," A Revolutionary Moment: Women's Liberation in the Late 1960s and Early 1970s Conference, March 29, 2014.

35 For a full description of this, see Fahs, *Valerie Solanas*, 156–195.

36 Dunbar-Ortiz, in conversation with Densmore and Fahs, "Oral History of Cell 16."

37 Ibid.

38 Dunbar-Ortiz, letter to Jean-Louis, July 5, 1968.

39 Dunbar-Ortiz, in conversation with Densmore and Fahs, "Oral History of Cell 16."

40 Ibid.

41 Dunbar-Ortiz and Densmore, interview by Fahs, March 29, 2014.

42 Martin Puchner, *Poetry of the Revolution: Marx, Manifestos, and the Avant-Gardes* (Princeton, NJ: Princeton University Press, 2005); Mary Ann Caws, *Manifesto: A Century of Isms* (Lincoln: University of Nebraska Press, 2001); Franca Tani, Carole Peterson, and Martina Smorti, "The Words of Violence: Autobiographical Narratives of Abused Women," *Journal of Family Violence* 31, no. 7 (2016): 885–96; and Johan Siebers, "What Cannot Be Said: Speech and Violence," *Journal of Global Ethics* 6, no. 2 (2010): 89–102.

43 Judith Butler, *Excitable Speech: A Politics of the Performative* (New York: Routledge 1997); and Antoine Buyse, "'Fear Speech,' or How Violent Conflict Escalation Relates to the Freedom of Expression," *Human Rights Quarterly* 36, no. 4 (2014): 779–97.

44 For an example of how comedy can work as symbolic rage, see Kyra Pearson, "Words Should Do the Work of Bombs: Margaret Cho as Symbolic Assassin," *Women and Language* 32, no. 1 (2009): 36–43.

45 Dunbar-Ortiz, in Dunbar-Ortiz and Densmore, interview by Fahs, March 29, 2014.

46 Ibid.

47 Densmore, in Dunbar-Ortiz and Densmore, interview by Fahs, March 29, 2014.

48 Digitized versions of several issues of the journal can be found in the Sallie Bingham Center for Women's History and Culture digital archives at Duke University. See http://library.duke.edu/digitalcollections/wlmpc_wlmms01029.

49 Densmore, in Dunbar-Ortiz and Densmore, interview by Fahs, March 29, 2014.

50 Dunbar-Ortiz, in Dunbar-Ortiz and Densmore, interview by Fahs, March 29, 2014.

51 Densmore, in Dunbar-Ortiz and Densmore, interview by Fahs, March 29, 2014.

52 Dunbar-Ortiz, in Dunbar-Ortiz and Densmore, interview by Fahs, March 29, 2014.

53 Densmore, in Dunbar-Ortiz and Densmore, interview by Fahs, March 29, 2014.

54 Fahs, with Avital Ronell, Lisa Duggan, and Karen Finley, "Feminist Rage: A Discussion about Valerie Solanas," public forum, New York University, New York, April 11, 2014.

55 Dunbar-Ortiz, *Outlaw Woman*, 138.

2. RADICALISM AND REFUSAL

1 "Radical," *Encyclopedia Britannica*, www.britannica.com/topic/radical-ideologist.

2 Industrial Workers of the World, "Industrial Workers of the World: What Everyone Should Know," Seattle Joint Branches, Industrial Workers of the World, 1957, www.iww.org/culture/official/qanda.

3 Densmore, in Dunbar-Ortiz and Densmore, interview by Fahs, March 29, 2014.

4 Dunbar-Ortiz, in Dunbar-Ortiz and Densmore, interview by Fahs, March 29, 2014.

5 Densmore, in Dunbar-Ortiz and Densmore, interview by Fahs, March 29, 2014.

6 Ibid.

7 Dunbar-Ortiz, in Dunbar-Ortiz and Densmore, interview by Fahs, March 29, 2014.

8 Densmore, in Dunbar-Ortiz and Densmore, interview by Fahs, March 29, 2014.

9 Dunbar-Ortiz, in Dunbar-Ortiz and Densmore, interview by Fahs, March 29, 2014.

10 Densmore, interview by Fahs, October 24, 2009.

11 See Bair, *Simone de Beauvoir*; and Krizman, *Politics, Philosophy, Culture*.

12 Dunbar-Ortiz, in Dunbar-Ortiz and Densmore, interview by Fahs, March 29, 2014.

13 Ibid.

14	The phrase "politically correct" is another example of a phrase that the left has had to grapple with and combat.

15	Sarachild, "Feminist Revolution," March 26, 2013.

16	Ibid.

17	Ibid.

18	Ibid.

19	Pete Seeger (1919–2014) was an American folk artist and social activist who was originally a member of the Weavers in the 1950s. He was blacklisted by the FBI and shunned by the American public for his early involvement in the Communist party. He refused to answer questions of the House Un-American Activities Committee and was charged with ten counts of contempt (later dismissed in appeals court). Seeger's protest songs, including "If I Had a Hammer" and "We Shall Overcome," would become a rallying cry of the civil rights movement. See Jon Pareles, "Pete Seeger, Champion of Folk Music and Social Change, Dies at 94," *New York Times*, January 28, 2014. Odetta Holmes (1930–2008) was a jazz, soul, and folk singer whose music would become the soundtrack of the civil rights movement, inspiring everyone from Rosa Parks to Martin Luther King Jr. She performed on the steps of the Lincoln Memorial during the March on Washington in 1963. See Tim Weiner, "Odetta, Voice of Civil Rights Movement, Dies at 77," *New York Times*, December 3, 2008. The Weavers (formed in 1948 in Greenwich Village) were an American folk band that rose to fame in the early 1950s, comprising Pete Seeger, Ronnie Gilbert, Lee Hays, and Fred Hellerman. Paul Robeson (1898–1976) was an athlete, singer, and civil rights activist best known for being blacklisted from the entertainment industry for his alleged Communist activities by the House Un-American Activities Committee. See Jessica Duchen, "Paul Robeson: The Story of How an American Icon Was Driven to Death to Be Told in Film," *Independent*, November 20, 2014.

20	Sarachild, "Feminist Revolution," March 26, 2013.

21	Sarachild, with Fahs and Atkinson, "Feminist Provocations."

22	Shulamith "Shulie" Firestone (1945–2012) was born in Ottawa, Canada, and raised in Saint Louis, Missouri. She originally became involved in civil rights and antiwar activism while studying at the Art Institute of Chicago, and later developed groundbreaking theories about women's roles in society. She was a founding member of Chicago's Westside Group, New York Radical Women, Redstockings, and New York Radical Feminists. She published *The Dialectic of Sex* in 1970, outlining a feminist theory of politics, and later published a fictional collection of stories entitled *Airless Spaces* in 1998. She was famously reclusive and struggled with mental illness; in 2012 she was found dead in her New York City apartment. See Margalit Fox, "Shulamith Firestone, Feminist Writer, Dies at 67," *New York Times*, August 30, 2012; and Martha Ackelsberg, "Shulamith Firestone," Jewish Women's Archive, http://jwa.org/encyclopedia /article/firestone-shulamith.

23	Rosalyn ("Ros") Baxandall (1939–2015) was a feminist historian and activist who helped to create Liberation Nursery, the first feminist day care center in New York City. She participated in the Miss America pageant protest and was active in abortion activism in the late 1960s. She authored, with Linda Gordon, *America's Working Women*. See William Grimes, "Rosalyn Baxandall, Feminist Historian and Activist, Dies at 76," *New York Times*, October 14, 2015.

24 Sarachild, with Fahs and Atkinson, "Feminist Provocations."

25 Atkinson, with Fahs and Sarachild, "Feminist Provocations."

26 Willis, "Radical Feminism and Feminist Radicalism," 91–118; see also Redstockings, "About Redstockings of the Women's Liberation Movement."

27 Willis, "Radical Feminism and Feminist Radicalism," 91–118.

28 Dunbar-Ortiz, interview by Fahs, Tempe, AZ, April 9, 2015.

29 Monique Wittig, *The Straight Mind and Other Essays* (Boston: Beacon Press 1992), xiii; and Louise Turcotte, "Changing the Point of View," foreword to *The Straight Mind and Other Essays*, x.

30 Dunbar-Ortiz, interview by Fahs, April 9, 2015.

31 Martha Nussbaum, *Sex and Social Justice* (New York: Oxford University Press, 1999), 10.

32 Alison M. Jaggar, *Feminist Politics and Human Nature* (Totowa, NJ: Rowman and Allanheld, 1983).

33 Dunbar-Ortiz, interview by Fahs, April 9, 2015.

34 Ibid.

35 Atkinson, interview by Fahs, Cambridge, MA, June 4, 2015.

36 Ibid.

37 Victoria Woodhull (1838–1927) was an American leader of the women's suffrage movement and the first woman to run for president in the United States (1873) alongside running mate Frederick Douglass. She later became the first woman to open a brokerage firm on Wall Street (with her sister Tennessee Claflin); the pair also started a newspaper.

38 Atkinson, interview by Fahs, June 4, 2015.

39 Dunbar-Ortiz, interview by Fahs, April 9, 2015.

40 Ibid.

41 Ibid.

42 Fahs, "'Freedom To' and 'Freedom From': A New Vision for Sex Positive Politics," *Sexualities* 17, no. 3 (2014): 267–90.

43 Dunbar-Ortiz, interview by Fahs, April 9, 2015.

44 Ibid.

45 The occupation of Wounded Knee, a standoff that lasted seventy-one days, began as a protest over the corruption of tribal council chairman Richard "Dick" Wilson, whose tenure was marked by extreme violence and corruption. Frustrated by the failure of Wilson's impeachment as president of the Oglala Lakota (Sioux) and fueled by anger over the US government's failure to fulfill treaties with the Native Americans, activists from the American Indian Movement (AIM), as well as members of the Oglala Sioux Civil Rights Organization,

began an occupation in the area known in the Lakota language as Cankpe Opi Wakpala ("Wounded Knee Creek"). The federal government cut off protesters with roadblocks, but the occupying group was supported by sympathetic Native Americans who poured in from across the country. Led by Russell Means and Dennis Banks, two hundred activists grew to two thousand activists; regular gunfighting and standoffs occurred during the protest, which ended after a local Oglala Lakota tribe member, Buddy Lamont, was killed and AIM begrudgingly reached an agreement with the federal government. See Mary Brave Bird [Mary Crow Dog] and Richard Erdoes, *Lakota Woman* (New York: Grove Weidenfeld, 1990).

46   The occupation of Alcatraz began on November 20, 1969, when eighty-nine Native Americans descended onto the island of Alcatraz, a former federal penitentiary. The protesters laid claim to the island (it had recently been declared "surplus property" and could therefore be returned to the Native Americans under the Treaty of Fort Laramie from 1868). Led by Richard Oakes, LaNada Means, and John Trudell, the protestors occupied the island for nearly nineteen months, until protesters were forcibly removed from the island in June 1971. See Evan Andrews, "Native American Activists Occupy Alcatraz Island, 45 Years Ago," History.com, November 20, 2014, www.history.com/news/native-american -activists-occupy-alcatraz-island-45-years-ago.

47   On March 18, 1970, one hundred feminists began a sit-in at the New York City offices of the *Ladies' Home Journal*. Outraged at the magazine's depictions of women's interests, the protesters occupied the office for eleven hours and brought a list of demands that included hiring a female editor-in-chief, having women write the columns and articles that were currently written by men, and getting a new editor. They successfully lobbied to secure their own issue of the magazine and, a few years later, Lenore Hershey became the first female editor-in-chief of the magazine. See Annelise Orleck, *Rethinking American Women's Activism* (New York: Routledge, 2015).

48   Dunbar-Ortiz, interview by Fahs, April 9, 2015.

49   Ibid.

50   Sarachild, "Feminist Revolution," March 26, 2013.

51   Ibid.

52   Atkinson, interview by Fahs, June 4, 2015.

53   Atkinson, email to Fahs, September 23, 2016. In a follow-up email that same night, Ti-Grace wrote: "I believe I first saw this phrase ("double-role institution") in Kenneth Stampp's *The Peculiar Institution: Slavery in the Ante-Bellum South* (1956). Then I saw this notion referenced again in John Rawls's article "Justice as Fairness" (this initial article published in 1965, later developed into his famous book, *A Theory of Justice* [1971]). Again, this notion was only applied to slavery. Back in the mid- to late 1960s, I was friendly with John Rawls and discussed this analogy with him. My guess is that he wasn't thrilled with the comparison but told me at the time that he could find no logical fault with the

analogy. So I read Beauvoir's *Second Sex* in I believe 1962 and was taken with her institutional analysis generally. This led me to read on in various literatures (this is when I came upon Kenneth Stampp's work). This analogy seemed a good fit to me. I still think it works."

54 Atkinson, email to Fahs, April 22, 2017.

55 Atkinson, interview by Fahs, June 4, 2015.

56 For a number of radical queer critiques of marriage, see Michael Warner, *The Trouble with Normal: Sex, Politics, and the Ethic of Queer Life* (New York: Free Press, 1999); Richard Kim and Lisa Duggan, "Beyond Gay Marriage," *Nation*, July 18, 2005; and Matthew Hays, "Some on the Radical Queer Left Still Think Gay Marriage Is Bad for the LGBTQ Community," *Vice*, September 16, 2015, www .vice.com/en_us/article/some-on-the-radical-queer-left-still-think-gay-marriage -is-bad-for-the-lgbtq-community.

57 Jason Ruiz, "The Violence of Assimilation: An Interview with Mattilda aka Matt Bernstein Sycamore," *Radical History Review* 100 (2008), 238.

58 Atkinson, interview by Fahs, June 4, 2015.

59 Ibid.

60 Ibid.

61 Ibid.

62 Dunbar-Ortiz, interview by Fahs, April 9, 2015.

63 Ibid.

3. TACTICS

1 Sarachild, "Feminist Revolution."

2 Heather Booth (1945–) is a women's rights activist and one of the founding members of Jane, an organization dedicated to helping women obtain abortions before they became legalized by *Roe v. Wade* in 1973. Booth became involved in the reproductive rights movement in 1965, after a friend told her she was pregnant and wanted an abortion; Booth used her connections in the civil rights movement to find a doctor willing to help her. Booth told women seeking abortions to ask for "Jane," and would prep the women before their procedures and do follow-up with the doctors. See Jewish Women's Archive, "Heather Booth," http://jwa.org/feminism/booth-heather. Naomi Weisstein (1939–2015) fought against the sexist oppression women faced in higher education in order to get her doctorate in psychology from Yale. She was a founding member of the Chicago independent consciousness-raising group the Westside Group, as well as the Chicago Women's Liberation Union. She contributed to the 1970 anthology *Sisterhood Is Powerful* (edited by Robin Morgan), and she started a feminist rock group, the Chicago Women's Liberation Rock Band, to rebel against the male-dominated genre. See Stephanie Austin, "Naomi Weisstein," Society for the Psychology of Women, www.apadivisions.org/division-35/about/heritage/naomi -weisstein-biography.aspx.

3   The National Conference for New Politics, a male-led New Left organization dedicated to the overthrow of existing power structures in the United States via "creative disorder," brought together over two thousand revolutionaries in August 1967 to discuss priorities for combating white supremacy and militarization. Speakers included Stokely Carmichael and Martin Luther King Jr.; the conference was held at the Palmer House in Chicago. See Chesly Manly, "'New Politics' Convention to Open Here," *Chicago Tribune*, August 27, 1967.

4   Simon Hall, *American Patriotism, American Protest: Social Movements since the Sixties* (Philadelphia: University of Pennsylvania Press, 2011), 61; and Jo Freeman, "On the Origins of Social Movements," in *Waves of Protest: Social Movements since the Sixties*, ed. Freeman and Victoria Johnson (New York: Rowman and Littlefield, 1999), 7–24.

5   Suzanne Staggenborg, "Social Movement Communities and Cycles of Protest: The Emergence and Maintenance of a Local Women's Movement," *Social Problems* 45, no. 2 (1998): 180–204.

6   Lord Byron (George Gordon Byron, 1788–1824) was a Romantic poet most well known for his satiric poem *Don Juan* and for his poetry on unrequited love.

7   Frederick Douglass (1818–1895) was a former slave turned human rights activist who fought to abolish slavery. He was the first African American to hold a high-ranking government position, and the first African American to be nominated as vice president. He was active in the abolitionist movement and wrote numerous antislavery writings. Douglass's famed autobiography, *Narrative of the Life of Frederick Douglass, an American Slave* (1845), was a foundational text in African American history.

8   Sarachild, "Feminist Revolution."

9   Ibid.

10   Ibid.

11   *Notes from the First Year*, published in 1968, was a collective work of feminist writings that included many now-classic essays from second-wave radical feminism: Anne Koedt's "Myth of the Vaginal Orgasm," Jennifer Gardner's "Woman as Child," and Shulamith Firestone's "The Women's Rights Movement in the U.S.: A New View." New York Radical Women (founded in 1967 by Firestone and Pam Allen) wrote the text and charged women fifty cents and men one dollar for the journal. See Echols, *Daring to Be Bad*, 51–109.

12   On January 15, 1968, five thousand women descended on Washington, DC, to protest the Vietnam War. Inspired by the life and work of Jeanette Rankin, an ardent antiwar activist and the first woman elected to Congress, the group called themselves the Jeanette Rankin Brigade. The brigade illuminated the generation gaps between older suffragettes and younger feminists and would later become a marker for the beginning of second-wave feminism. See Anne M. Valk, *Radical Sisters: Second-Wave Feminism and Black Liberation in Washington, D.C.* (Urbana: University of Illinois Press, 2008).

13   The *Voice of the Women's Liberation Movement* newsletter began in Chicago in

response to the entrenched sexism of the New Left and its dismissal of women's issues. Jo Freeman published the newsletter from March 1968 to March 1969 to facilitate conversations about women's oppression. See Echols, *Daring to Be Bad*, 53.

14 Sarachild, "Feminist Revolution."

15 Ibid.

16 Stokely Carmichael (1941–1998) was a prominent organizer for the SNCC; he organized for voting rights and registered black voters. He had been active in the Congress for Racial Equality (CORE) during his time at school, and participated in freedom rides and nonviolent protests. He eventually became honorary prime minister of the Black Panther Party, where he advocated for black power and coined the term "Black Is Beautiful." Because of his increasing militancy, Carmichael found it difficult to live in the United States and eventually moved to West Africa in 1969; from there, he traveled the world to speak about Pan-Africanism and socialism until his death. See Karen G. Bates, "Stokely Carmichael, a Philosopher Behind the Black Power Movement," *Code Switch*, National Public Radio, March 10, 2014, www.npr.org/sections/codeswitch /2014/03/10/287320160/stokely-carmichael-a-philosopher-behind-the-black -power-movement.

17 Sarachild, "Feminist Revolution."

18 Ibid.

19 Atkinson, interview by Fahs, June 4, 2015.

20 Ibid.

21 Ibid.

22 Kimberlé Crenshaw, "Mapping the Margins: Intersectionality, Identity Politics, and Violence against Women of Color," *Stanford Law Review* 43, no. 6 (1991): 1241–99. See also Patricia Hill Collins, "Black Feminist Thought in the Matrix of Domination," in *Social Theory: The Multicultural and Classic Readings*, ed. Charles Lemert (Boulder, CO: Westview Press, 2017), 413–20; and Gerda Lerner, *Why History Matters: Life and Thought* (Oxford: Oxford University Press, 1998).

23 Atkinson, interview by Fahs, June 4, 2015.

24 Billie Holliday (1915–1959), nicknamed "Lady Day," was a legendary blues singer known for her famous song "Strange Fruit." Flo Kennedy helped her in 1956 with legal troubles related to her drug habit. Charlie Parker (1920–1955), also known as "Yardbird" or "Bird," was a famed American jazz saxophonist. Flo worked with him on cases of copyright infringement and theft of intellectual property in 1962. See Florynce Kennedy Papers, 1915–2004. Flo later said that working as a lawyer showed her the limits of enacting "within-system" social justice: "'Handling the Holiday and Parker estates taught me more than I was really ready for about government and business delinquency and the hostility and helplessness of the courts. . . . Not only was I not earning a decent living, there began to be a serious question in my mind whether practicing law could ever be an effective means of changing society or even of simple resistance to

oppression." See *New York Times*, "Flo Kennedy, Feminist, Civil Rights Advocate and Flamboyant Gadfly, Is Dead at 84," December 23, 2000.

25 *New York Times*, "Flo Kennedy."

26 Randolph, *Florynce "Flo" Kennedy.*

27 *New York Times*, "Flo Kennedy."

28 Atkinson, interview by Fahs, February 1, 2008.

29 Ibid.

30 Vietnam Veterans Against the War is a national veterans' organization, founded in 1967. It originally was organized as a way to voice growing opposition to the war in Vietnam and expose treatment of veterans by the US government; it has since turned into an organization that rights for the rights and needs of veterans in general. See Vietnam Veterans Against the War, "About VVAW," www.vvaw.org/about.

31 Atkinson, interview by Fahs, February 1, 2008.

32 Ibid.

33 Ibid.

34 Ibid.

35 Marie Stopes (1880–1958) was a British paleobotanist who campaigned for women's rights and pioneered the movement for family planning. She opened the UK's first family planning clinic in London in 1921; it provided free services to married women, dispensed birth control to the poor, and gathered scientific data on contraception. She later formed the National Birth Control Council and famously opposed abortion by instead claiming that prevention of pregnancy was sufficient. See British Broadcasting Corporation, "Marie Stopes: A Brief Biography," www.bbc.co.uk/history/historic_figures/stopes_marie_carmichael.shtml.

36 Margaret Sanger (1879–1966) was an American birth control advocate who coined the term "birth control" and helped to push for the creation of the birth control pill. She founded the American Birth Control League (a precursor to Planned Parenthood) and worked as a nurse in the Lower East Side of New York City, where she assisted women who had undergone botched abortions. She fled the United States in 1915 while facing a five-year jail term for distributing information about contraceptive methods, and later played a pivotal role in procuring research funding for the first birth control pill approved by the FDA, in 1960. See *American Experience*, "People and Events: Margaret Sanger," www.pbs.org/wgbh/amex/pill/peopleevents/p_sanger.html.

37 Leslie J. Reagan, *When Abortion Was a Crime: Women, Medicine, and Law in the United States, 1867–1973* (Berkeley: University of California Press, 1998).

38 Rachel Benson Gold, "Lessons from before Roe: Will Past Be Prologue?" *Guttmacher Policy Review* 6, no. 1 (2003), www.guttmacher.org/about/gpr/2003/03/lessons-roe-will-past-be-prologue. See also FactCheck.org, "Abortion Distortions," Annenberg Public Policy Center, http://dev.factcheck.org/2005/07/abortion-distortions/#.

39 Atkinson, interview by Fahs, February 1, 2008.

40 Ibid.

41 Ibid.

42 Ibid.

43 Ibid.

44 Quoted in University of Chicago Law School, *Justice Ruth Bader Ginsburg and Geoffrey Stone*, "Roe *at 40*," May 19, 2013, www.youtube.com/ watch?v=-pVnvBCzTyI.

45 David Helscher, "*Griswold v. Connecticut* and the Unenumerated Right of Privacy," *Northern Illinois University Law Review* 33 (1994–1995): 33–62. See also the Guttmacher Institute (www.guttmacher.org) for updates on abortion laws under attack.

46 Atkinson, with Fahs and Sarachild, "Feminist Provocations."

47 Myra Marx Ferree, "Resonance and Radicalism: Feminist Framing in the Abortion Debate of the United States and Germany," *American Journal of Sociology* 109, no. 2 (2003): 304–44.

48 Eva R. Rubin, *Abortion, Politics, and the Courts:* Roe v. Wade *and Its Aftermath* (Westport, CT: Greenwood Press, 1982).

49 Atkinson, with Fahs and Sarachild, "Feminist Provocations."

50 Sarachild, with Fahs and Atkinson, "Feminist Provocations."

51 Loretta Ross, "Understanding Reproductive Justice: Transforming the Pro-Choice Movement," *Off Our Backs* 36, no. 4 (2006): 14–19; and Loretta J. Ross, Sarah L. Brownlee, Dázon Dixon Diallo, Luz Rodriguez, and Latina Roundtable, "The 'SisterSong Collective': Women of Color, Reproductive Health and Human Rights," *American Journal of Health Studies* 17, no. 2 (2001): 79–88.

52 Lauren Kelley, "Nearly 400 Anti-Abortion Laws Introduced Last Year," *Rolling Stone*, January 4, 2016.

53 Dana Densmore, "Cell 16: Gender and Agency, with Digressions into Naming," paper presented at A Revolutionary Moment: Women's Liberation in the Late 1960s and Early 1970s Conference, March 29, 2014.

54 Brownmiller, *In Our Time*, 51.

55 Kathie Sarachild, "Who Are We? The Redstockings Position on Names," in *Feminist Revolution*, 53.

56 Brownmiller, *In Our Time*, 21, 78.

57 Sarachild, "Consciousness-Raising," 145.

58 Ibid.

59 Jo Reger, "Organizational 'Emotion Work' Through Consciousness-Raising: An Analysis of a Feminist Organization," *Qualitative Sociology* 27, no. 2 (2004): 205–22.

60 Sarachild, "Consciousness-Raising," 149.

61 Ibid., 145.

62 Ibid.

63 Ibid., 145–46.

64   Emmeline Pankhurst, *My Own Story* (London: Virago, 1914), 38.

65   Patricia Searles and Ronald J. Berger, "The Feminist Self-Defense Movement: A Case Study," *Gender and Society* 1, no. 1 (1987), 61–84.

66   Densmore, "Cell 16."

67   Dunbar-Ortiz, interview by Fahs, April 9, 2015.

68   Densmore, interview by Fahs, October 24, 2009.

69   Jocelyn A. Hollander, "'I Can Take Care of Myself': The Impact of Self-Defense Training on Women's Lives," *Violence against Women* 10, no. 3 (2004): 205–35.

70   Laura Kipnis, *Unwanted Advances: Sexual Paranoia Comes to Campus* (New York: Harper, 2017).

71   Densmore, interview by Fahs, October 24, 2009.

72   Atkinson, interview by Fahs, June 4, 2015.

73   Orleck, *Rethinking American Women's Activism*, 105-136.

74   John Mack Carter (1928–2014) was the editor-in-chief of three major women's magazines: *McCall's, Ladies Home Journal*, and *Good Housekeeping*. See *Los Angeles Times*, "John Mack Carter Dies at 86: Hearst Editor Led Top Women's Magazines," September 29, 2014.

75   Atkinson, interview by Fahs, February 1, 2008.

76   Orleck, *Rethinking American Women's Activism*.

77   Atkinson, interview by Fahs, February 1, 2008.

78   See Ruth Simpson and Cheryl Jacques, *From the Closet to the Courts: The Lesbian Transition* (New York: Take Roots Media, 2007), 121. See also *Morning Record*, "Two Feminists Arrested in N.Y. Protest," October 24, 1972.

79   Atkinson, email to Fahs, April 23, 2017.

80   Mary Ellen Snodgrass, *Civil Disobedience: An Encyclopedic History of Dissidence in the United States* (New York: Routledge, 2015).

81   Atkinson, email to Fahs, April 23, 2017.

82   Atkinson, interview by Fahs, February 1, 2008.

83   Ibid.

4. SEX, LOVE, AND BODIES

1   Elizabeth Grosz, *Volatile Bodies: Toward a Corporeal Feminism* (Bloomington: Indiana University Press, 1994), 14. See also Kathleen Lennon, "Feminist Perspectives on the Body," *Stanford Encyclopedia of Philosophy*, http://plato.stanford.edu/entries/feminist-body.

2   Dunbar-Ortiz, interview by Fahs, April 9, 2015.

3   Ibid.

4   Atkinson, interview by Fahs, June 4, 2015.

5   Marilyn Bender, "The Feminists Are on the March Once More," *New York Times*, December 14, 1967.

6 Sara Davidson, "An 'Oppressed Majority' Demands Its Rights: The Cause of Women's Equality Draws a Growing Number of Active-and-Angry Female Militants," *Life*, December 12, 1969, www.maryellenmark.com/text/magazines/life/905W-000-004.html. Davidson's profile of the movement goes on to offer other sexist comments: "Even the most radical feminists, however, retain many female character traits: soft-spokenness; talkiness (interviews and phone calls are difficult to terminate); and a proclivity for handwork. There was hardly a meeting I attended where someone was not knitting. While they condemn seductiveness, many want to look attractive. Pam Kearon of The Feminists said, 'People like to look nice for other people. It's a statement of respect. It's just not true that we want to look like ugly freaks.'"

7 Ruby Rohrlich (1913–1999) was an anthropologist who studied women across cultures. She wrote *Resisting the Holocaust, Women in Search of Utopia*, and *Women Cross-Culturally*. See Phyllis Chesler, Esther D. Rothblum, and Ellen Cole, *Feminist Foremothers in Women's Studies, Psychology, and Mental Health* (New York: Haworth Press, 1995), 391–404.

8 Atkinson, interview by Fahs, June 4, 2015.

9 Atkinson, interview by Fahs, February 1, 2008.

10 Sarachild, with Fahs and Atkinson, "Feminist Provocations," March 27, 2013.

11 Atkinson, with Fahs and Sarachild, "Feminist Provocations," March 27, 2013.

12 Karli June Cerankowski and Megan Milks, "New Orientations: Asexuality and Its Implications for Theory and Practice," *Feminist Studies* 36, no. 3 (2010): 650–64.

13 Atkinson, "Vaginal Orgasm as a Mass Hysterical Survival Response," *Amazon Odyssey*, 5–7.

14 Ibid., 6.

15 Ibid., 7.

16 Atkinson, interview by Fahs, February 1, 2008.

17 Atkinson, interview by Fahs, June 4, 2015.

18 Ibid.

19 Ibid.

20 Ibid.

21 Atkinson, interview by Fahs, February 1, 2008.

22 Atkinson, interview by Fahs, June 4, 2015.

23 Ibid.

24 Ibid.

25 Atkinson, interview by Fahs, February 1, 2008.

26 Ibid.

27 Ibid.

28 bell hooks, *All About Love: New Visions* (New York: William Morrow, 2000), xix.

29 Ibid., 19–20.

30 Ai-jen Poo, "Organizing with Love: Lessons from the New York Domestic

Workers Bill of Rights Campaign," *Left Turn*, December 1, 2010, www.leftturn .org/Organizing-with-Love.

31 Atkinson, "The Autonomous Woman."

32 Ibid.

33 Ibid.

34 Arthur Schopenhauer (1788–1860) was a German philosopher who wrote about people's desire to rationalize everything they perceived as real, thus concluding that the world is not a rational place. In his essay "Metaphysics of Love," he argued that love is a hindrance that stems from the inherent will to live and reproduce; even the most intelligent of people allow powerful feelings of love to control them because of this will. See Schopenhauer, "Metaphysics of Love," in *Essays of Schopenhauer*, trans. Rudolf Dirks (Gloucestershire: Dodo Press, 2008).

35 Atkinson, "The Autonomous Woman."

36 Ibid.

37 Ibid.

38 Ibid.

39 Atkinson, interview by Fahs, June 4, 2015.

40 Atkinson, interview by Fahs, February 1, 2008.

41 Nicola Gavey, *Just Sex? The Cultural Scaffolding of Rape* (London and New York: Routledge, 2008).

42 Ela Przybylo, *Asexual Erotics: Intimate Readings of Compulsory Sexuality*, forthcoming with Ohio State University Press.

43 Cerankowski and Milks, "New Orientations," 656.

44 Przybylo, "Crisis and Safety: The Asexuality in Sexusociety," *Sexualities* 14, no. 4 (2011): 456.

45 Densmore, "Cell 16."

46 Densmore, in Dunbar-Ortiz and Densmore, interview by Fahs, March 29, 2014.

47 Ibid.

48 Densmore, interview by Fahs, October 24, 2009.

49 Ibid.

50 Dunbar-Ortiz, interview by Fahs, April 9, 2015.

51 Ibid.

52 Ibid.

53 Atkinson, interview by Fahs, June 4, 2015.

54 Ibid.

55 Kathie Sarachild apparently never had a negative view of marriage. She wrote, "I was never against marriage. I had the Redstockings view of marriage, exemplified by Jenny Gardner's article on the subject in *Notes from the Second Year* (and the quote from me in *Notes from the Second Year* in 'Hot Flashes'). Also the Random House edition of *Feminist Revolution* had Pat Mainardi's article on marriage and Barbara Leon's 'The Male Supremacist Attack on Monogamy.'" Kathie Sarachild, email to Breanne Fahs, April 7, 2017.

56 Dunbar-Ortiz, in Dunbar-Ortiz and Densmore, interview by Fahs, March 29, 2014.

57 Ibid.

58 Densmore, in Dunbar-Ortiz and Densmore, interview by Fahs, March 29, 2014.

59 Ibid.

60 Dunbar-Ortiz, in Dunbar-Ortiz and Densmore, interview by Fahs, March 29, 2014.

61 Densmore, in Dunbar-Ortiz and Densmore, interview by Fahs, March 29, 2014.

62 Dunbar-Ortiz, in Dunbar-Ortiz and Densmore, interview by Fahs, March 29, 2014.

63 Densmore, in Dunbar-Ortiz and Densmore, interview by Fahs, March 29, 2014.

64 Ibid.

65 Evans, *Personal Politics*.

66 Dunbar-Ortiz, in Dunbar-Ortiz and Densmore, interview by Fahs, March 29, 2014.

67 The International Wages for Housework Campaign was a global social movement, founded in 1972 in Italy, that argued that childcare and housework should be compensated as paid wage labor.

68 Dunbar-Ortiz, in Dunbar-Ortiz and Densmore, interview by Fahs, March 29, 2014.

69 Densmore, in Dunbar-Ortiz and Densmore, interview by Fahs, March 29, 2014.

70 Dunbar-Ortiz, in Dunbar-Ortiz and Densmore, interview by Fahs, March 29, 2014.

71 Densmore, in Dunbar-Ortiz and Densmore, interview by Fahs, March 29, 2014.

72 Densmore, interview by Fahs, October 24, 2009.

5. WOMEN AS A SOCIAL AND POLITICAL CLASS

1 This chapter will forgo the asterisk after the word *trans*. While *trans** initially meant a more inclusive sense of those who fell under the umbrella of *trans* and *queer*, more recent scholarship has argued against the use of the asterisk because *trans* is already inclusive, the asterisk is widely misused and misunderstood, and it distracts from the fluid qualities of gender identity already embodied in trans identities. See Hugh Ryan, "What Does *Trans** Mean, and Where Did It Come From?" *Slate*, October 1, 2014, www.slate.com/blogs/outward/2014/01/10/trans_what_does_it_mean_and_where_did_it_come_from.html; and Nat Titman, "About That Often Misunderstood Asterisk," *Practical Androgyny*, October 31, 2013, http://practicalandrogyny.com/2013/10/31.

2 Ellen Willis (1941–2006) was a radical feminist journalist and cultural critic, known for her columns on music and culture as well as her militant radical feminist activism. An early member of New York Radical Women, she famously

split from socialist feminists by joining Shulamith Firestone and other radical feminist groups to eventually form Redstockings. In the early 1980s, Willis founded No More Nice Girls, a pro-abortion street theater group in New York City, and was known for her complicated writings on pornography. See Jenny Gotwals, "Ellen Willis," *American National Biography Online*, www.anb.org /articles/16/16-03903.html.

3   Willis, "Radical Feminism and Feminist Radicalism," 91.
4   Valerie Purdie-Vaughns and Richard P. Eibach, "Intersectional Invisibility: The Distinctive Advantages and Disadvantages of Multiple Subordinate-Group Identities," *Sex Roles* 59, no. 5–6 (2008): 377–91.
5   Densmore, in Dunbar-Ortiz and Densmore, interview by Fahs, March 29, 2014.
6   Ibid.
7   Ibid.
8   Katie McLaughlin, "Five Things Women Couldn't Do in the 1960s," CNN, August 25, 2014, www.cnn.com/2014/08/07/living/sixties-women-5-things; and Jill Elaine Hasday, "Contest and Consent: A Legal History of Marital Rape," *California Law Review* 88, no. 5 (2000): 1373–505.
9   Densmore, "Cell 16."
10 Ibid.
11 Butler, *Gender Trouble: Feminism and the Subversion of Identity* (New York: Routledge, 1990).
12 Lorber, *Paradoxes of Gender* (New Haven, CT: Yale University Press, 1994).
13 De Beauvoir, *The Second Sex* (New York: Vintage, 1973), 301.
14 Sarachild, "Feminist Revolution," March 26, 2013.
15 Sarachild, with Fahs and Atkinson, "Feminist Provocations."
16 Ibid.
17 Linda Alcoff, "Cultural Feminism versus Post-Structuralism: The Identity Crisis in Feminist Theory," *Signs* 13, no. 3 (1988): 405–36.
18 Atkinson, with Fahs and Sarachild, "Feminist Provocations."
19 Shulamith Firestone, *The Dialectic of Sex: The Case for Feminist Revolution* (New York: William Morrow and Company, 1970).
20 Atkinson, with Fahs and Sarachild, "Feminist Provocations."
21 The term *TERF* originated in 2008 as a means to address the perception that some radical feminists wanted to exclude trans people (particularly trans women) from feminism. The term is often used as a slur and is widely contested in its utility, accuracy, and impact, particularly given that radical feminism has long embraced and supported gender fluidity and trans identities. See Cristan Williams, "Radical Inclusion: Recounting the Trans Inclusive History of Radical Feminism," *TSQ: Transgender Studies Quarterly* 3, no. 1–2 (2016): 254–58.
22 Willis, "Radical Feminism and Feminist Radicalism," 91–118; Echols, *Daring to Be Bad.*
23 Echols, *Daring to Be Bad.*

24 Ibid.

25 Willis, "Radical Feminism and Feminist Radicalism," 91–118; Rose Coursey, "The Radical Feminist Politics of Trans Identification," unpublished thesis, Arizona State University, 2014.

26 Coursey, "Radical Feminist Politics," 4.

27 Willis, "Radical Feminism and Feminist Radicalism," 91–118.

28 Ibid., 93.

29 Ibid., 91–118; Coursey, "Radical Feminist Politics," 4.

30 Coursey, "Radical Feminist Politics," 6.

31 Williams, "Radical Inclusion," 254–58.

32 Atkinson, with Fahs and Sarachild, "Feminist Provocations."

33 Sarachild, with Fahs and Atkinson, "Feminist Provocations."

34 Atkinson, interview by Fahs, June 4, 2015.

35 Ibid.

36 Ibid.

37 Ibid.

38 Ibid.

39 Ibid.

40 Ibid.

41 Dunbar-Ortiz, interview by Fahs, April 9, 2015.

42 *New York Times*, "Transcript: Donald Trump's Taped Comments About Women," October 8, 2016.

43 Female Collective, "Pussy Grabs Back," 2016, www.femalecollective.org/product /pussy-grabs-back.

44 Presidential Gender Watch, "Presidential Polling Data," November 10, 2016, http://presidentialgenderwatch.org/polls/womens-vote-watch/presidential -polling-data.

45 Lorde, "Age, Race, Class, and Sex: Women Redefining Difference," in *Sister Outsider: Essays and Speeches* (Freedom, CA: Crossing Press, 1984): 114–23.

46 Crenshaw, "Mapping the Margins," 1241–99.

47 Atkinson, interview by Fahs, June 4, 2015.

48 Ibid.

49 Dunbar-Ortiz, interview by Fahs, April 9, 2015.

50 Ibid.

51 Ibid.

52 Kathie Amatniek (Sarachild), "Funeral Oration for the Burial of Traditional Womanhood," in *Notes from the First Year*, 1968, Duke University Libraries, http://library.duke.edu/digitalcollections/wlmpc_wlmms01037.

53 Frye, "Some Reflections," 91.

54 Atkinson, interview by Fahs, June 4, 2015.

55 Ibid.

56 Dunbar-Ortiz, interview by Fahs, April 9, 2015.

57 Ibid.

58 Carolyn Gage, *Hotter than Hell: More Sermons for a Lesbian Tent Revival* (Amazon Digital Services, 2011), 140–41.

59 Lisa Vogel, "Michfest Responds: We Have a Few Demands of Our Own," *Pride-Source*, August 18, 2014, www.pridesource.com/article.html?article=67561.

60 Kath Brown, "Womyn's Separatist Spaces: Rethinking Spaces of Difference and Exclusion," *Transactions of the Institute of British Geographers* 34, no. 4 (2009), 541. See also Kath Brown, "Lesbian Separatist Feminism at the Michigan Womyn's Music Festival," *Feminism & Psychology* 21, no. 2 (2011): 248–56; and Joshua Gamson, "Messages of Exclusion: Gender, Movements, and Symbolic Boundaries," *Gender & Society* 11, no. 2 (1997): 178–99.

61 Dunbar-Ortiz, interview by Fahs, April 9, 2015.

62 Ibid.

63 Carol Hanisch, Kathy Scarbrough, Ti-Grace Atkinson, and Kathie Sarachild, "Forbidden Discourse: The Silencing of Feminist Criticism of 'Gender': An Open Statement from Thirty-Seven Radical Feminists from Five Countries," August 12, 2013 (full text: https://womensspace.wordpress.com/2013/08/20/forbidden-discourse-the-silencing-of-feminist-criticism-of-gender-an-open-statement-from-37-radical-feminists-from-five-countries-with-biographical-information-about-each-signat/). The letter was also signed by Roberta Salper (MA), Marjorie Kramer (VT), Jean Golden (MI), Marisa Figueiredo (MA), Maureen Nappi (NY), Sonia Jaffe Robbins (NY), Tobe Levin (Germany), Marge Piercy (MA), Barbara Leon (CA), Anne Forer (AZ), Anselma Dell'Olio (Italy), Carla Lesh (NY), Laura X (CA), Gabrielle Tree (Canada), Christine Delphy (France), Pam Martens (FL), Nellie Hester Bailey (NY), Colette Price (NY), Candi Churchhill (FL), Peggy Powell Dobbins (GA), Annie Tummino (NY), Margo Jefferson (NY), Jennifer Sunderland (NY), Michele Wallace (NJ), Allison Guttu (NY), Sheila Michaels (MO), Carol Giardina (NY), Nicole Hardin (FL), Merle Hoffman (NY), Linda Stein (NY), Margaret Stern (NY), Faith Ringgold (NJ), and Joanne Steele (NY).

64 For a fuller exploration of the controversies surrounding Deep Green Resistance and radical feminist communities, see Michelle Goldberg, "What Is a Woman? The Dispute between Radical Feminism and Transgenderism," *New Yorker*, August 4, 2014.

65 Dunbar-Ortiz, interview by Fahs, April 9, 2015.

66 Ibid.

6. INTERGENERATIONAL DIALOGUES AND THE FUTURE OF RADICAL FEMINISM

1 The Shulamith Firestone Women's Liberation Conference on What Is to Be Done was held in New York City on October 5, 2013, almost a year after Shulamith Firestone's death. The conference gathered "a range of radical and feminist female organizers to take a hard look at how much progress had really been

made in the thinking and the concrete gains toward freedom for humanity's 'second sex.'" It featured talks by Ti-Grace Atkinson, Loretta Ross, Rachel Ivy, Gail Dines, Peggy Dobbins, Bai Di, and many members of Redstockings. See Redstockings, "Shulamith Firestone Conference, 2013," *What Is to Be Done*, https://womenwhatistobedone.wordpress.com/shulamith-firestone-conference-2013.

2   National Center for Education Statistics, "College Enrollment Rates of High School Graduates, by Sex: 1960 to 1998," 1999, https://nces.ed.gov/programs/digest/d99/d99t187.asp.

3   John W. Curtis, "Persistent Inequity: Gender and Academic Employment," paper presented at the New Voices in Pay Equity Panel, Washington, DC, April 11, 2011, www.aaup.org/NR/rdonlyres/08E023AB-E6D8-4DBD-99A0 -24E5EB73A760/0/persistent_inequity.pdf.

4   Mikaila Mariel Lemonik Arthur, *Student Activism and Curricular Change in Higher Education* (New York: Routledge, 2016).

5   Roberta Salper, "San Diego State 1970: The Initial Year of the Nation's First Women's Studies Program," *Feminist Studies* 37, no. 3 (2011): 658–82.

6   Marilyn J. Boxer, "Women's Studies as Women's History," *Women's Studies Quarterly* 30, no. 3–4 (2002): 42–51.

7   Ibid.

8   Sarachild, with Fahs and Atkinson, "Feminist Provocations."

9   Ibid.

10   Ibid.

11   Ibid.

12   Ibid.

13   Densmore, interview by Fahs, October 24, 2009.

14   Ibid.

15   Atkinson, with Fahs and Sarachild, "Feminist Provocations."

16   Ibid.

17   Ibid.

18   The Sears, Roebuck and Company class action lawsuit was a major lawsuit, filed in the 1970s by the EEOC, that alleged that Sears had discriminated against women in commission sales jobs and certain managerial positions. Sears won the case after Charles Morgan Jr., the former head of the American Civil Liberty Union, was hired to fight the charges. *New York Times* writer Tamar Lewin explained that Morgan drew from testimony by women's historian Rosalind Rosenberg (then at Barnard College and later at Columbia University) to create an unusual "women's history" defense "based on the premise that women in the workforce behave differently from men. The paucity of women in higher-paying commission sales jobs, Sears argued, was not due to discrimination but rather to women's preference for less competitive jobs." Despite the fact that the EEOC provided statistical evidence that women were not hired or promoted into commission sales jobs as frequently as men, Sears won the case. Further, Clarence Thomas, who oversaw the commission, said he did not believe in

statistics as one of the reasons for ruling in favor of Sears. (See Lewin, "Statistics Have Become Suspect in Sex Discrimination Cases," *New York Times*, February 9, 1986.) Rosenberg drew heavy criticism from opposing historian Alice Kessler-Harris, who argued, "This issue is purely this. . . . You would not lie in your testimony, but you also would not say or write something as a historian solely to hurt a group of people. And the consequences of Rosalind's testimony can be interpreted that way." See Samuel G. Freedman, "Of History and Politics: Bitter Feminist Debate," *New York Times*, June 6, 1986.

19 Stephanie Riger, "Women's History Goes to Trial: *EEOC v. Sears, Roebuck and Company*," *Signs* 13, no. 4 (1988): 897–903.

20 Atkinson, with Fahs and Sarachild, "Feminist Provocations."

21 Catharine Stimpson (1936–) is a professor and dean of the graduate school of arts and sciences at New York University. She was a founding editor of *Signs: Journal of Women in Culture and Society* from 1974 to 1980 and served as chair of the New York State Council for the Humanities and the National Council for Research on Women. See New York University, "Catharine R. Stimpson," http://its.law.nyu.edu/facultyprofiles/index.cfm?fuseaction=profile.biography&personid=20538.

22 Atkinson, interview by Fahs, February 1, 2008.

23 Atkinson, email to Fahs, April 11, 2017.

24 Sarachild, with Fahs and Atkinson, "Feminist Provocations."

25 Kate Eichhorn, *The Archival Turn in Feminism: Outrage in Order* (Philadelphia: Temple University Press, 2013).

26 Abigail J. Stewart, Jayati Lal, and Kristin McGuire, "Expanding the Archives of Global Feminisms: Narratives of Feminism and Activism," *Signs* 36, no. 4 (2011): 889–914; Griselda Pollock, *Encounters in a Virtual Feminist Museum: Time, Space, and the Archive* (London: Routledge, 2007); Jacqueline Wernimont and Julia Flanders, "Feminism in the Age of Digital Archives: The Women Writers Project," *Tulsa Studies in Women's Literature* 29, no. 2 (2010): 425–35; Danielle Cooper, "Imagining Something Else Entirely: Metaphorical Archives in Feminist Theory," *Women's Studies* 45, no. 5 (2016): 444–56; and Ela Przybylo and Danielle Cooper, "Asexual Resonances: Tracing a Queerly Asexual Archive," *GLQ* 20, no. 3 (2014): 297–318.

27 In yet another twist of power, many early radical feminists have also started to sell parts of their archives to powerful institutions like the Schlesinger Library at Harvard University or the Sallie Bingham Center for Women's History and Culture at Duke University. These payments then help these activists to survive in an economy that neglects older women without large retirement funds.

28 Redstockings, "About the Archives," www.redstockings.org/index.php/about-the-archives.

29 Ibid.

30 Redstockings, *Feminist Revolution*.

31 Kathie Sarachild, "The Power of History," in *Feminist Revolution*, 15.

32 Ibid., 42.

33 Sarachild, with Fahs and Atkinson, "Feminist Provocations."

34 Press coverage of the strike appeared across a variety of media outlets, including *Gothamist, New York* magazine, *AM New York, Bustle, Mic,* the *Huffington Post,
Jacobin, ThinkProgress, In These Times,* the *Village Voice,* and the *New York Observer.*

35 The official strike website noted: "Women had many good reasons to strike
before this election, but now we have a president-elect who openly disrespects
and assaults women, and wants to limit our roles to servant, mother, or sexual
plaything. This strike comes from anger at men in our lives who didn't vote, or
who voted for Trump, or who aren't taking seriously the threat that his presidency represents. And it is a reaction to an election campaign that—apart from
Bernie Sanders in the primary—ignored the universal programs that women
and all people need, and that work well in so many other countries, from paid
family leave to childcare to national health care. The Democrats didn't pursue
these plans when they could have, and now the Republican-majority Congress
is promising to cut, undermine, privatize, or eliminate every social contract
from public schools to Medicare to Social Security. They expect the family (that
is, WOMEN) to fill in the gaps and pick up the pieces. NO WE WON'T. This
strike is a warning. Our work can no longer be taken for granted." National
Women's Liberation, "1.20.17 to 1.21.17—Women Strike," www.womenslibera
tion.org/index.php/events/350-1-20-2017-to-1-21-2017-women-strike.

36 Redstockings, "About Redstockings of the Women's Liberation Movement."

37 Dunbar-Ortiz, interview by Fahs, April 9, 2015.

38 Ibid.

39 Ibid.

40 Ibid.

41 Ibid.

42 Atkinson, "The Autonomous Woman."

43 Frantz Fanon (1925–1961) was a West Indian psychoanalyst, revolutionary, and
social philosopher best known for his work on colonialism. His 1952 book *Black
Skin, White Masks* focused on the impact of colonialism on racial consciousness,
while his 1961 book *The Wretched of the Earth* helped cement Fanon as a prominent
scholar of decoloniality. He supported the Algerian National Liberation Front.
(See also the discussion of Fanon in this book's first chapter.) Albert Memmi
(1920–) is a French writer and novelist who focused on the sociological study of
human oppression. His work *The Colonizer and the Colonized* examined the primary
focus of colonial oppression. He taught sociology at the University of Paris.

44 Atkinson, "The Autonomous Woman."

45 Georg W. F. Hegel, *The Phenomenology of Mind* (London: Allen & Unwin, 1977).

46 Atkinson, "The Autonomous Woman."

47 Atkinson, interview by Fahs, February 1, 2008.

48 Atkinson, interview by Fahs, June 4, 2015.

49 Atkinson, interview by Fahs, February 1, 2008.

50   Atkinson, interview by Fahs, June 4, 2015.

51   Atkinson, interview by Fahs, February 1, 2008.

52   See Chapter 3 of this book for details about Florynce "Flo" Kennedy.

53   Atkinson, interview by Fahs, February 1, 2008.

54   The Weather Underground was an American militant radical-left-wing organization founded on the Ann Arbor campus of the University of Michigan. Originally called the Weathermen in honor of the Bob Dylan song lyric, the group emerged in 1969 as a faction of Students for a Democratic Society; they sought to overthrow the US government and were well known for a campaign of bombings of government buildings and banks in the mid-1970s. See Dan Berger, *Outlaws of America: The Weather Underground and the Politics of Solidarity* (San Francisco: AK Press, 2006).

55   The phrase "good German" emerged during World War II to describe individuals who choose to ignore obvious facts, including crimes against humanity and human rights abuses by governments. Citizens of Germany, for example, failed to acknowledge and fight against concentration camps. See Frank Rich, "The 'Good Germans' among Us," *New York Times*, October 14, 2007.

56   Atkinson, interview by Fahs, February 1, 2008.

57   Ibid.

58   Ibid.

59   Ibid.

60   Ibid.

61   Densmore, interview by Fahs, October 24, 2009.

62   Atkinson, interview by Fahs, June 4, 2015.

63   Many prominent feminists have argued against the Bible for its misogynistic claims about subordinating women. Elizabeth Cady Stanton famously argued in her nonfiction book *The Woman's Bible* that women should rewrite the Bible as a form of resistance. See Shira Wolosky, "Women's Bibles: Biblical Interpretation in Nineteenth-Century American Women's Poetry," *Feminist Studies* 28, no. 1 (2002): 191–211.

64   Elizabeth Cady Stanton (1815–1902) was a prominent suffragette and activist in the early women's movement. She helped to organize and lead the first protest for women's suffrage in the United States in 1848 and gave a speech that helped pass legislation to allow women to keep their wages and have equal guardianship of their children. Susan B. Anthony (1820–1906) was also a prominent suffragette and activist in the early US women's movement; she helped make it possible for the Nineteenth Amendment to be enacted. She was involved in antislavery movements during the 1850s and 1860s as well, and she formed the National Woman Suffrage Association with Stanton.

65   Atkinson, interview by Fahs, June 4, 2015.

66   Ibid.

67   Ibid.

68   Atkinson, interview by Fahs, February 1, 2008.

69   Ibid.

70   For a systematic description of continuity between feminists of different gen-
     erations, see Pauline Cullen and Clara Fischer, "Conceptualizing Generational
     Dynamics in Feminist Movements: Political Generations, Waves, and Affective
     Economies," *Sociology Compass* 8, no. 3 (2014): 282–93; see also Nancy Whittier,
     "Political Generations, Micro-Cohorts, and the Transformation of Social Move-
     ments," *American Sociological Review* 62, no. 5 (1997): 760–78.

71   Atkinson, interview by Fahs, June 4, 2015.

72   Dunbar-Ortiz, interview by Fahs, April 9, 2015.

73   Ibid.

74   Ibid.

75   Wolfgang Saxon, "Donna Allen, 78, a Feminist and an Organizer," *New York
     Times*, July 26, 1999.

76   Dunbar-Ortiz, interview by Fahs, April 9, 2015.

77   Angela Davis (1944–) is a radical black feminist activist icon who was arrested
     for conspiracy and imprisoned from 1970 to 1972. She had well-known ties to
     the Black Panther Party and the Communist Party. She later became a professor
     at the University of California, Los Angeles, where she taught history, and cur-
     rently teaches at the University of California, Santa Cruz. She was on the most-
     wanted list during the 1970s but was later acquitted of charges for murder and
     conspiracy.

78   Dunbar-Ortiz, interview by Fahs, April 9, 2015. For more information about
     compelling antimilitarization work, see Nadine Puechguirba and Cynthia Enloe,
     "The Damning Effects of Militarization," *Feminist Activism*, May 12, 2011, https://
     feministactivism.com/2011/05/12/the-damning-effects-of-militarization.

79   See Rachel V. Kutz-Flamenbaum, "Code Pink, Raging Grannies, and the Missile
     Dick Chicks: Feminist Performance Activism in the Contemporary Anti-War
     Movement," *NWSA Journal* 19, no. 1 (2007): 89–105.

80   Dunbar-Ortiz, interview by Fahs, April 9, 2015.

81   ACORN stands for the Association of Community Organization for Reform
     Now; it was a grassroots nonprofit that focused on the "economic and political
     needs of lower-income Americans, and [lobbied] on behalf of the disadvan-
     taged." The organization was widely attacked by Republicans (including Sarah
     Palin), and was dissolved in 2010. See Robert North Roberts, Scott J. Ham-
     mond, and Valerie A. Sulfaro, *Presidential Campaigns, Slogans, Issues, and Plat-
     forms: The Complete Encyclopedia, Volume 1* (Santa Barbara, CA: ABC-CLIO, 2012).

82   Atkinson, interview by Fahs, June 4, 2015.

83   Atkinson, interview by Fahs, February 1, 2008.

84   Ibid.

85   Ibid.

86   Ibid.

EPILOGUE

1 Erica Chenoweth and Jeremy Pressman, "This Is What We Learned by Counting the Women's Marches," *Washington Post*, February 7, 2017, www.washington post.com/news/monkey-cage/wp/2017/02/07/this-is-what-we-learned-by -counting-the-womens-marches/?utm_term=.58bf915e5b32.

2 Alicia Garza, "A Herstory of the #BlackLivesMatter Movement," *Feminist Wire*, October 7, 2014, www.thefeministwire.com/2014/10/blacklivesmatter-2.

3 Julia Sudbury, *Global Lockdown: Race, Gender, and the Prison-Industrial Complex* (New York: Routledge, 2014).

4 Kristin A. Goss and Michael T. Heaney, "Organizing Women as Women: Hybridity and Grassroots Collective Action in the 21st Century," *Perspectives on Politics* 8, no. 1 (2010): 27–52.

5 Jenny Pickerill and John Krinsky, "Why Does Occupy Matter?" *Social Movement Studies* 11, no. 3–4 (2012): 279–87.

6 See Jeska Rees, "A Look Back at Anger: The Women's Liberation Movement in 1978," *Women's History Review* 19, no. 3 (2010): 337–56; Nancy A. Naples, "Transnational Activism, Feminist Praxis, and Cultures of Resistance," in *Globalizing Cultures: Theories, Paradigms, Actions*, eds. Vincenzo Mele and Marina Vujnovic (Leiden, Netherlands: Brill Press, 2015): 143–73; and Eli R. Green, "Debating Trans Inclusion in the Feminist Movement: A Trans-Positive Analysis," *Journal of Lesbian Studies* 10, no. 1–2 (2006): 231–48.

7 For more on the importance of having a radical flank in progressive social movements, see Lorna Weir, "Left Popular Politics in Canadian Feminist Abortion Organizing, 1982–1991," *Feminist Studies* 20, no. 2 (1994): 249–74; Holly J. McCammon, Sandra C. Arch, and Erin M. Bergner, "A Radical Demand Effect: Early US Feminists and the Married Women's Property Acts," *Social Science History* 38, no. 1–2 (2014): 221–50; and Erica Chenoweth and Maria J. Stephan, *Why Civil Resistance Works: The Strategic Logic of Nonviolent Conflict* (New York: Columbia University Press, 2011).

8 James Baldwin, "Unnameable Objects, Unspeakable Crimes," *BlackState*, http:// blackstate.com/baldwin1.html.

BIBLIOGRAPHY |

Ackelsberg, Martha. "Shulamith Firestone." Jewish Women's Archive. Accessed March 1, 2009. http://jwa.org/encyclopedia/article/firestone-shulamith.

Akchurin, Maria, and Lee Cheol-Sung. "Pathways to Empowerment: Repertoires of Women's Activism and Gender Earnings Equality." *American Sociological Review* 78, no. 4 (2013): 679–701.

Alcoff, Linda. "Cultural Feminism versus Post-Structuralism: The Identity Crisis in Feminist Theory." *Signs* 13, no. 3 (1988): 405–36.

Alterman, Eric. *Why We're Liberals*. New York: Viking, 2008.

Amatniek (Sarachild), Kathie. "Funeral Oration for the Burial of Traditional Womanhood." *Notes from the First Year*, 1968. Duke University Libraries. http://library.duke.edu/digitalcollections/wlmpc_wlmms01037.

Andrews, Evan. "Native American Activists Occupy Alcatraz Island, 45 Years Ago." History.com. November 20, 2014. www.history.com/news/native-american-activists-occupy-alcatraz-island-45-years-ago.

American Experience. "People and Events: Margaret Sanger." Accessed November 25, 2016. www.pbs.org/wgbh/amex/pill/peopleevents/p_sanger.html.

Arthur, Mikaila Mariel Lemonik. *Student Activism and Curricular Change in Higher Education*. New York: Routledge, 2016.

Atkinson, Ti-Grace. *Amazon Odyssey: The First Collection of Writings by the Political Pioneer of the Women's Movement*. New York: Links Books, 1974.

———. "Catholic University." Speech, Washington, DC, March 10, 1971.

———. "How to Defang a Movement: Replacing the Political with the Personal." Paper presented at A Revolutionary Moment: Women's Liberation in the Late 1960s and the Early 1970s Conference, Boston, MA, March 29, 2014.

———. Interview by Breanne Fahs. Cambridge, MA, February 1, 2008.

———. Interview by Breanne Fahs. Boston, MA, March 29, 2014.

———. Interview by Breanne Fahs. Cambridge, MA, June 4, 2015.

———. "The Autonomous Woman: Sex, Love, and Feminism." Lecture, Arizona State University, Phoenix, March 27, 2013.

———. "Vaginal Orgasm as a Mass Hysterical Survival Response." Public speech, Philadelphia, PA, April 6, 1968.

Atkinson, Ti-Grace, with Breanne Fahs and Kathie Sarachild. "Feminist Provocations." Public forum, Arizona State University, Phoenix, AZ, March 27, 2013.

Austin, Stephanie. "Naomi Weisstein." Society for the Psychology of Women. www.apadivisions.org/division-35/about/heritage/naomi-weisstein-biography.aspx.

Ayers, Bill, Bernardine Dohrn, and Jeff Jones, eds. *Sing a Battle Song: The Revolutionary Poetry, Statements, and Communiqués of the Weather Underground, 1970–1974*. New York: Seven Stories Press, 2011.

Bair, Deirdre. *Simone de Beauvoir: A Biography*. New York: Summit Books, 1990.

Baldwin, James. *The Fire Next Time*. New York: Dial Press, 1963.

———. "Unnameable Objects, Unspeakable Crimes." *BlackState*. http://blackstate.com/baldwin1.html.

Banaszak, Lee Ann, and Heather L. Ondercin. "Public Opinion as a Movement Outcome: The Case of the US Women's Movement." *Mobilization* 21, no. 3 (2016): 361–78.

Bates, Karen G. "Stokely Carmichael, a Philosopher behind the Black Power Movement." *Code Switch*, National Public Radio, March 10, 2014. www.npr.org/sections/codeswitch/2014/03/10/287320160/stokely-carmichael-a-philosopher-behind-the-black-power-movement.

Baxandall, Rosalyn, and Linda Gordon. "Second-Wave Feminism." In *A Companion to American Women's History*, edited by Nancy A. Hewitt, 414–32. New York: John Wiley and Sons, 2008.

Becker, Mary. "Patriarchy and Inequality: Towards a Substantive Feminism." *University of Chicago Legal Forum* 1 (1999): 21–22.

Bender, Marilyn. "The Feminists Are on the March Once More." *New York Times*, December 14, 1967.

Benson Gold, Rachel. "Lessons from before Roe: Will Past Be Prologue?" *Guttmacher Policy Review* 6, no. 1 (2003). www.guttmacher.org/about/gpr/2003/03/lessons-roe-will-past-be-prologue.

Berger, Dan. *Outlaws of America: The Weather Underground and the Politics of Solidarity*. San Francisco: AK Press, 2006.

Bernstein, Adam. "Patricia Buckley Bozell, 81; Activist Founded a Catholic Opinion Journal." *Washington Post*, July 15, 2008.

Bornat, Joanna, and Hanna Diamond. "Women's History and Oral History: Developments and Debates." *Women's History Review* 16, no. 1 (2007): 19–39.

Boxer, Marilyn J. "Women's Studies as Women's History." *Women's Studies Quarterly* 30, no. 3–4 (2002): 42–51.

Bradley, Patricia. *Mass Media and the Shaping of American Feminism, 1963–1975*. Jackson: University Press of Mississippi, 2004.

Crow Dog, Mary [Mary Brave Bird], and Richard Erdoes. *Lakota Woman*. New York: Grove Weidenfeld, 1990.

Brine, Ruth. "The New Feminists: Revolt against 'Sexism.'" *Time*, November 21, 1969, 53–56.

British Broadcasting Corporation. "Marie Stopes." Accessed November 25, 2016. www
.bbc.co.uk/history/historic_figures/stopes_marie_carmichael.shtml.

Brown, Kath. "Lesbian Separatist Feminism at the Michigan Womyn's Music Festival."
Feminism and Psychology 21, no. 2 (2011): 248–56.

———. "Womyn's Separatist Spaces: Rethinking Spaces of Difference and Exclusion."
Transactions of the Institute of British Geographers 34, no. 4 (2009): 541–56.

Brownmiller, Susan. *In Our Time: Memoir of a Revolution*. New York: Penguin/Random
House, 2000.

Butler, Judith. *Excitable Speech: A Politics of the Performative*. New York: Routledge, 1997.

———. *Gender Trouble: Feminism and the Subversion of Identity*. New York: Routledge, 1990.

Buyse, Antoine. "'Fear Speech,' or How Violent Conflict Escalation Relates to the
Freedom of Expression." *Human Rights Quarterly* 36, no. 4 (2014): 779–97.

Callarman, Michelle. "A Daughter's Story," in *The Conversation Begins*, edited by Christina Looper Baker and Christina Baker Kline. New York: Bantam Books, 1996.

Caws, Mary Anne. *Manifesto: A Century of Isms*. Lincoln: University of Nebraska Press,
2001.

Cerankowski, Karli June, and Megan Milks. "New Orientations: Asexuality and Its
Implications for Theory and Practice." *Feminist Studies* 36, no. 3 (2010): 650–64.

Chenoweth, Erica, and Jeremy Pressman. "This Is What We Learned by Counting
the Women's Marches." *Washington Post*, February 7, 2017.

Chenowith, Erica, and Maria J. Stephan. *Why Civil Resistance Works: The Strategic Logic
of Nonviolent Conflict*. New York: Columbia University Press, 2011.

Chesler, Phyllis, Esther D. Rothblum, and Ellen Cole. *Feminist Foremothers in Women's
Studies, Psychology, and Mental Health*. New York: Haworth Press, 1995.

Civil Rights Digital Library. "Kathie Sarachild." October 23, 2016. http://crdl.usg.edu
/people/s/sarachild_kathie/?Welcome.

Cobble, Dorothy Sue, Linda Gordon, and Astrid Henry. *Feminism Unfinished: A Short,
Surprising History of American Women's Movements*. New York: W. W. Norton, 2014.

Collier-Thomas, Bettye, and V. P. Franklin, editors. *Sisters in the Struggle; African American Women in the Civil Rights–Black Power Movement*. New York: New York University
Press, 2001.

Collins, Patricia Hill. "Black Feminist Thought in the Matrix of Domination." In *Social
Theory: The Multicultural and Classic Readings*, edited by Charles Lemert, 413–20.
Boulder, CO: Westview Press, 2017.

Cooper, Danielle. "Imagining Something Else Entirely: Metaphorical Archives in Feminist Theory." *Women's Studies* 45, no. 5 (2016): 444–56.

Costain, Anne N., and Steven Majstorovic. "Congress, Social Movements, and Public
Opinion: Multiple Origins of Women's Rights Legislation." *Political Research Quarterly* 47, no.1 (1994): 111–35.

Coursey, Rose. "The Radical Feminist Politics of Trans Identification." Unpublished
thesis, Arizona State University, 2014.

Crenshaw, Kimberlé. "Mapping the Margins: Intersectionality, Identity Politics, and
Violence against Women of Color." *Stanford Law Review* 43, no. 6 (1991): 1241–99.

Crow, Barbara A. *Radical Feminism: A Documentary Reader*. New York: New York University Press, 2000.

Cullen, Pauline, and Clara Fischer. "Conceptualizing Generational Dynamics in Feminist Movements: Political Generations, Waves, and Affective Economies." *Sociology Compass* 8, no. 3 (2014): 282–93.

Curtis, John W. "Persistent Inequity: Gender and Academic Employment." Paper presented at the New Voices in Pay Equity Panel, Washington, DC, April 11, 2011. www.aaup.org/NR/rdonlyres/08E023AB-E6D8-4DBD-99A0-24E5EB73A760/0/persistent_inequity.pdf.

Davidson, Sara. "An 'Oppressed Majority' Demands Its Rights: The Cause of Women's Equality Draws a Growing Number of Active-and-Angry Female Militants." *Life*, December 12, 1969. www.maryellenmark.com/text/magazines/life/905W-000-004.html.

De Beauvoir, Simone. *The Second Sex*. Translated by Constance Borde and Sheila Malovany-Chevallier. New York: Random House/Alfred A. Knopf, 1949.

———. *The Second Sex*. New York: Vintage, 1973.

Densmore, Dana. "Cell 16: Gender and Agency, with Digressions into Naming." Paper presented at A Revolutionary Moment: Women's Liberation in the Late 1960s and Early 1970s Conference, Boston, MA, March 29, 2014.

———. Interview by Breanne Fahs. Santa Fe, NM, October 24, 2009.

———. Interview by Breanne Fahs. Boston, MA, March 29, 2014.

Densmore, Dana, Roxanne Dunbar-Ortiz, and Breanne Fahs. "Oral History of Cell 16, Female Liberation." Public forum, A Revolutionary Moment: Women's Liberation in the Late 1960s and Early 1970s Conference, Boston, MA, March 29, 2014.

Donohue, Kathleen G. *Freedom from Want: American Liberalism and the Idea of the Consumer*. Baltimore: Johns Hopkins University Press, 2003.

Duchen, Jessica. "Paul Robeson: The Story of How an American Icon Was Driven to Death to Be Told in Film." *Independent*, November 20, 2014.

Dunbar-Ortiz, Roxanne. *An Indigenous Peoples' History of the United States*. Boston: Beacon Press, 2014.

———. *Blood on the Border: A Memoir of the Contra War*. Boston: South End Press, 2005.

———. "From the Cradle to the Boat: A Feminist Historian Remembers Valerie Solanas." *San Francisco Bay Guardian*, January 5, 2000.

———. Interview by Breanne Fahs. San Francisco, CA, December 11, 2008.

———. Interview by Breanne Fahs. Boston, MA, March 29, 2014.

———. Interview by Breanne Fahs. Tempe, AZ, April 9, 2015.

———. Letter to Jean-Louis. July 5, 1968.

———. "Outcasts and Outlaws: Cell 16, Valerie Solanas, and the History of Radical Feminism." Panel presented with Dana Densmore and Breanne Fahs at A Revolutionary Moment: Women's Liberation in the Late 1960s and the Early 1970s Conference, Boston, MA, March 29, 2014.

———. *Outlaw Woman: A Memoir of the War Years, 1960–1975*. San Francisco: City Lights Press, 2001.

———. *Outlaw Woman: A Memoir of the War Years, 1960–1975*. Norman: University of Oklahoma Press, 2014.

———. *Red Dirt: Growing Up Okie*. Norman: University of Oklahoma Press, 2006.

———. *Roots of Resistance: A History of Land Tenure in New Mexico*. Norman: University of Oklahoma Press, 2007.

———. *The Great Sioux Nation: An Oral History of the Sioux Nation and Its Struggle for Sovereignty*. New York: Random House, 1977.

———. *The Great Sioux Nation: Sitting in Judgment on America*. Lincoln: University of Nebraska Press, 2013.

Dunbar-Ortiz, Roxanne, and Dana Densmore. Interview by Breanne Fahs. Boston, MA, March 29, 2014.

Dunbar-Ortiz, Roxanne, and Dina Gilio-Whitaker. *"All the Real Indians Died Off" and 20 Other Myths about Native Americans*. Boston: Beacon Press, 2016.

Duncan, Lauren E., and Abigail J. Stewart. "A Generational Analysis of Women's Rights Activists." *Psychology of Women Quarterly* 24, no. 4 (2000): 297–308.

Echols, Alice. *Daring to Be Bad: Radical Feminism in America, 1967–1975*. New York: Vintage Books, 1979.

Eichorn, Kate. *The Archival Turn in Feminism: Outrage in Order*. Philadelphia: Temple University Press, 2013.

Evans, Sara M. *Personal Politics: The Roots of Women's Liberation in the Civil Rights Movement and the New Left*. New York: Vintage Books, 1976.

———. "Women's Liberation: Seeing the Revolution Clearly." *Feminist Studies* 41, no. 1 (2015): 138–59.

FactCheck.org. "Abortion Distortions." Annenberg Public Policy Center. Accessed November 25, 2016. http://dev.factcheck.org/2005/07/abortion-distortions/#.

Fahs, Breanne. "Breaking Body Hair Boundaries: Classroom Exercises for Challenging Social Constructions of the Body and Sexuality." *Feminism and Psychology* 22, no. 4 (2012): 482–506.

———. "Dreaded 'Otherness': Heteronormative Patrolling in Women's Body Hair Rebellions." *Gender and Society* 24, no. 4 (2011): 451–72.

———. "'Freedom To' and 'Freedom From': A New Vision for Sex Positive Politics." *Sexualities* 17, no. 3 (2014): 267–90.

———. "Perilous Patches and Pitstaches: Imagined Versus Lived Experiences of Women's Body Hair Growth." *Psychology of Women Quarterly* 38, no. 2 (2014): 167–80.

———. *Valerie Solanas: The Defiant Life of the Woman Who Wrote SCUM (and Shot Andy Warhol)*. New York: Feminist Press, 2014.

Fahs, Breanne, with Avital Ronell, Lisa Duggan, and Karen Finley. "Feminist Rage: A Discussion about Valerie Solanas." Public forum, New York University, New York, April 11, 2014.

Faludi, Susan. "Facebook Feminism, Like It or Not." *Baffler* 23 (2013). http://thebaffler.com/articles/facebook-feminism-like-it-or-not#.

Female Collective. "Pussy Grabs Back." 2016. www.femalecollective.org/product/pussy-grabs-back.

Feminists Against Trump (Facebook community). Accessed December 1, 2016. www
.facebook.com/FeministsAgainstTrump.

Ferree, Myra Marx. "Resonance and Radicalism: Feminist Framing in the Abortion
Debate of the United States and Germany." *American Journal of Sociology* 109, no. 2
(2003): 304–44.

Firestone, Shulamith. *The Dialectic of Sex: The Case for Feminist Revolution*. New York:
William Morrow and Company, 1970.

Fitz, Caroline C., Alyssa N. Zucker, and Laina Bay-Cheng. "Not All Nonlabelers
Are Created Equal: Distinguishing between Quasi-Feminists and Neoliberals."
Psychology of Women Quarterly 36, no. 3 (2012): 274–85.

Florence Morning News. "Feminist Consulted Columbo." August 22, 1974. www.news
papers.com/newspage/68522437.

Florynce Kennedy Papers, 1915–2004. Schlesinger Library, Radcliffe Institute, Harvard
University, Cambridge, MA. http://oasis.lib.harvard.edu/oasis/deliver/~sch01221.

Fox, Margalit. "Betty Friedan, Who Ignited Cause in *Feminine Mystique*, Dies at 85."
New York Times, February 5, 2006.

———. "Shulamith Firestone, Feminist Writer, Dies at 67." *New York Times*,
August 30, 2012.

Freedman, Estelle. *No Turning Back: The History of Feminism and the Future of Women*. New
York: Random House, 2007.

Freedman, Samuel G. "Of History and Politics: Bitter Feminist Debate." *New York
Times*, June 6, 1986.

Freeman, Jo. "The Tyranny of Structurelessness." *Women's Studies Quarterly* 41, no. 3–4
(2013): 231–46.

Freeman, Jo, and Victoria Johnson. *Waves of Protest: Social Movements since the Sixties*.
New York: Rowman and Littlefield, 1999.

Friedan, Betty. *The Feminine Mystique*. New York: W. W. Norton, 1963.

Frye, Marilyn. "Some Reflections on Separatism and Power." In *The Lesbian and Gay
Studies Reader*, edited by Henry Abelove, Michele Aina Barale, and David M.
Halperin, 91–98. New York: Routledge, 1993.

Gage, Carolyn. *Hotter than Hell: More Sermons for a Lesbian Tent Revival*. Amazon Digital
Services, 2011.

Gamson, Joshua. "Messages of Exclusion: Gender, Movements, and Symbolic Boundaries." *Gender and Society* 11, no. 2 (1997): 178–99.

Garza, Alicia. "A Herstory of the #BlackLivesMatter Movement." *Feminist Wire*, October 7, 2014. www.thefeministwire.com/2014/10/blacklivesmatter-2.

Gavey, Nicola. *Just Sex? The Cultural Scaffolding of Rape*. London and New York: Routledge, 2008.

Geiger, Susan. "What's So Feminist about Women's Oral History?" *Journal of Women's
History* 2, no. 1 (1990): 169–82.

George Washington University. "National Committee for a SANE Nuclear Policy."
www2.gwu.edu/~erpapers/teachinger/glossary/nat-com-sane-nuc-pol.cfm.

Gilmore, Stephanie. "The Dynamics of Second-Wave Feminist Activism in Memphis,

1971–1982: Rethinking the Liberal/Radical Divide." *NWSA Journal* 15, no. 1 (2003): 94–117.

Gluck, Sherna Berger. "Has Feminist Oral History Lost Its Radical/Subversive Edge?" *Oral History* 39, no. 2 (2011): 63–72.

Gluck, Sherna Berger, and Daphne Patai. *Women's Words: The Feminist Practice of Oral History*. New York: Routledge, 2013.

Goldberg, Michelle. "What Is a Woman? The Dispute Between Radical Feminism and Transgenderism." *New Yorker*, August 4, 2014.

Goss, Kristin A., and Michael T. Heaney. "Organizing Women as Women: Hybridity and Grassroots Collective Action in the 21st Century." *Perspectives on Politics* 8, no.1 (2010): 27–52.

Gotwals, Jenny. "Ellen Willis." *American National Biography Online*, April 2014. www .anb.org/articles/16/16-03903.html.

Green, Eli R. "Debating Trans Inclusion in the Feminist Movement: A Trans-Positive Analysis." *Journal of Lesbian Studies* 10, no. 1–2 (2006): 231–48.

Grimes, William. "Rosalyn Baxandall, Feminist Historian and Activist, Dies at 76." *New York Times*, October 14, 2015.

Grosz, Elizabeth. *Volatile Bodies: Toward a Corporeal Feminism*. Bloomington: Indiana University Press, 1994.

Hall, Simon. *American Patriotism, American Protest: Social Movements since the Sixties*. Philadelphia: University of Pennsylvania Press, 2011.

Hanisch, Carol. "Women's Liberation: Looking Back, Looking Forward." *On the Issues*, Winter 2011. http://ontheissuesmagazine.com/2011winter/2011_winter_Hanisch .php.

Hanisch, Carol, Kathy Scarbrough, Ti-Grace Atkinson, and Kathie Sarachild. "Forbidden Discourse: The Silencing of Feminist Criticism of 'Gender'; An Open Statement from Thirty-Seven Radical Feminists from Five Countries." August 12, 2013. https://womensspace.wordpress.com/2013/08/20/forbidden-discourse-the-silenc ing-of-feminist-criticism-of-gender-an-open-statement-from-37-radical-feminists -from-five-countries-with-biographical-information-about-each-signat.

Hasday, Jill Elaine. "Contest and Consent: A Legal History of Marital Rape." *California Law Review* 88, no. 5 (2000): 1373–505.

Hays, Matthew. "Some on the Radical Queer Left Still Think Gay Marriage Is Bad for the LGBTQ Community." *Vice*, September 16, 2015. www.vice.com/en_us/article /some-on-the-radical-queer-left-still-think-gay-marriage-is-bad-for-the-lgbtq -community.

Hegel, Georg W. F. *The Phenomenology of Mind*. London: Allen & Unwin, 1977.

Helscher, David. "*Griswold v. Connecticut* and the Unenumerated Right of Privacy." *Northern Illinois University Law Review* 33 (1994–1995): 33–62.

Henley, Nancy M., Karen Meng, Delores O'Brien, William J. McCarthy, and Robert J. Sockloskie. "Developing a Scale to Measure the Diversity of Feminist Attitudes." *Psychology of Women Quarterly* 22, no. 3 (1998): 317–48.

Hesford, Victoria. *Feeling Women's Liberation*. Durham, NC: Duke University Press, 2013.

Hollander, Jocelyn A. "'I Can Take Care of Myself': The Impact of Self-Defense Training on Women's Lives." *Violence against Women* 10, no. 3 (2004): 205–35.

hooks, bell. *All about Love: New Visions*. New York: William Morrow, 2000.

———. "Dig Deep: Beyond 'Lean In.'" *Feminist Wire*, October 23, 2013. http://thefeministwire.com/2013/10/17973.

———. *Feminist Theory: From Margin to Center*. New York: Routledge, 2015.

Htun, Mala, and S. Laurel Weldon. "The Civic Origins of Progressive Policy Change: Combatting Violence against Women in Global Perspective, 1975–2005." *American Political Science Review* 106, no. 3 (2012): 548–69.

Industrial Workers of the World. "Industrial Workers of the World: What Everyone Should Know." Seattle Joint Branches, Industrial Workers of the World, 1957. www.iww.org/culture/official/qanda.

Jaggar, Alison M. *Feminist Politics and Human Nature*. Totowa, NJ: Rowman and Allanheld, 1983.

Jewish Women's Archive. "Heather Booth." Accessed November 25, 2016. http://jwa.org/feminism/booth-heather.

Kaplan, Judy, and Linn Shapiro. *Red Diapers: Growing Up in the Communist Left*. Urbana: University of Illinois Press, 1998.

Kelley, Lauren. "Nearly 400 Anti-Abortion Laws Introduced Last Year." *Rolling Stone*, January 4, 2016.

Kim, Richard, and Lisa Duggan. "Beyond Gay Marriage." *Nation*, July 18, 2005.

Kipnis, Laura. *Unwanted Advances: Sexual Paranoia Comes to Campus*. New York: Harper, 2017.

Krizman, Lawrence D., ed. *Politics, Philosophy, Culture: Interviews and Other Writings, 1977–1984*. New York: Routledge, 1990.

Kutz-Flamenbaum, Rachel V. "Code Pink, Raging Grannies, and the Missile Dick Chicks: Feminist Performance Activism in the Contemporary Anti-War Movement." *NWSA Journal* 19, no. 1 (2007): 89–105.

Kwon, Sarah. "Ti-Grace Atkinson, at Home in Cambridge, Adds Cause to Radical Feminism: Housing." *Cambridge Day*, January 6, 2016. www.cambridgeday.com/2016/01/06/ti-grace-atkinson-at-home-in-cambridge-adds-cause-to-radical-feminism-housing.

Lear, Martha Weinman. "The Second Feminist Wave." *New York Times Magazine*, March 10, 1968.

Lennon, Kathleen. "Feminist Perspectives on the Body." *Stanford Encyclopedia of Philosophy*. http://plato.stanford.edu/entries/feminist-body.

Lerner, Gerda. *Why History Matters: Life and Thought*. Oxford: Oxford University Press, 1998.

Lewin, Tamar. "Statistics Have Become Suspect in Sex Discrimination Cases." *New York Times*, February 9, 1986.

Lorber, Judith. *Paradoxes of Gender*. New Haven, CT: Yale University Press, 1994.

Lorde, Audre. "Age, Race, Class, and Sex: Women Redefining Difference." In *Sister Outsider: Essays and Speeches*, 114–23. Freedom, CA: Crossing Press, 1984.

Los Angeles Times. "John Mack Carter Dies at 86: Hearst Editor Led Top Women's Magazines." September 29, 2014.

Love, Barbara. *Feminists Who Changed America, 1963–1975.* Chicago: University of Illinois Press, 2006.

Mackay, Finn. *Radical Feminism: Feminist Activism in Movement.* London: Palgrave, 2015.

Malatesta, Errico. *L'Anarchia.* London: Freedom Press, 1974.

Mallard, Aida. "Fame Recipient Fought for Equal Rights." *Gainesville Sun,* January 7, 2010.

Manly, Chesly. "'New Politics' Convention to Open Here." *Chicago Tribune,* August 27, 1967.

McCammon, Holly J., Sandra C. Arch, and Erin M. Bergner. "A Radical Demand Effect: Early US Feminists and the Married Women's Property Acts." *Social Science History* 38, no. 1–2 (2014): 221–50.

McCammon, Holly J., Erin M. Bergner, and Sandra C. Arch. "'Are You One of Those Women?': Within-Movement Conflict, Radical Flank Effects, and Social Movement Political Outcomes." *Mobilization* 20, no. 2 (2015): 157–78.

McLaughlin, Katie. "Five Things Women Couldn't Do in the 1960s." CNN, August 25, 2014. www.cnn.com/2014/08/07/living/sixties-women-5-things.

Moran, Rachel F. "How Second-Wave Feminism Forgot the Single Woman." *Hofstra Law Review* 33 (2004): 223–34.

Morgan, Robin, ed. *Sisterhood Is Powerful: An Anthology of Writings from the Women's Liberation Movement.* New York: Random House, 1970.

Morning Record (Meriden, CT). "Two Feminists Arrested in N.Y. Protest." October 24, 1972.

Morrison, Toni. *The Bluest Eye.* New York: Holt McDougal, 1970.

Naples, Nancy A. "Transnational Activism, Feminist Praxis, and Cultures of Resistance." In *Globalizing Cultures: Theories, Paradigms, Actions,* edited by Vincenzo Mele and Marina Vujnovic, 143–73. Leiden, Netherlands: Brill Press, 2015.

National Center for Education Statistics. "College Enrollment Rates of High School Graduates, by Sex: 1960 to 1998." 1999. https://nces.ed.gov/programs/digest/d99/d99t187.asp.

National Organization for Women. "About the NOW Foundation." Accessed November 13, 2016. http://now.org/now-foundation/about-now-foundation.

Native Times. "Activist, Author Roxanne Dunbar-Ortiz Addresses Standing Room Only Crowd at University of Tulsa." May 5, 2013. www.nativetimes.com/life/people/8695-activist-author-roxanne-dunbar-ortiz-addresses-standing-room-only-crowd-at-university-of-tulsa.

New York Radical Women. *Notes from the First Year.* New York, 1968.

———. *Notes from the Second Year.* New York, 1970.

New York Times. "Flo Kennedy, Feminist, Civil Rights Advocate and Flamboyant Gadfly, Is Dead at 84." December 23, 2000.

———. "Transcript: Donald Trump's Taped Comments About Women." October 8, 2016.

New York University. "Catharine R. Stimpson." Accessed November 1, 2016. http://
its.law.nyu.edu/facultyprofiles/index.cfm?fuseaction=profile.biography&
personid=20538.

Nussbaum, Martha. *Sex and Social Justice.* New York: Oxford University Press, 1999.

Organise! for Revolutionary Anarchism. "Safe, Free, Diverse and Consensual: Anarchism
and Sex." December 21, 2002. www.afed.org.uk/org/org59.pdf.

Orleck, Annelise. *Rethinking American Women's Activism.* New York: Routledge, 2015.

Pankhurst, Emmeline. *My Own Story.* London: Virago, 1914.

Pareles, Jon. "Pete Seeger, Champion of Folk Music and Social Change, Dies at 94."
New York Times, January 28, 2014.

Paul, Alice. "Women's Party to Call a Convention." *New York Times,* September 11,
1920.

Pearson, Kyra. "Words Should Do the Work of Bombs: Margaret Cho as Symbolic
Assassin." *Women and Language* 32, no. 1 (2009): 36–43.

Pickerill, Jenny, and John Krinsky. "Why Does Occupy Matter?" *Social Movement
Studies* 11, no. 3–4 (2012): 279–87.

Piven, Frances Fox, and Richard A. Cloward. *Poor People's Movements: Why They Succeed,
and How They Fail.* New York: Vintage, 1979.

Pollock, Griselda. *Encounters in a Virtual Feminist Museum: Time, Space, and the Archive.*
London: Routledge, 2007.

Poo, Ai-jen. "Organizing with Love: Lessons from the New York Domestic Workers
Bill of Rights Campaign." *Left Turn,* December 1, 2010. www.leftturn.org/Organiz
ing-with-Love.

Portelli, Alessandro. "What Makes Oral History Different." In *Oral History, Oral Culture, and Italian Americans,* edited by Luisa Del Giudice, 21–30. London: Palgrave,
2009.

Presidential Gender Watch. "Presidential Polling Data." November 10, 2016. http://
presidentialgenderwatch.org/polls/womens-vote-watch/presidential-polling
-data.

Przybylo, Ela. *Asexual Erotics: Intimate Readings of Compulsory Sexuality.* Forthcoming
with Ohio State University Press.

———. "Crisis and Safety: The Asexuality in Sexusociety." *Sexualities* 14, no. 4 (2011):
444–61.

Przybylo, Ela, and Danielle Cooper. "Asexual Resonances: Tracing a Queerly Asexual
Archive." *GLQ* 20, no. 3 (2014): 297–318.

Puchner, Martin. *Poetry of the Revolution: Marx, Manifestos, and the Avant-Gardes.* Princeton, NJ: Princeton University Press, 2005.

Puechguirba, Nadine, and Cynthia Enloe. "The Damning Effects of Militarization."
Feminist Activism, May 12, 2011. https://feministactivism.com/2011/05/12/the
-damning-effects-of-militarization.

Purdie-Vaughns, Valerie, and Richard P. Eibach. "Intersectional Invisibility: The
Distinctive Advantages and Disadvantages of Multiple Subordinate-Group
Identities." *Sex Roles* 59, no. 5–6 (2008): 377–91.

Randolph, Sherie M. *Florynce "Flo" Kennedy: The Life of a Black Feminist Radical*. Chapel Hill: University of North Carolina Press, 2015.

Rawls, John. *A Theory of Justice*. Cambridge, MA: Harvard University Press, 1971.

Reagan, Leslie. *When Abortion Was a Crime: Women, Medicine, and Law in the United States, 1867–1973*. Berkeley: University of California Press, 1998.

Redstockings. "About Redstockings of the Women's Liberation Movement." Accessed October 22, 2016. www.redstockings.org/index.php/about-redstockings.

———. "About the Archives." www.redstockings.org/index.php/about-the-archives.

———. "June 1969: A Blast of Redstockings Feminism." www.redstockings.org/index .php/june-1969-a-blast-of-redstockings-feminism.

———. *Feminist Revolution*. New York: Random House, 1978.

———. *Redstockings Women's Liberation Archive for Action Packet: Some Documents from and Media Responses to Redstockings Abortion Speakouts, 1969 and 1989*. New York: Archives Distribution Project.

———. "Shulamith Firestone Conference, 2013." *What Is to Be Done?* https://women whatistobedone.wordpress.com/shulamith-firestone-conference-2013.

Rees, Jeska. "A Look Back at Anger: The Women's Liberation Movement in 1978." *Women's History Review* 19, no. 3 (2010): 337–56.

———. "'Are You a Lesbian?': Challenges in Recording and Analysing the Women's Liberation Movement in England." *History Workshop Journal* 69, no. 1 (2007): 177–87.

Red Dirt Site. "About Roxanne Dunbar-Ortiz." Accessed November 2, 2016. www .reddirtsite.com/about.htm.

Reger, Jo. "Organizational 'Emotion Work' Through Consciousness-Raising: An Analysis of a Feminist Organization." *Qualitative Sociology* 27, no. 2 (2004): 205–22.

Rich, Frank. "The 'Good Germans' among Us." *New York Times*, October 14, 2007.

Riger, Stephanie. "Women's History Goes to Trial: *EEOC v. Sears, Roebuck and Company.*" *Signs* 13, no. 4 (1988): 897–903.

Robert, Slayton. "Don't Mourn, Organize!" *Huffington Post*, November 9, 2016. www .huffingtonpost.com/robert-slayton/dont-mourn-organize_b_12876600.html.

Roberts, Robert North, Scott J. Hammond, and Valerie A. Sulfaro. *Presidential Campaigns, Slogans, Issues, and Platforms: The Complete Encyclopedia, Volume 1*. Santa Barbara, CA: ABC-CLIO, 2012.

Rosen, Ruth. *The World Split Open: How the Modern Women's Movement Changed America*. New York: Penguin Books, 2006.

Ross, Loretta. "Understanding Reproductive Justice: Transforming the Pro-Choice Movement." *Off Our Backs* 36, no. 4 (2006): 14–19.

Ross, Loretta J., Sarah L. Brownlee, Dázon Dixon Diallo, Luz Rodriguez, and Latina Roundtable. "The 'SisterSong Collective': Women of Color, Reproductive Health and Human Rights." *American Journal of Health Studies* 17, no. 2 (2001): 79–88.

Rottenberg, Catherine. "The Rise of Neoliberal Feminism." *Cultural Studies* 28, no. 3 (2014): 418–37.

Rubin, Eva R. *Abortion, Politics, and the Courts:* Roe v. Wade *and Its Aftermath.* Westport, CT: Greenwood Press, 1982.

Ruiz, Jason. "The Violence of Assimilation: An Interview with Mattilda aka Matt Bernstein Sycamore." *Radical History Review* 100 (2008): 237–47.

Ryan, Hugh. "What Does *Trans** Mean, and Where Did It Come From?" *Slate*, January 10, 2014. Last modified October 1, 2014. www.slate.com/blogs/outward /2014/01/10/trans_what_does_it_mean_and_where_did_it_come_from.html.

Salper, Roberta. "San Diego State 1970: The Initial Year of the Nation's First Women's Studies Program." *Feminist Studies* 37, no. 3 (2011): 658–82.

Sandberg, Sheryl. *Lean In: Women, Work, and the Will to Lead.* New York: Knopf, 2013.

Sarachild, Kathie. "A Program for Feminist 'Consciousness Raising.'" *Notes from the Second Year: Women's Liberation,* 1970. Digital Collections, Duke University Libraries. http://library.duke.edu/digitalcollections/wlmpc_wlmms01039.

———. "Consciousness-Raising: A Radical Weapon." In *Feminist Revolution,* edited by Redstockings, 144–50. New York: Random House, 1978.

———. "Feminist Revolution: Toward a Science of Women's Freedom." Lecture, Arizona State University, Phoenix, March 26, 2013.

———. "The Power of History." In *Feminist Revolution,* 12–43.

———. "Who Are We? The Redstockings Position on Names." In *Feminist Revolution,* 53–55.

Sarachild, Kathie, with Breanne Fahs and Ti-Grace Atkinson. "Feminist Provocations." Public forum, Arizona State University, Phoenix, AZ, March 27, 2013.

Saxon, Wolfgang. "Donna Allen, 78, a Feminist and an Organizer." *New York Times,* July 26, 1999.

Schopenhauer, Arthur. "Metaphysics of Love." In *Essays of Schopenhauer,* translated by Rudolf Dirks. Gloucestershire: Dodo Press, 2008.

Searles, Patricia, and Ronald J. Berger. "The Feminist Self-Defense Movement: A Case Study." *Gender and Society* 1, no. 1 (1987): 61–84.

Sherman, Amy. "Hillary Clinton's Changing Position on Same-Sex Marriage." PolitiFact, June 17, 2015. www.politifact.com/truth-o-meter/statements/2015/jun/17 /hillary-clinton/hillary-clinton-change-position-same-sex-marriage.

Siebers, Johan. "What Cannot Be Said: Speech and Violence." *Journal of Global Ethics* 6, no. 2 (2010): 89–102.

Simpson, Ruth, and Cheryl Jacques. *From the Closet to the Courts: The Lesbian Transition.* New York: Take Roots Media, 2007.

Smith, Howard. "The Shot That Shattered the Velvet Underground." *Village Voice,* June 6, 1968.

Snodgrass, Mary Ellen. *Civil Disobedience: An Encyclopedic History of Dissidence in the United States.* New York: Routledge, 2015.

Solanas, Valerie. *SCUM Manifesto.* New York: Olympia Press, 1968 (first self-published in 1967).

Staggenborg, Suzanne. "Social Movement Communities and Cycles of Protest: The

Emergence and Maintenance of a Local Women's Movement." *Social Problems* 45, no. 2 (1998): 180–204.

Staggenborg, Suzanne, and Verta Taylor. "Whatever Happened to the Women's Movement?" *Mobilization* 10, no. 1 (2005): 37–52.

Stampp, Kenneth. *The Peculiar Institution: Slavery in the Ante-Bellum South*. New York: Vintage, 1956.

Steinem, Gloria. *My Life on the Road*. New York: Penguin Random House, 2016.

Stewart, Abigail J., Jayati Lal, and Kristin McGuire. "Expanding the Archives of Global Feminisms: Narratives of Feminism and Activism." *Signs* 36, no. 4 (2011): 889–914.

Stoper, Emily. "The Student Nonviolent Coordinating Committee: Rise and Fall of a Redemptive Organization." *Journal of Black Studies* 8, no. 1 (1977): 13–34.

Sudbury, Julia. *Global Lockdown: Race, Gender, and the Prison-Industrial Complex*. New York: Routledge, 2014.

Tani, Franca, Carole Peterson, and Martina Smorti. "The Words of Violence: Autobiographical Narratives of Abused Women." *Journal of Family Violence* 31, no. 7 (2016): 885–96.

Thompson, Denise. *Radical Feminism Today*. London: Sage, 2001.

Titman, Nat. "About That Often Misunderstood Asterisk." *Practical Androgyny*, October 31, 2013. http://practicalandrogyny.com/2013/10/31.

Valk, Anne M. *Radical Sisters: Second-Wave Feminism and Black Liberation in Washington, D.C.* Urbana: University of Illinois Press, 2008.

Van Dyke, Nella. "Crossing Movement Boundaries: Factors That Facilitate Coalition Protest by American College Students, 1930–1990." *Social Problems* 50, no. 2 (2003): 226–50.

Vietnam Veterans Against the War. "About VVAW." Accessed November 25, 2016. www.vvaw.org/about.

Vogel, Lisa. "Michfest Responds: We Have a Few Demands of Our Own." *PrideSource*, August 18, 2014. www.pridesource.com/article.html?article=67561.

Wada, Kayomi. "National Black Feminist Organization (1973–1976)." *Black Past*. www.blackpast.org/aah/national-black-feminist-organization-1973-1976#sthash.T9Lj8kTA.dpuf.

Walzer, Michael. "The Communitarian Critique of Liberalism." *Political Theory* 18, no. 1 (1990): 6–23.

Warner, Michael. *The Trouble with Normal: Sex, Politics, and the Ethic of Queer Life*. New York: Free Press, 1999.

Weiner, Tim. "Odetta, Voice of Civil Rights Movement, Dies at 77." *New York Times*, December 3, 2008.

Weir, Lorna. "Left Popular Politics in Canadian Feminist Abortion Organizing, 1982–1991." *Feminist Studies* 20, no. 2 (1994): 249–74.

Wernimont, Jacqueline, and Julia Flanders. "Feminism in the Age of Digital Archives: The Women Writers Project." *Tulsa Studies in Women's Literature* 29, no. 2 (2010): 425–35.

Whittier, Nancy. *Feminist Generations: The Persistence of the Radical Women's Movement.* Philadelphia: Temple University Press, 2010.

———. "Political Generations, Micro-Cohorts, and the Transformation of Social Movements." *American Sociological Review* 62, no. 5 (1997): 760–78.

Williams, Cristan. "Radical Inclusion: Recounting the Trans Inclusive History of Radical Feminism." *Transgender Studies Quarterly* 3, no. 1–2 (2016): 254–58.

Willis, Ellen. "Radical Feminism and Feminist Radicalism." *Social Text* 3, no. 3 (1984): 91–118.

———. "Women and the Left." *Notes from the Second Year: Women's Liberation*, 1970. http://library.duke.edu/digitalcollections/wlmpc_wlmms01039.

Wittig, Monique. *The Straight Mind and Other Essays.* Foreword by Louise Turcotte. Boston: Beacon Press, 1992.

Wolosky, Shira. "Women's Bibles: Biblical Interpretation in Nineteenth-Century American Women's Poetry." *Feminist Studies* 28, no. 1 (2002): 191–211.

INDEX |

Freeman, Jo, 82–83, 85
free speech, 6, 163
Friedan, Betty, 10, 17, 19, 31, 38, 44, 85, 89, 113–14
friendship, xii, 3–4, 117–18, 123, 178, 180, 194
Frye, Marilyn, 154–55

Gage, Carolyn, 157
Gamergate, 192
Gavey, Nicola, 127
Geiger, Susan, xiii
gender: binary, 138; continuum, 147; essentialism, 138, 145; expression, 140, 158; fluidity, 147; roles, 30–31, 72, 74, 154
Gender Trouble, 143
generations, xii, xv, 34, 69, 79, 128, 140, 153, 159, 175, 179–81, 184–85
gentrification, 77
Ginsburg, Ruth Bader, 96
girl power, 9, 11
glass ceiling, 7
Great Sioux Nation, The, 28, 30
Griswold v. Connecticut, 96
Grosz, Elizabeth, 111–12
Guevara, Che, 50, 62

Hall, Jacqueline, xiii
Hanisch, Carol, 159, 172
Harmeling, Daniel, 22
health care, 7, 77, 191
Hefner, Hugh, 175
Hegel, G. W. F., 176
Heidegger, Martin, 69
heterosexuality, 66, 127
history, xv, 5, 11–13, 34–35, 42–44, 104, 164, 170–74, 193–94. *See also* black history; oral history
Hollander, Jocelyn, 106
Honduras, 29
hooks, bell, 6–7, 122
hookup culture, 120–21

housework, 5, 45, 72, 74, 103, 136, 153
housing, 77
human rights, 28

ideology, 8, 26, 75, 128–29, 143
immigration, 70
imperialism, 77, 174, 185
independence, 17, 23, 33, 79, 121, 153, 159–60, 183, 187
indigenous rights, 11–12, 30, 73
Industrial Workers of the World, 8, 22–23, 59
inequality, 6, 20, 78, 147, 193
injustice, vii, 8, 55, 57, 59, 131, 143
intergenerational dialogue, xi, 34
International Indian Treaty Council, 28
International Women's Day, 173
intersectionality theory, 12, 88, 139, 151
ISIS, 61

Jeannette Rankin Brigade, 20, 84
justice, 20, 34, 52, 122, 131, 137; criminal, 192; reproductive, 97–98, 190; social, 22, 32, 122, 138, 150, 159, 162

karate, 11, 26
Kelly, Megyn, 192
Kennedy, Bobby, 46
Kennedy, Florynce, 10, 19, 47–48, 82, 88–93, 108, 178, 180, 182–83, 188–89
Kessler-Harris, Alice, 168–69
King, Martin Luther, Jr., 25
kinship structures, 75, 193
Kipnis, Laura, 106
KKK, 23
Koedt, Anne, 19, 20, 66, 127
Kollontai, Alexandra, 42
Kritzler, Helen, 38

labor movement, 20, 192
Lacan, Jacques, 52–53
Ladies Home Journal, 18, 73, 107–8
Lafferty, Jeanne, 38